PRAISE FOR *WHEN HELPING HURTS*

For over fifteen years I've worked alongside other Christians in efforts to effectively address poverty at home and abroad. I can honestly report that *When Helping Hurts* is the single best book I've seen on this topic. While accessible to beginners, it is rich with insight for veterans, too. With solid biblical exegesis, engaging stories from the front lines, and practical, no-nonsense advice, Corbett and Fikkert offer essential wisdom desperately needed in today's church. The book will make many readers uncomfortable: it reveals the unhealthy and frankly unbiblical ways congregations have undertaken to help the poor in their local communities and abroad through short-term missions. But it quickly offers hope in the form of understandable, feasible new strategies that better grasp the dignity and promise of the materially poor. This book deserves a #1 spot on the reading list of every Christian who wants to follow Jesus in genuine, mutually transforming love of neighbor.

> —**AMY L. SHERMAN, PHD,** *Senior Fellow and Director, Sagamore Institute Center on Faith in Communities; author of* Restorers of Hope

What an opportunity evangelicals have to make a difference in our world through the church as we move deeper into the third millennium! Corbett and Fikkert build on the growing momentum of holistic witness that's sweeping our country and globe. Given their work nationally and internationally both personally and through the Chalmers Center, Corbett and Fikkert are eminently qualified and positioned to take motivated kingdom citizens on a Christ-centered and comprehensive journey that will pay huge dividends for impoverished people and for Christians in our broken world. *When Helping Hurts* will help the hurting—and us as well.

> —**DR. RONALD J. SIDER,** *President, Evangelicals for Social Action Professor of Theology, Holistic Ministry, and Public Policy; Palmer Theological Seminary; author of* Rich Christians in an Age of Hunger

From the early pages, where the authors promptly and humbly confess how they have "messed up" in their own efforts to alleviate poverty, to the last chapters where their vast experience and on-the-street wisdom show through so helpfully, this is a book that wonderfully combines heavy-duty thinking with practical tools. As a journalist, I appreciate the authors' storytelling and descriptive abilities. As a churchman, I appreciate their zeal to root all strategies in the institution God has ordained to bring about His goals. No donor should invest another dollar in any kind of relief effort before digesting the last page of this important book.

> —**JOEL BELZ,** *Founder and writer,* World *magazine*

Steve Corbett and Brian Fikkert are zealous to make sure that we honor the gospel not only in word but also in deed by caring for "the least of these" as Christ instructed. But how can a local church make a difference, and how do individual Christians meaningfully reflect Christ's grace, when the disparities of wealth and power in our world are so great? And how do we show material care without drifting into a social gospel devoid of spiritual priorities? *When Helping Hurts* explores biblical principles in terms of real-life situations to offer real help and grace-filled answers for such questions.

—**DR. BRYAN CHAPELL,** *President, Covenant Theological Seminary*

Corbett and Fikkert fill some important gaps in our thinking and acting about poverty as Christians. Churches in North America will find this a helpful way to educate congregations and then motivate them to action, both globally and in their neighborhoods. A biblical framework for thinking about poverty is presented in an engaging way. More importantly, the authors shift the conversation away from the needs of the poor to a call to build on what the poor already have—willing hearts and minds that just need an opportunity. The book closes with a compelling call to support ministries of micro-enterprise development.

—**BRYANT L. MYERS, PHD,** *Professor of International Development School of Intercultural Studies, Fuller Theological Seminary*

Steve and Brian have rung the bell—a clarion call to rethink how we apply the gospel to a broken world. *When Helping Hurts* lays out the principles and practice for transforming our good intentions into genuine, lasting change. I couldn't recommend this book more highly.

—**STEPHAN J. BAUMAN,** *Senior Vice President of Programs, World Relief*

We live at a time when it has become popular to be an activist for the poor. But before we all run over to Africa to "do something," this book is a must-read! The impact of good but uninformed intentions leads to unintended consequences that can be damaging to everyone involved. This book will help all of us—churches, mission agencies, Christian relief and development organizations, and donors—to establish the right foundation for our ministry to the "least of these" and for the church to do this work as God intended.

—**DARYL HEALD,** *Senior Vice President, The Maclellan Foundation*

Corbett and Fikkert have done a masterful job integrating insights from Scripture, social science research, and community development practice to give readers sound, practical, and effective strategies for equipping people to have more effective ministry to the poor. In this excellent book you'll discover new ways of approaching short-term missions (that truly help the poor rather than hurt them) as well as new ways of providing long-term economic empowerment of poor people both in North America and across the world. *When Helping Hurts* should be required reading for all church leaders, academics, and church members.

—**DR. STEVEN L. CHILDERS,** *President and CEO, Global Church Advancement; Associate Professor of Practical Theology, Reformed Theological Seminary-Orlando*

This is a book that every church leader should read. It takes the church beyond the common Band-Aid ministries to ministries that truly make a difference in the lives of the people they seek to serve. For too long the church in America has kept people in a relief mode by their well-intentioned attempts at assistance. By reading this book, church leaders can help their churches move past relief to recovery and development. I highly recommend this book!

—**DR. L. JEAN WHITE,** *Coordinator for Church and Community Ministries, Ministry Evangelism Team, North American Mission Board*

When Helping Hurts offers a timely message to the North American church that being well-meaning and well-resourced and even amply generous does not mean all is well! As North American churches and individuals move more and more toward hands-on involvement with communities and churches in the developing world, there will be a natural tendency toward creating asymmetrical relationships where Global South counterparts are not viewed as equals and partners with invaluable talents, resources, and funds. As two men who have walked their talk over many years of holistic engagement with developing-world communities, Steve and Brian provide a credible and humbly toned corrective to this unhealthy and unbiblical dynamic. This book is a must-read for any Christian who hopes to be globally aware, biblically grounded, and thoughtfully engaged in international relief and development.

—**PAUL PARK,** *Executive Director, First Fruit, Inc.*

When Helping Hurts is the most important book for the church to read as it seeks to serve the poor in ways that make a lasting difference. Corbett and Fikkert biblically define poverty, highlight why past initiatives haven't always lived up to expectations, and provide practical ways for extending the kingdom of God in inner cities and to the ends of the earth.

—**PETER GREER,** *President, HOPE International*

Becoming more and more aware of the poverty in the world, the North American church is responding and ministering to the poor in unprecedented numbers. But this is easier said than done, as poverty is a complex problem. Good intentions are not enough, for faulty assumptions can result in strategies that do considerable harm.

If churches truly want to help, this book is a must-read. It presents a biblically based framework for understanding poverty and its alleviation. The principles and strategies will help the church build an effective ministry for a hurting world, both at home and abroad.

—**DR. PAUL KOOISTRA,** *Executive Director, Mission to the World*

Globalization, immigration, and suburbanization are bringing new opportunities to minister to the poor to the front doorsteps of many North American churches. We must not repeat the mistakes of the past by running away from those whom Jesus loves so deeply. Rather, we must learn how to walk with our new neighbors in highly transformative relationships. There is no simple route to success, but this book provides a marvelous compass to guide our steps. I highly recommend it to any church that wants to be "the body" to the world outside its doors.

—**JIM BLAND,** *Executive Director, Mission to North America*

When Helping Hurts is an important resource for Christians who are concerned about seeing people's lives transformed in a way that goes beyond paternalism and embraces a Christlike, whole-person approach to loving our neighbor. Steve Corbett and Brian Fikkert share insights that will help those of us who care for the poor understand that our own brokenness might be our greatest asset in our quest to be wounded healers in a world desperate for hope.

—NOEL CASTELLANOS, *CEO, Christian Community Development Association*

Corbett and Fikkert provide readers with an introductory yet realistic examination of the problem of poverty. Avoiding an "us" versus "them" mentality that recognizes the brokenness in both poor and rich people, the authors encourage evangelicals to engage in biblically based, kingdom-focused mission that avoids a "one-size-fits-all" response to local and global poverty. From their lofty heights on Lookout Mountain, Corbett and Fikkert use down-to-earth language that is straightforward and simple without offering simplistic solutions. They note the relatively new phenomenon of poverty's shift from urban centers to suburbs, and suggest effective and up-to-date strategies such as asset-based ministry, appreciative inquiry, asset mapping, and microenterprise development.

—REV. PHIL OLSON, *Pastor, Church on the Mall, Plymouth Meeting, PA; Affiliate Staff, Evangelicals for Social Action; Coauthor,* Churches That Make a Difference: Reaching Your Community with Good News and Good Works

I confess to becoming irritated when I read something—such as *When Helping Hurts*—that makes me reconsider my methods and ministry, but am usually thankful when it helps me be more effective in serving the Lord. The authors struggle with an ambivalence that arises from the desperation of poor people around the world and the often stumbling efforts of those of us who try to help them. Poor people need help, but what is the best way to help them, and how do we keep from hurting them? These are the issues at stake.

This book has wonderful stories that illustrate the dilemma faced by those who would do good. It may be a bitter pill to swallow that, having invested in a worthy cause, you hear that the results have caused damage to the very people you meant to bless. Please see this book as an encouragement to do things right and not as a condemnation of anyone's sincere motive to help the needy.

Though the authors are men of education, knowledge, and experience, they confess their own struggles in the application of these principles. As someone who has been poor, and has worked all of his years in ministry to help the poor, I encourage you to read and ponder the principles in *When Helping Hurts*.

—RANDY NABORS, *Pastor of New City Fellowship, Chattanooga, Tennessee, Presbyterian Church in America*

WHEN HELPING HURTS

How to Alleviate Poverty without Hurting the Poor... and Yourself

STEVE CORBETT and BRIAN FIKKERT

MOODY PUBLISHERS

CHICAGO

All Scripture quotations, unless otherwise indicated, are taken from the *Holy Bible, New International Version®*, NIV®. Copyright ©1973, 1978, 1984 by Biblica, Inc.™ Used by permission of Zondervan. All rights reserved worldwide. www.zondervan.com

Scripture quotations marked KJV are taken from the King James Version.

Edited by Cheryl Dunlop
Cover design: Faceout Studio, Emily Weigel
Cover image: Shutterstock #92598721
Interior design: Smartt Guys design

Library of Congress Cataloging-in-Publication Data
Corbett, Steve.
    When helping hurts: how to alleviate poverty without hurting the
    poor—and yourself / Steve Corbett and Brian Fikkert.
        p. cm.
    Includes bibliographical references.
    ISBN 978-0-8024-0998-0
    1. Church work with the poor. 2. Poverty—Religious
aspects—Christianity. I. Fikkert, Brian. II. Title.
BV639.P6C67 2009
261.8'325—dc22
                2009009076

We hope you enjoy this book from Moody Publishers. Our goal is to provide high-quality, thought-provoking books and products that connect truth to your real needs and challenges. For more information on other books and products written and produced from a biblical perspective, go to www.moodypublishers.com or write to:

Moody Publishers
820 N. LaSalle Boulevard
Chicago, IL 60610

7 9 10 8 6

Printed in the United States of America

CONTENTS

FOREWORD – 2009

Have you ever done anything to help poor people? It was not too many years ago that most North American evangelicals would have answered no to this question. Let me explain.

I grew up as the son of a sharecropper in rural Mississippi, where I experienced violent racism and grinding poverty from the day I was born. I left Mississippi looking for a better life. But Jesus Christ took hold of me, and in 1960 He called me to go back to Mississippi to help my people. Soon thereafter I started Voice of Calvary Ministries to address the spiritual, physical, and social needs of the poor. Many evangelical Christians were leery of me in those days. My concern for the poor and for social justice made many evangelicals suspect that I was theologically liberal. I never did understand those folks. I never questioned that the Bible was totally true. In fact, I really believed such passages as Matthew 25:31–46 and 1 John 3:17–18.

Evangelicals have come a long way since those days. Many now agree that as followers of Jesus Christ we must show compassion for the poor. Indeed, there is a good chance that you have volunteered at a soup kitchen, donated to a food pantry, or gone on a short-term mission trip to a poor country. At the very least you have put money in the offering plate, money that was then used to support the local homeless shelter or a missionary working in an AIDS clinic in Africa. While we are not doing nearly enough, many of us evangelicals are now doing something. This is good news, but it leads to my second question.

Have you ever done anything to hurt poor people? Most of you would probably answer no to this question, but the reality is that you may have done considerable harm to poor people in the very process of trying to help them. The federal government made this mistake for decades. Well-intentioned welfare programs penalized work, undermined families, and created dependence. The government hurt the very people it was trying to help. Unfortunately, the same is true for many Christian ministries today. By focusing on symptoms rather than on the underlying disease, we are often hurting the very people we are trying to help. Surprisingly, we are also hurting ourselves in the process. As followers of Jesus Christ, we simply must do better.

I have devoted most of my life to helping Christians minister effectively to poor people. The following book builds on that tradition in a profound way. The authors combine sound theology, solid research, foundational principles, and proven strategies to prepare you for transformational ministry amongst "the least of these" both at home and around the world. But it would be a mistake to think that the power of this book lies in the tools and techniques it presents. Rather, the central message of this book is that we need the person of Jesus Christ to transform not just the poor but also ourselves.

Hence, I urge you to approach this book not just with your mind but also with your heart. Meditate on the Bible passages. Reflect on the questions and exercises. Pray for the Holy Spirit to break you and to change you. And then do not be just a hearer of the Word but a doer. Ask God what you and your church can do to truly engage in helping the poor without hurting them . . . and yourselves.

—DR. JOHN PERKINS

Founder and President Emeritus of the Christian Community
Development Association

FOREWORD – 2012

We live in a world of urgent spiritual and physical need.

Nearly three billion people are living on less than two dollars a day, and over a billion of them dwell in desperate poverty. They are starving in slums, sold into slavery, orphaned due to AIDS, and dying of preventable diseases. Some of them are our Christian brothers and sisters while others of them have never even heard of Christ.

So what are we to do? In light of massive need in the world and in view of God's merciful concern for the poor, how are we in the church to respond? This question forms the foundation for the pages that lie ahead. Steve Corbett and Brian Fikkert have undertaken a mammoth task in this book, and I praise God for how they have carried it out.

They start with the Word of God, which is where we must begin. A book filled with practical thoughts and economic tips would be vain apart from eternal truth. This book is saturated with Scripture as the authors continually ground their assertions in God-breathed authority. They address poverty alleviation through the lens of redemptive history, and in so doing they rightly exalt Christ as the supreme healer of every human heart, whether rich or poor.

The authors move from God's Word to God's people, specifically the local church. Their conviction (which I share) that the local church has a unique role to play in poverty alleviation affects everything they write. In a real sense, they are writing to the church and for the church; they want to see local churches carry out the commands of Christ in ways that are gracious to the poor, good for God's people, and glorifying to God's name.

But this book does not stall in the sphere of the theological and theoretical. It moves wonderfully from timeless truth to contemporary application. As you read, you won't just learn about problems in the world; you will discover how poverty in the world can actually be addressed. In the process of reading case studies, exploring critical questions, and analyzing current events, you will realize that God has given you—and your church—a unique opportunity to be a part of His global plan to make His great mercy known in your community and among all the nations.

For all of these reasons (and more), this book is virtually required reading for everyone in our church who is intentionally engaging the poor here and around the world. I cannot recommend it highly enough for anyone who is passionate about spreading and showing the love of Christ to the "least of these."

Simply put, I have never read a better book on practically serving the poor, and I pray that God will use this new edition to equip his people to accomplish His purposes in a world of urgent spiritual and physical need for the glory of His great name.

—DAVID PLATT
Pastor, Church at Brook Hills, Birmingham, AL and author of Radical: Taking Back Your Faith from the American Dream

PREFACE

The average North American enjoys a standard of living that has been unimaginable for most of human history. Meanwhile, 40 percent of the earth's inhabitants eke out an existence on less than two dollars per day. And from inner-city ghettos to rural Appalachia, poverty continues to inflict pain, loss, and despair on the North American continent itself. Indeed, the economic and social disparity between the "haves" and the "have-nots" is on the rise both within North America and between North America and much of the Majority World (Africa, Asia, and Latin America).

If you are a North American *Christian*, the reality of our society's vast wealth presents you with an enormous responsibility, for throughout the Scriptures God's people are commanded to show compassion to the poor. In fact, doing so is simply part of our job description as followers of Jesus Christ (Matt. 25:31–46). While the biblical call to care for the poor transcends time and place, passages such as 1 John 3:17 should weigh particularly heavy on the minds and hearts of North American Christians: "If anyone has material possessions and sees his brother in need but has no pity on him, how can the love of God be in him?"

Of course, there is no "one-size-fits-all" recipe for how each Christian should respond to this biblical mandate. Some are called to pursue poverty alleviation as a career, while others are called to do so as volunteers. Some are called to engage in hands-on, relational ministry, while others are better suited to support frontline workers through financial donations, prayer, and other types of support. Each Christian has a unique set of gifts, callings, and responsibilities that influence the scope and manner in which to fulfill the biblical mandate to help the poor.

Furthermore, the institutional context greatly influences both the type and scale of various poverty-alleviation efforts. Some Christians are called to work at a government level, seeking to promote justice for the poor through public policy. Others are called to work in the business world where they can provide job opportunities for the unemployed. Many Christians work with churches or parachurch ministries, allowing them to communicate openly the love of Jesus Christ through both words and deeds. And some Christians simply minister as individuals, walking across the street to help a neighbor in need.

Finally, no single sector can alleviate poverty on its own. Like all human beings, poor people have a range of physical, emotional, social, and spiritual needs. Hence, appropriate interventions for poor people include such diverse sectors as economic development, health, education, agriculture, spiritual formation, etc.

In summary, while all Christians have a responsibility to help the poor, there is enormous diversity in the ways that each Christian is to fulfill this biblical mandate.

THE SCOPE OF THIS BOOK

How can one book deal with all of this diversity? All North American Christians have one thing in common: Each one of us is called to participate in the life of a local church. While this participation can be in leadership or membership, each of us is responsible to participate at some level in helping our congregation to be everything Scripture calls it to be, including fulfilling its biblical mandate to care for the poor.

Moreover, we believe the local church has a unique role to play in poverty alleviation, and we are delighted to see the recent resurgence in church-based, holistic ministry to the poor both at home and abroad. At the same time, we are grieved when we see churches using poverty-alleviation strategies that are grounded in unbiblical assumptions about the nature of poverty and that violate "best practice" methodologies developed by theorists and practitioners over the course of many decades.

For all of these reasons, this book focuses on appropriate ways for a North American congregation—and its missionaries—to participate in poverty alleviation at home and abroad, taking into account the God-ordained mission of the church and the typical church's organizational capacity. However, the concepts, principles, and interventions described in this book are applicable for a wide range of settings. In particular, nonprofit organizations and individuals will find that the principles and strategies described in this book transfer very easily to their ministries.

Part 1 of this book lays a foundation for all poverty-alleviation efforts by discussing the fundamental nature of poverty and then drawing out some initial implications. Part 2 builds on this foundation by discussing three key issues that should be considered in the design and implementation of any poverty-alleviation strategy. Part 3 applies all of these concepts to "economic development," a set of strategies designed to alleviate material poverty through increasing people's income and wealth. Part 4, which is new to the second edition, describes steps that can be taken to get started in applying the book's principles in a variety of contexts.

NEW FEATURES OF THE SECOND EDITION

We are deeply grateful to God for all of the ways that He used the first edition of this book to equip His people for more effective ministry. By God's grace alone, we have received reports from all over the world that God is changing the paradigms of churches and ministries, helping them to walk with people who are poor in more empowering ways. We praise God for this, and we give the glory to Him and to Him alone.

Unfortunately, we have also heard some readers of the first edition say that they are not quite sure what to do next. They want to "help without hurting," but they are not sure how to get started. Some have even said that they feel a bit paralyzed, being so worried about doing harm that they are afraid to do anything at all. And in a few rare but disturbing cases, some have used the first edition to argue—erroneously—that nothing should be done to help people who are poor, as all efforts are likely to do harm.

Hence, we want to say as loudly and as clearly as we can: GET MOVING! We believe that the coexistence of agonizing poverty and unprecedented wealth—even just within the household of faith—is an affront to the gospel. You see, what is at stake is not just the well-being of poor people—as important at that is—but rather the very authenticity of the church's witness to the transforming power of the kingdom of God. Hence, the North American church should have a profound sense of urgency to spend ourselves "in behalf of the hungry and satisfy the needs of the oppressed" (Isa. 58:10).

That having been said, good intentions are not enough. It is possible to hurt poor people, and ourselves, in the process of trying to help them. But do not let that truth paralyze you. Read this book and other resources, study, learn, pray, repent, try to do something, evaluate, and then repent again. And then trust that a sovereign God is more than able to take our feeble acts and turn them into something that He can use for His glory.

In summary, our message to you is this: Quadruple your efforts to help the poor and do so immediately. Just consider doing things differently than you have in the past.

Because our desire is to unleash and to equip and not to paralyze, we have written this second edition, adding Part 4 to enable you to get started in more effective approaches to poverty alleviation. Although it is impossible to provide a "one-size-fits-all" pathway to success, it is our prayer that Part 4 will provide readers with sufficient principles, resources, and steps to get moving in the right direction.

We have also made a few small changes to the original chapters from the first edition, the most notable being an expanded discussion in chapter 3 of the role of worldview in shaping the thoughts and actions of North Americans.

HOW TO USE THIS BOOK

We want this book to be used by God to affect your heart, your mind, and your actions. Such impact is less likely to happen if you simply read through the book. Toward that end, we have included the following: pre-chapter questions called "Initial Thoughts," post-chapter "Reflection Questions and Exercises," and several longer exercises. It is very important that you take the time to prayerfully and thoughtfully complete all of these questions and exercises, as they are an integral part of engaging with the material and applying it to your own life. The book is appropriate for both individual and group study. Groups might include Sunday school classes, small groups, staff or ministry team meetings, etc.

If used in a group setting, it is important that the facilitator give adequate time for discussion, as there is enormous power in having people wrestle with questions and issues together. Participants should read the chapter and complete assigned questions and exercises before the meeting, and the majority of the time together should be spent discussing the questions and exercises for each chapter. It is extremely important that the facilitator create a safe atmosphere so that participants feel comfortable sharing their ideas, weaknesses, questions, and concerns.

Below we suggest formats for the group meetings, including the time that should be allocated to each component. However, the minutes allocated below are only a suggestion, and the group facilitator should adapt the time allocation to fit the context and needs of the particular group.

We suggest the following format for the *first* meeting:

- To avoid biasing people's responses, do *not* start the meeting with an introduction to the content of the book.
- Immediately divide the group into subgroups of approximately five people each and ask the subgroups to complete the "Opening Exercise" about the tsunami that precedes the introduction. The subgroups should write down their plans, ideally on large poster paper (25 minutes).
- Ask the subgroups to share their plans for the trip to Indonesia with the larger group. The facilitator should collect each subgroup's written plan, keeping them all in a safe place so that they can be reexamined during the "Extended Exercise: Indonesia Reconsidered" at the end of chapter 6 (15 minutes).
- The facilitator should ask the group to complete both the introduction and chapter 1 before the next meeting, including the pre-chapter "Initial Thoughts" and the post-chapter "Reflection Questions and Exercises" for chapter 1.

For all subsequent meetings, we suggest the following format:

- Group members should come to the meeting having read the chapter for that week and having completed the pre-chapter "Initial Thoughts" and the post-chapter "Reflection Questions and Exercises."
- The facilitator should ask group members to share the answers that they wrote to the "Initial Thoughts" *before* they read the chapter (5 minutes).
- The facilitator should then ask the group members to summarize the main points of the chapter, clarifying ideas and filling in any key points that the group fails to mention (10–15 minutes).
- The facilitator should then lead a discussion of the post-chapter "Reflection Questions and Exercises" (25–30 minutes).

The only exception to this pattern occurs in chapter 6, where the "Extended Exercise: Indonesia Reconsidered" at the end of the chapter requires additional time. Hence, we suggest that you allocate two meetings for chapter 6 to allow sufficient time for discussion of this exercise.

Additional Resources

This book is only an introduction to some very complex issues. Throughout the text and the notes, we refer you to additional books, articles, websites, and organizations that can help you to dig deeper. In addition, the Chalmers Center for Economic Development at Covenant College, with which we are affiliated, provides additional resources and learning opportunities related to all of the topics introduced in this book. Go to www.chalmers.org.

About the Stories

To the best of our knowledge, all of the stories included in this book are completely true. The only exceptions are several stories (Mary on pages 59–61, Creekside Community Church on pages 62–64, Grace Fellowship Church on pages 186–187, and Parkview Fellowship on pages 205–206) that are "based on one or more true events" but in which a few details have been added to illustrate various points.

The names of individuals, churches, and organizations in the stories have been changed to protect their identity, unless those names have been previously revealed in other publications from which the stories were taken.

OPENING EXERCISE

Consider the following scenario:

The tsunami that hit Indonesia in December 2004 wiped out many of the small businesses. These small businesses are owned by poor people and serve as their primary source of income. Most of the shops, equipment, materials, and inventory were destroyed. Four months after the tsunami, your church has decided to send a team to assist with the restarting of these small businesses.

Discuss the following questions in groups of approximately five people. If you are reading this book individually, then consider these questions on your own.

1. What will you do to plan and prepare for your trip?
2. What resources will you bring with you?
3. Whom will you choose from your church to go on this trip?
4. What will your team do once it gets there?
5. What will be the specific components of your ministry?
6. How will you implement each component?

Please write down your responses to these questions and store them in a safe place. You will be asked to reflect upon your responses later in the book.

INTRODUCTION

MZUNGU

The smoke curled its way up from the floor and headed straight for me (Brian), standing just a few feet away. As the smoke from the witch doctor's burning herbs made its way into my nostrils, I wondered, *If the demons leave when the herbs are burned, does that mean they are in the smoke?*

I grew up as a pastor's kid in a rural Wisconsin village that consisted of twelve hundred no-nonsense, fourth-generation Dutch immigrants. I have been a member of theologically conservative Presbyterian churches my entire life. Hence, I am understandably a bit weak on my demonology. *What happens if I inhale?* Thinking this was absurd but not wanting to take any chances, I plugged my nose as inconspicuously as I could and prayed for God's protection.

This was the second week of a small-business training class held in St. Luke's Church, deep in the heart of a slum in Kampala, the capital city of Uganda. The class consisted of refugees who had fled unspeakable suffering from the civil war in the north and were trying to eke out a living by selling used clothing, drying fish, or making charcoal. I was on a teaching sabbatical from my college and was living in Uganda for five months with my wife and three children.

Elizabeth, the director of women's ministries for a major Ugandan denomination, had kindly agreed to help me test the biblically based small-business training curriculum that I was writing, so we ventured into this slum every Monday. The plan was for Elizabeth to translate my lessons and to teach the classes. I would observe the sessions and administer follow-up questionnaires. But now somehow we'd moved from dollars and cents to demons and smoke. This is how it all happened . . .

Elizabeth started today's class by asking, "Has God done anything in your lives as a result of last week's lesson?" A rugged lady raised her hand and said, "I am a witch doctor. After last week's lesson, I went back to church for the first time in twenty years. What do I do now?"

Elizabeth firmly ordered her, "Go and get your herbs and medicines, and we will burn them up right here on the floor of the church!"

After running home, the witch doctor marched to the front of St. Luke's Church and dropped her bag of herbs on the floor. She then confessed her sins publicly. "I have a demon living inside of me who drinks 50,000 Ugandan shillings [approximately $27 US] of alcohol per day. I feed him through the profits from my witchcraft business. My specialty is keeping husbands faithful to their wives. I sell these herbs to women and instruct them to rub them over the intimate parts of their bodies. When the women are with their husbands, the herbs rub off onto their husbands' bodies, and this makes the husbands remain faithful. Some of my best customers are in this church. But I want to forsake my witchcraft and become a follower of Jesus Christ."

Forsaking her business was no small sacrifice, as her profits were quite large by slum standards. Indeed, the value of the alcohol she was consuming *every day* was greater than the *monthly* income of the average refugee sitting in the audience.

Elizabeth lit a match and dropped it onto the bag of herbs. "The demons will leave if we burn the herbs," she said. Elizabeth then started to pray. With her booming voice, piercing glare, and pointing finger, Elizabeth commanded the demons to leave the witch doctor alone. The Bible says demons are afraid of Jesus. I think they might have been afraid of the fierce look on Elizabeth's face as well!

When Elizabeth finished praying, she hugged the witch doctor and said, "From now on, your name will be 'Grace.'" It was a dramatic event, but the drama wasn't over.

A NEW CRISIS

For the next five weeks, Grace never missed a lesson. Her face became brighter, she smiled regularly, and she seemed to be at peace. Grace gave regular testimony to the ways that God was transforming her life. Only the Lord knows for certain, but I fully expect to see Grace in heaven someday.

But then one week Grace was absent. "Where is the witch doctor today?" I asked. We were all still struggling to remember to call her "Grace." A murmur went through the group of seventy-five refugees. Finally, the leader of the refugees spoke up, "One of the ladies says the witch doctor is sick. Maybe somebody should go and visit her to make sure she is all right."

Elizabeth and I immediately left the church and trudged through the slum to find Grace's house. As our guide led us deep into the slum, we carefully stepped over small streams that flowed between the shacks, streams teeming with human sewage, all types of trash, and a mysterious green slime. We passed children covered with sores. We walked past clusters of men gambling as they sipped the local brew and inhaled smoke through long tubes. Few "mzungus" (white people) ever venture into these parts, and with my height of 6'10", I am a walking conversation piece even in my own culture. All along the way children yelled "Mzungu!" and ran up to touch my strangely colored skin and to pull the hair on my arms.

After about a ten-minute walk, we entered Grace's one-room shack. Grace was lying on a mat on the dirt floor and writhing in agony. A plate with a few morsels of food covered with fleas was the only other thing in the place. Grace could not lift her head and could barely whisper. Elizabeth bent over and got close to try to understand Grace's faint words. Elizabeth then stood up and explained the situation to me.

Grace had developed tonsillitis. Because she is poor and has HIV, the local hospital refused to treat her. Desperate for relief, Grace paid her neighbor to cut out her tonsils with a kitchen knife. *We are in the very bowels of hell,* I thought to myself.

Elizabeth asked me to pray, so I led all of us in whatever a conservative Presbyterian prays for ex–witch doctors with HIV who live in crowded slums and who get their neighbors to cut out their tonsils with kitchen knives.

Elizabeth and I then started to walk back toward St. Luke's, where the class of refugees was still gathered. "I am afraid she will die of an infection. Can we get her some penicillin?" I asked, feeling quite helpless.

"Yes we can, but we'll need 15,000 Uganda shillings, about eight dollars US," Elizabeth said. I immediately reached into my pocket and handed Elizabeth the money. I did not return to the church that day, as my taxi was waiting for me out on the main road and the sun was going down. I wanted to get out of there before dark. Elizabeth and her driver went to the nearest pharmacy and bought the penicillin for Grace.

A week later I could hardly believe my eyes when Grace walked through the door of St. Luke's for the next session of the small-business training class. She looked better than ever. I believe Elizabeth and I probably saved Grace's life with the penicillin that day.

UPON FURTHER REVIEW

Two weeks later, my family and I boarded an airplane to return to the United States. It had been a remarkable sabbatical, and my adrenaline was still pumping. We had been used by God to bring a witch doctor to Christ! And then we got the chance to save her life! Totally awesome!

But as the adrenaline began to subside, the analytical part of my personality began to kick in. I reviewed the entire situation in the slum, thinking about each of the characters and institutions and the roles they had played in these dramatic events.

There was St. Luke's Church and its faithful pastor, trying to shed light in the darkness with a congregation full of extremely poor refugees. The pastor was always welcoming, and he was very supportive of the small-business training classes, although I do not think he ever attended any of them. He did come to the graduation ceremony, a ceremony at which the refugees showered my entire family with all sorts of gifts that they could not afford. He sensed my discomfort at this and whispered in my ear, "Don't feel bad. Take their gifts with joy. This is how they show their love for you." He always thanked Elizabeth and me profusely every time he saw us.

There were the refugees in the small-business class, the vast majority of whom were women. Each of them had suffered enormous loss at the hands of the Lord's Resistance Army (LRA), a rebel group that has terrorized the villages in northern Uganda for more than twenty years. The LRA is notorious for kidnapping children, using the boys as soldiers and the girls as sex slaves. As part of a brainwashing process, kidnapped children are often forced to kill or torture their parents, relatives, or peers. Chopping off limbs, ears, lips, and noses is standard procedure for the LRA. Unfortunately, the people of Kampala have not welcomed the refugees with open arms, often discriminating against them for being from an "inferior" tribe.

There was the witch doctor, who was simultaneously revered and despised. On the one hand, local women coveted her power and paid a handsome price for her services. On the other hand, she was notorious for erupting into violent rages when she was drunk. Slum residents often subdued her during these outbursts by beating her into submission, and her body was bruised and scarred as a result. By forsaking her witchcraft, she was accepting a substantial drop in income and leaving herself vulnerable to any enemies she had accumulated as a result of her previous lifestyle.

There was Elizabeth, who was really the key figure in everything that had happened. Ten years earlier, she had been instrumental in starting St. Luke's, but she now held a prestigious position in the headquarters of her denomination. Elizabeth was from the same tribe as the refugees, and she herself had lost friends and relatives to the LRA. The refugees absolutely adored her, but her superior level of education, middle class income, and successful career made her an outsider to this community. Like me, she left the slum every Monday evening when the class was over and drove to a nice home.

Finally, there was me, the mzungu, and all which that word represents: money, power, money, education, money, superiority, and money.

Suddenly, I felt sick, and the flight attendant hadn't even brought the food yet. Yes, Elizabeth and I had led the witch doctor to Christ and had saved her life. But I suddenly realized that we might have done an enormous amount of harm in the process—harm to St. Luke's Church and its pastor, harm to the refugees in the small-business class, and even harm to Grace herself. I kicked myself for violating several basic principles of poverty alleviation, principles that I regularly teach to others. But this was not the first time I had messed up. In fact, I have done far dumber things in my attempts to help the poor, some of which will be shared later in this book.

What did I do wrong? How could I have hurt the poor in the process of trying to help them? We cannot answer these questions in a sound bite, which is the reason we are writing this book. After laying some groundwork, we will return to the case of the witch doctor in a later chapter.

WHY WE WRITE THIS BOOK

My coauthor and I have spent most of our adult lives trying to learn how to improve the lives of poor people. Steve worked for many years with a major Christian relief and development agency, serving in roles ranging from grassroots community developer, to country director, to serving on the global management team. I took the academic route, spending my time as a researcher and a professor. About ten years ago our lives converged as we began working together at the Chalmers Center for Economic Development at Covenant College, a research and training initiative that seeks to equip churches around the world to minister to the economic and spiritual needs of low-income people. We also teach together in an undergraduate major in Community Development at Covenant College, a degree program that tries to prepare Christian young people to make a difference in the lives of low-income people in North America and around the world.

Steve and I still have a lot to learn, as the problems of poverty continue to confound us. Moreover, we do not pretend that the material in this book is unique to us. Rather, the following pages are simply a way of synthesizing and organizing the ideas of many others into a framework that audiences in a variety of settings have found helpful. We are deeply indebted to the many authors, researchers, and practitioners who have produced a vast range of principles, resources, and tools for us to draw upon. We hope that this book will help—in some small way—to make their ideas and tools more accessible to others.

Unless noted otherwise, the "I" in this book refers to me, Brian, as I did nearly all of the actual writing; however, Steve has played a crucial role in this book. For the past seven years, Steve has helped me and the rest of the Chalmers Center staff to understand and apply many of the concepts in this book to our work, serving as a tremendous mentor to our entire team. In addition, Steve participated in planning the content of the book and carefully reviewed every word.

We write this book with a great deal of excitement about the renewed interest in helping low-income people that is so apparent among North American Christians. While materialism, self-centeredness, and complacency continue to plague all of us, nobody can deny the upswing in social concern among North American evangelicals in the past two decades. There is perhaps no better illustration of this trend than the exploding short-term mission movement, much of which has focused on ministering to the poor at home and abroad.

But our excitement about these developments is seriously tempered by two convictions. First, North American Christians are simply not doing enough. We are the richest people ever to walk the face of the earth. Period. Yet, most of us live as though there is nothing terribly wrong in the world. We attend our kids' soccer games, pursue our careers, and take beach vacations while 40 percent of the world's inhabitants struggle just to eat every day. And in our own backyards, the homeless, those residing in ghettos, and a wave of immigrants live in a world outside the economic and social mainstream of North America. We do not necessarily need to feel guilty about our wealth. But we do need to get up every morning with a deep sense that something is terribly wrong with the world and yearn and strive to do something about it. There is simply not enough yearning and striving going on.

Second, many observers, including Steve and I, believe that when North American Christians *do* attempt to alleviate poverty, the methods used often do considerable harm to both the materially poor and the materially non-poor. Our concern is not just that these methods are wasting human, spiritual, financial, and organizational resources but that these methods are actually exacerbating the very problems they are trying to solve.

Fortunately, there is hope, because God is at work. By renewing our commitment, by adjusting our methods, and by repenting daily, we North American Christians can play a powerful role in alleviating poverty at home and abroad. It is our prayer that God will use the following pages to play some small role in helping the church of Jesus Christ to increase both the level and the effectiveness of our efforts to minister to a hurting world.

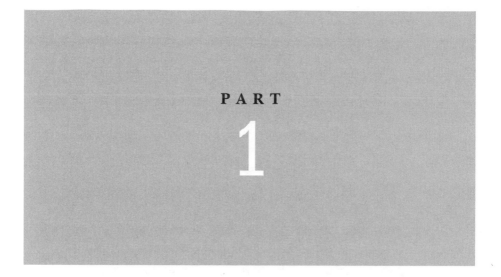

PART

1

FOUNDATIONAL CONCEPTS
for HELPING
WITHOUT HURTING

WHY DID **JESUS**
COME TO EARTH?

Why did Jesus come to earth?[1] Most Christians have a ready answer to this question. However, there are actually nuanced differences in how Christians think about this most basic issue, and those small differences can have dramatic consequences for all endeavors, including how the church responds to the plight of the poor. Let's examine how Jesus Himself understood His mission.

Jesus' earthly ministry began one Sabbath day in a synagogue in Nazareth. Week in and week out, Jews gathered in this synagogue to worship under the chafing yoke of the Roman Empire. Aware of Old Testament prophecy, these worshipers were longing for God to send the promised Messiah who would restore the kingdom to Israel, reigning on David's throne forever. But centuries had gone by with no Messiah, and the Romans were running the show. Hope was probably in short supply. It is in this context that the son of a carpenter from that very town stood up and was handed a scroll from the prophet Isaiah.

> Unrolling it, he found the place where it is written: "The Spirit of the Lord is on me, because he has anointed me to preach good news to the poor. He has sent me to proclaim freedom for the prisoners and recovery of sight for the blind, to release the oppressed, to proclaim the year of the Lord's favor." . . .

The eyes of everyone in the synagogue were fastened on him, and he began by saying to them, "Today this scripture is fulfilled in your hearing." *(Luke 4:17–21)*

A shiver must have gone down the spine of the worshipers that day. Isaiah had prophesied that a King was coming who would usher in a kingdom unlike anything the world had ever seen. Could it be that Isaiah's prophecies were really about to come true? Could it really be that a kingdom whose domain would increase without end was about to begin (Isa. 9:7)? Was it really possible that justice, peace, and righteousness were about to be established forever? Would this King really bring healing to the parched soil, the feeble hands, the shaky knees, the fearful hearts, the blind, the deaf, the lame, the mute, the brokenhearted, the captives, and the sinful souls, and would proclaim the year of jubilee for the poor (Isa. 35:1–6; 53:5; 61:1–2)? Jesus' answer to all these questions was a resounding "yes," declaring, "*Today* this scripture is fulfilled in your hearing."

In the same chapter, Jesus summarized His ministry as follows: "I must preach the good news of the *kingdom of God* to the other towns also, because that is why I was sent" (Luke 4:43, italics added). The mission of Jesus was and is to preach the good news of the kingdom of God, to say to one and all, "I am the King of kings and Lord of lords, and I am using My power to fix everything that sin has ruined." As pastor and theologian Tim Keller states, "The kingdom is the renewal of the whole world through the entrance of supernatural forces. As things are brought back under Christ's rule and authority, they are restored to health, beauty, and freedom."[2]

Of course there is both a "now" and a "not yet" to the kingdom. The full manifestation of the kingdom will not occur until there is a new heaven and a new earth. Only then will every tear be wiped from our eyes (Rev. 21:4). But two thousand years ago, Jesus clearly stated that there is a "now" to the kingdom, saying, "*Today* this scripture is fulfilled in your hearing" (Luke 4:21).

A FULLER ANSWER TO THE QUESTION

We have asked thousands of evangelical Christians in numerous contexts this most basic question—why did Jesus come to earth?—and the vast majority of people say something like, "Jesus came to die on the cross to save us from our sins so that we can go to heaven." While this answer is true, Jesus' message is an even more grand and sweeping epic than that: "The kingdom of heaven is at hand. I am the King who is bringing healing to the entire cosmos. If—and only if—you repent and believe in me, you will someday enjoy all of the many benefits that my kingdom brings."

Contrast the response of most evangelicals with the following passage concerning the nature and work of Jesus Christ:

> He is the image of the invisible God, the firstborn over all creation. For by him all things were created: things in heaven and on earth, visible and invisible, whether thrones or powers or rulers or authorities; all things were created by him and for him. He is before all things, and in him all things hold together. And he is the head of the body, the church; he is the beginning and the firstborn from among the dead, so that in everything he might have the supremacy. For God was pleased to have all his fullness dwell in him, and through him to reconcile to himself all things, whether things on earth or things in heaven, by making peace through his blood, shed on the cross. *(Col. 1:15–20)*

In this passage Jesus Christ is described as the Creator, Sustainer, and Reconciler of *everything*. Yes, Jesus died for our souls, but He also died to reconcile—that is, to put into right relationship—all that He created. This is what we sing every year in the Christmas carol, "He comes to make His blessings known far as the curse is found." The curse is cosmic in scope, bringing decay, brokenness, and death to every speck of the universe. But as King of kings and Lord of lords, Jesus is making all things new! This is the good news of the gospel.

When she was three years old, my daughter Anna bowed her head one night and prayed, "Dear Jesus, please come back soon, because we have lots of owies, and they hurt." I got all choked up listening to her, for she had captured the essence of the comprehensive healing of the kingdom and was longing for this healing to happen to her. She was praying—in three-year-old language—"Thy kingdom come. Thy will be done in earth, as it is in heaven" (Matt. 6:10 KJV). Yes, come quickly Lord Jesus, for we do have lots of owies, and they really hurt.

Is Jesus Really the Messiah?

Jesus claimed to be the promised King, but how do we know His claims were true? This question has perplexed everyone from the lepers of Jesus' day to the greatest minds of the twenty-first century. But it is a bit surprising that at the end of his life, John the Baptist himself was still uncertain about the authenticity of Jesus. John had spent his entire career eating locusts and wild honey, wearing strange clothes, hanging out in the desert, and preaching to one and all that Jesus was the promised Messiah, the King who would reign on David's throne. But now John found himself in Herod's prison about to have his head chopped off. He was likely thinking to himself, *If Jesus is really the Messiah, surely He would start the coup against King Herod before I, his secretary of state, get executed!* But there was no coup attempt, and John understandably developed some doubt.

So John sent two of his disciples to ask Jesus, "Are you the one who was to come, or should we expect someone else?" (Luke 7:19). There are so many ways that Jesus could have answered this question. He could have pointed out that His birth in Bethlehem from the line of David was consistent with prophecies about the Messiah. Or Jesus could have referred to His remarkable knowledge of the Scriptures and to His unparalleled teaching abilities. Or Jesus could have reminded John that they had both witnessed the Holy Spirit descend upon Jesus in the form of a dove and had heard God the Father say, "This is my Son, whom I love; with him I am well pleased" (Matt. 3:17). If this latter event couldn't convince John, it would seem that nothing could! But Jesus chose not to point to any of these signs. John was already aware of these and apparently needed something else to comfort him. So Jesus said:

> Go back and report to John what you have seen and heard: The blind receive sight, the lame walk, those who have leprosy are cured, the deaf hear, the dead are raised, and the good news is preached to the poor. Blessed is the man who does not fall away on account of me. *(Luke 7:22–23)*

In essence, Jesus was saying to John, "John, you have not run the race in vain. I am the promised Messiah. And you can be sure because of what your disciples are *both hearing Me say and seeing Me do*. I am preaching the good news of the kingdom, *and* I am showing the good news of the kingdom, just as Isaiah said I would."

How useless it would have been if Jesus had only used words and not deeds to declare the kingdom. Imagine reading the story in Luke 18:35–43 about the blind beggar who was sitting along the roadside. Learning that Jesus was walking by, he called out, "Jesus, Son of David, have mercy on me!" What if Jesus had said, "I am the fulfillment of all prophecy. I am the King of kings and Lord of lords. I have all the power in heaven and earth. I could heal you today of your blindness, but I only care about your soul. Believe in Me"? Who would have believed that Jesus was the promised King if He had not given any evidence to prove it? As Peter stated at Pentecost, "Men of Israel, listen to this: Jesus of Nazareth was a man accredited by God to you by miracles, wonders and signs, which God did among you through him, as you yourselves know" (Acts 2:22). Jesus' deeds were essential to proving that He truly was the promised Messiah. Jesus preached the good news of the kingdom, and He showed the good news of the kingdom.

What Would Jesus Do?

In his book *The Last Days: A Son's Story of Sin and Segregation at the Dawn of the New South*, Charles Marsh describes growing up in Laurel, Mississippi, during the 1960s. Racial tensions were high as the federal government sought to end segregation. Civil rights workers, many of whom came from the North, poured into the region, seeking to end centuries of discrimination against African Americans. Charles's father was the well-known pastor of First Baptist Church in Laurel and was a pillar of the community. Beloved for his outstanding preaching and godly living, Reverend Marsh was to his parishioners the model Christian.

Also living in Laurel, Mississippi, was Sam Bowers, the Imperial Wizard of the White Knights of the Ku Klux Klan of Mississippi, who terrorized African Americans throughout the region. Bowers was suspected of plotting at least nine murders of African Americans and civil rights workers, seventy-five bombings of African-American churches, and numerous beatings and physical assaults.

How did Reverend Marsh, the model Christian, respond to this situation? Charles explains:

There is no doubt my father loathed the Klan when he thought about them at all. In his heart of hearts, he considered slavery a sin, racisms like Germany's or South Africa's an offense to the faith, and he taught me as much in occasional pronouncements on Southern history over homework assignments. "There is no justification for what we did to the Negro. It was an evil thing and we were wrong." Nevertheless, the work of the Lord lay elsewhere. "Be faithful in church attendance, for your presence can, if nothing else, show that you are on God's side when the doors of the Church are opened," he advised in the church bulletin. Of course, packing the pews is one of any minister's fantasies—there's always the wish to grow, grow, grow. But the daily installments of Mississippi burning, the crushing poverty of the town's Negro inhabitants, the rituals of white supremacy, the smell of terror pervading the streets like Masonite's stench, did not figure into his sermons or in our dinner-table conversations or in the talk of the church. These were, to a good Baptist preacher like him, finally matters of politics, having little or nothing to do with the spiritual geography of a pilgrim's journey to paradise. Unwanted annoyances? Yes. Sad evidences of our human failings? Certainly. But all of these would be rectified in some eschatological future—"when we all get to Heaven, what a day of rejoicing that will be."[3]

Like many Christians then and now, Reverend Marsh's Christianity rightly emphasized personal piety but failed to embrace the social concern that should emanate from a kingdom perspective. He believed Christianity largely consisted in keeping one's soul pure by avoiding alcohol, drugs, and sexual impurity, and by helping others to keep their souls pure too. There was little "now" of the kingdom for Reverend Marsh, apart from the saving of souls.

Indeed, for many Christians James 1:27 says, "Religion that God our Father accepts as pure and faultless is this: . . . to keep oneself from being polluted by the world." Somehow, we often overlook the phrase that pure and faultless religion includes "look[ing] after orphans and widows in their distress."

While Reverend Marsh preached personal piety and the hope of heaven, African Americans were being lynched in Mississippi through the plotting of Sam Bowers. Less dramatic but even more pervasive was the entire social, political, and economic system designed to keep African Americans in their place. What would King Jesus do in this situation? Would He simply evangelize the African Americans, saying, "I have heard your cries for help, but your earthly plight is of no concern to Me. Believe in Me, and I will transport your soul to heaven someday. In the meantime, abstain from alcohol, drugs, and sexual impurity"? Is this how Jesus responded to the blind beggar who pleaded for mercy?

Reverend Marsh was under enormous pressure. If he spoke out against the Ku Klux Klan, he rightly feared that he would lose his job and that his family would be in danger of physical harm. Moreover, his theological lenses were more attuned to issues of personal piety than to "seeking justice and encouraging the oppressed" (Isa. 1:17). For all of these reasons, Reverend Marsh focused his attention and energies, not on fighting the Ku Klux Klan, but on the lack of personal piety and unbelief of some of the civil rights workers. This culminated in his writing a famous sermon, "The Sorrow of Selma," in which he lambasted the civil rights workers, calling them "unbathed beatniks," "immoral kooks," and "sign-carrying degenerates" who were hypocrites for not believing in God.[4]

In one sense, Reverend Marsh was right. Many of the civil rights protestors longed for the peace, justice, and righteousness of the kingdom, but they did not want to bend the knee to the King Himself, which is a prerequisite for enjoying the full benefits of the kingdom. In contrast, Reverend Marsh embraced King Jesus, but he did not understand the fullness of Christ's kingdom and its implications for the injustices in his community. Both Reverend Marsh and the civil rights workers were wrong, but in different ways. Reverend Marsh sought the King without the kingdom. The civil rights workers sought the kingdom without the King. The church needs a Christ-centered, fully orbed, kingdom perspective to correctly answer the question: "What would Jesus do?"

What Is the Task of the Church?

The task of God's people is rooted in Christ's mission. Simply stated, Jesus preached the good news of the kingdom in word and in deed, so the church must do the same. And as we have seen, Jesus particularly delighted in spreading the good news among the hurting, the weak, and the poor. Hence, it is not surprising that throughout history God's people have been commanded to follow their King's footsteps into places of brokenness.

In the Old Testament, God's chosen people, the nation of Israel, were to point forward to the coming King by foreshadowing what He would be like (Matt. 5:17; John 5:37–39, 45–46; Col. 2:16–17). Israel was to be a sneak preview of the coming attraction: King Jesus. Like any sneak preview, Israel was to give viewers an idea of what the main event would be like and to make viewers want to see the main event. When people looked at Israel, they were supposed to say to themselves, "Wow! These people are really different. I can't wait to meet their King. He must really be something special." Hence, since King Jesus would bring good news for the poor, it is not surprising that God wanted Israel to care for the poor as well.

In fact, God gave Moses numerous commands instructing Israel to care for the poor. The Sabbath guaranteed a day of rest for the slave and alien (Ex. 23:10–12). The Sabbath year canceled debts for Israelites, allowed the poor to glean from the fields, and set slaves free as well as equipping the slaves to be productive (Deut. 15:1–18). The Jubilee year emphasized liberty; it released slaves and returned land to its original owners (Lev. 25:8–55). Other laws about debt, tithing, and gleaning ensured that the poor would be cared for each day of the year (Lev. 25:35–38; Deut. 14:28–29; Lev. 19:9–10). The commands were so extensive that they were designed to achieve the ultimate goal of eradicating poverty among God's people: "There should be no poor among you," God declared (Deut. 15:4).

Unfortunately, Israel did not fulfill its task. She was a lousy sneak preview of the coming attraction, and God sent His chosen people into exile as a result. For what specific sins was Israel sent into captivity? Consider the following excerpts from passages in Isaiah in which God is indicting Israel for her sins and promising to send her into exile. What do you notice as you read these passages?

> Hear the word of the Lord, you rulers of Sodom; listen to the law of our God, you people of Gomorrah! "The multitude of your sacrifices—what are they to me?" says the Lord. "I have more than enough of burnt offerings, of rams and the fat of fattened animals; I have no pleasure in the blood of bulls and lambs and goats. When you come to appear before me, who has asked this of you, this trampling of my courts? Stop bringing meaningless offerings! Your incense is detestable to me. New Moons, Sabbaths, and convocations—I cannot bear your evil assemblies. . . . Stop doing wrong, learn to do right! Seek justice, encourage the oppressed. Defend the cause of the fatherless, plead the case of the widow. *(Isa. 1:10–13, 16b–17)*

Shout it aloud, do not hold back. Raise your voice like a trumpet. Declare to my people their rebellion and to the house of Jacob their sins. For day after day they seek me out; they seem eager to know my ways, as if they were a nation that does what is right and has not forsaken the commands of its God. They ask me for just decisions and seem eager for God to come near them. "Why have we fasted," they say, "and you have not seen it? Why have we humbled ourselves, and you have not noticed?" . . . Is this the kind of fast I have chosen, only a day for a man to humble himself? Is it only for bowing one's head like a reed and for lying on sackcloth and ashes? Is that what you call a fast, a day acceptable to the Lord? Is not this the kind of fasting I have chosen: to loose the chains of injustice and untie the cords of the yoke, to set the oppressed free and break every yoke? Is it not to share your food with the hungry and to provide the poor wanderer with shelter—when you see the naked, to clothe him, and not to turn away from your own flesh and blood? Then your light will break forth like the dawn, and your healing will quickly appear; then your righteousness will go before you, and the glory of the Lord will be your rear guard. Then you will call, and the Lord will answer; you will cry for help, and he will say: Here am I. If you do away with the yoke of oppression, with the pointing finger and malicious talk, and if you spend yourselves in behalf of the hungry and satisfy the needs of the oppressed, then your light will rise in the darkness, and your night will become like the noonday. (*Isa. 58:1–3, 5–10*)

Why was Israel sent into captivity? Many of us have a picture in our minds of the Israelites getting out of bed every morning and running off to the nearest shrine to worship idols. Indeed, numerous passages in the Old Testament indicate that idolatry was a problem in Israel. But these passages give a broader picture. Here Israel appears to be characterized by personal piety and the outward expressions of formal religion: worshiping, offering sacrifices, celebrating religious holidays, fasting, and praying. Translate this into the modern era, and we might say these folks were faithfully going to church each Sunday, attending midweek prayer meeting, going on the annual church retreat, and singing contemporary praise music. But God was disgusted with them, going so far as to call them "Sodom and Gomorrah"!

Why was God so displeased? Both passages emphasize that God was furious over Israel's failure to care for the poor and the oppressed. He wanted His people to "loose the chains of injustice," and not just go to church on Sunday. He wanted His people to "clothe the naked," and not just attend midweek prayer meeting. He wanted His people to "spend themselves on behalf of the hungry," and not just sing praise music.

Personal piety and formal worship are essential to the Christian life, but they must lead to lives that "act justly and love mercy" (Mic. 6:8).

In the New Testament, God's people, the church, are more than just a sneak preview of King Jesus. The church is the body, bride, and very fullness of Jesus Christ (Eph. 1:18–23; 4:7–13; 5:32). When people look at the church, they should see the very embodiment of Jesus! When people look at the church, they should see the One who declared—in word and in deed to the leper, the lame, and the poor—that His kingdom is bringing healing to every speck of the universe.

In fact, we see this from the very start of the church's ministry. When Jesus sent out His twelve disciples for the first time, we read, "He sent them out to preach the kingdom of God and to heal the sick" (Luke 9:2). Later, Jesus sent out seventy-two others, commanding them, "Heal the sick who are there and tell them, 'The kingdom of God is near you'" (Luke 10:9). The message was the kingdom of God, and it was to be communicated in both word and deed.

And in the very first passage concerning the gathering of the church, we read, "There were no needy persons among them" (Acts 4:34). Theologian Dennis Johnson explains that Luke, the author of Acts, is intentionally repeating the language we saw earlier in Deuteronomy 15:4 in which God told Israel: "There should be no poor among you."[5] Luke is indicating that while Israel had failed to care for the poor and was sent into captivity, God's people have been restored and are now embodying King Jesus and His kingdom, a kingdom in which there is no poverty (Rev. 21:1–4). Indeed, throughout the New Testament, care of the poor is a vital concern of the church (Matt. 25:31–46; Acts 6:1–7; Gal. 2:1–10; 6:10; James 1:27). Perhaps no passage states it more succinctly than 1 John 3:16–18:

> This is how we know what love is: Jesus Christ laid down his life for us. And we ought to lay down our lives for our brothers. If anyone has material possessions and sees his brother in need but has no pity on him, how can the love of God be in him? Dear children, let us not love with words or tongue but with actions and in truth.

The Bible's teachings should cut to the heart of North American Christians. By any measure, we are the richest people ever to walk on planet Earth. Furthermore, at no time in history has there ever been greater economic disparity in the world than at present.

Economic historians have found that for most of human history there was little economic growth and relatively low economic inequality. As a result, by the year 1820, after thousands of years of human development, the average income per person in the richest countries was only about four times higher than the average income per person in the poorest countries.[6] Then the Industrial Revolution hit, causing unprecedented economic growth in a handful of countries but leaving the rest of the world behind. As a result, while the average American lives on more than ninety dollars per day,[7] approximately one billion people live on less than one dollar per day and 2.6 billion—40 percent of the world's population—live on less than two dollars per day.[8] If God's people in both the Old and New Testaments were to have a concern for the poor during eras of relative economic equality, what are we to conclude about God's desire for the North American church today? "If anyone has material possessions and sees his brother in need but has no pity on him, how can the love of God be in him?"

What is the task of the church? We are to embody Jesus Christ by doing what He did and what He continues to do through us: declare—using both words and deeds—that Jesus is the King of kings and Lord of lords who is bringing in a kingdom of righteousness, justice, and peace. And the church needs to do this where Jesus did it, among the blind, the lame, the sick and outcast, and the poor.

AN ARMY OF OUTCASTS

Given the focus of Jesus' ministry, carried on through His body, it is not surprising that James makes the following observation about the early church: "Listen, my dear brothers: Has not God chosen those who are poor in the eyes of the world to be rich in faith and to inherit the kingdom he promised those who love him?" (James 2:5). Similarly, Paul drives this point home in his letter to the very unlovely Corinthian church when he says:

Brothers, think of what you were when you were called. Not many of you were wise by human standards; not many were influential; not many were of noble birth. But God chose the foolish things of the world to shame the wise; God chose the weak things of the world to shame the strong. He chose the lowly things of this world and the despised things—and the things that are not—to nullify the things that are, so that no one may boast before him. *(1 Cor. 1:26–29)*

Commenting on these passages, Mark Gornik, a theologian, pastor, and community developer in the United States, says, "Here then from both James and Paul is a central witness drawn from all of Scripture: God has sovereignly chosen to work in the world by beginning with the weak who are on the 'outside,' not the powerful who are on the 'inside.'"[9]

The claim here is not that the poor are inherently more righteous or sanctified than the rich. There is no place in the Bible that indicates that poverty is a desirable state or that material things are evil. In fact, wealth is viewed as a gift from God. The point is simply that, for His own glory, God has chosen to reveal His kingdom in the place where the world, in all of its pride, would least expect it, among the foolish, the weak, the lowly, and the despised.

It is strange indeed to place the poor at the center of a strategy for expanding a kingdom, but history indicates that this unconventional strategy has actually been quite successful. Sociologist Rodney Stark documents that the early church's engagement with suffering people was crucial to its explosive growth. Cities in the Roman Empire were characterized by poor sanitation, contaminated water, high population densities, open sewers, filthy streets, unbelievable stench, rampant crime, collapsing buildings, and frequent illnesses and plagues. "Life expectancy at birth was less than thirty years—and probably substantially less."[10] The only way for cities to avoid complete depopulation from mortality was for there to be a constant influx of immigrants, a very fluid situation that contributed to urban chaos, deviant behavior, and social instability.

Rather than fleeing these urban cesspools, the early church found its niche there. Stark explains that the Christian concept of self-sacrificial love of others, emanating from God's love for them, was a revolutionary concept to the pagan mind, which viewed the extension of mercy as an emotional act to be avoided by rational people. Hence, paganism provided no ethical foundation to justify caring for the sick and the destitute who were being trampled by the teeming urban masses. In contrast, Stark notes:

Christianity revitalized life in Greco-Roman cities by providing new norms and new kinds of social relationships able to cope with many urgent urban problems. To cities filled with the homeless and impoverished, Christianity offered charity as well as hope. To cities filled with newcomers and strangers, Christianity offered an immediate basis for attachments. To cities filled with orphans and widows, Christianity provided a new and expanded sense of family. To cities torn by violence and ethnic strife, Christianity offered a new basis for social solidarity. And to cities faced with epidemics, fires, and earthquakes, Christianity offered effective nursing services.[11]

God's kingdom strategy of ministering to and among the suffering was so powerful that other kings took note. In the fourth century AD, the Roman Emperor Julian tried to launch pagan charities to compete with the highly successful Christian charities that were attracting so many converts. Writing to a pagan priest, Julian complained, "The impious Galileans [i.e., the Christians] support not only their poor, but ours as well, everyone can see that our people lack aid from us."[12]

As Christianity expanded across the Roman world, the urban poor were on center stage of the drama. And the same is true today. Historian Philip Jenkins documents that Christianity is experiencing explosive growth in Africa, Latin America, and parts of Asia, regions of the world often called the "Majority World." For example, by 2025, in terms of numbers of adherents, Africa will have replaced Europe and the United States as the center of Christianity. By 2050, Uganda alone is expected to have more Christians than the largest four or five European nations combined. And like the early church, the growth in the church in the Majority World is taking place primarily with the poor on center stage. Jenkins observes: "The most successful new denominations target their message very directly at the have-nots, or rather, the have nothings."[13]

The Great Reversal

The idea that the church should be on the front lines of ministry to the poor is not a new concept in the North American context. As numerous scholars have noted, prior to the twentieth century, evangelical Christians played a large role in ministering to the physical and spiritual needs of the poor.[14] However, this all changed at the start of the twentieth century as evangelicals battled theological liberals over the fundamental tenets of Christianity. Evangelicals interpreted the rising social gospel movement, which seemed to equate all humanitarian efforts with bringing in Christ's kingdom, as part of the overall theological drift of the nation. As evangelicals tried to distance themselves from the social gospel movement, they ended up in large-scale retreat from the front lines of poverty alleviation. This shift away from the poor was so dramatic that church historians refer to the 1900–1930 era as the "Great Reversal" in the evangelical church's approach to social problems.[15]

It is important to note that the Great Reversal preceded the rise of the welfare state in America. Lyndon Johnson's War on Poverty did not occur until the 1960s, and even FDR's relatively modest New Deal policies were not launched until the 1930s. In short, the evangelical church's retreat from poverty alleviation was fundamentally due to shifts in theology and not—as many have asserted—to government programs that drove the church away from ministry to the poor. While the rise of government programs may have exacerbated the church's retreat, they were not the primary cause. Theology matters, and the church needs to rediscover a Christ-centered, fully orbed perspective of the kingdom.

An Important Task but Not an Exclusive Task

Although the Bible teaches that the local church must care for both the spiritual and physical needs of the poor, the Bible does not indicate that only the local church must care for the poor. There is evidence in Scripture that even in simple societies, individuals (Matt. 25:31–46), families (1 Tim. 5:8), and even governments (Dan. 4:27; Ps. 72) have responsibilities to the poor. Of course, in the highly complex societies of today, a wide range of parachurch ministries is capable of ministering to the poor as well. While the parachurch should never undertake tasks that are exclusively given to the church—for example administration of the sacraments—the Scriptures indicate that care of the poor is not an exclusive task of the church.

Hence, while the church must care for the poor, the Bible gives Christians some freedom in deciding the extent and manner in which the local church should do this, either directly or indirectly. Sometimes, the local church might feel it is wise to own and operate a ministry to the poor under the direct oversight of its leadership. In other situations, the local church might feel that it would be wiser to minister indirectly by starting or supporting a parachurch ministry or simply by encouraging individuals to reach out to the poor. Wisdom must be used to determine the best course of action in each situation. However, whenever God's people choose to minister outside of the direct oversight of the local church, they should always be seeking to partner with the local church, which has God-given authority over people's spiritual lives.

What Do Laurel, Mississippi, and Kigali, Rwanda, Have in Common?

I had just finished presenting much of the material in this chapter to an audience in Africa. A very tall and muscular African man in the audience approached me with tears in his eyes. He said, "This is not what the missionaries taught us. They told us just to do evangelism to save people's souls. But you are saying that Jesus cares about all of creation and that He wants us to minister to people's bodies and souls. I can't argue with the Bible passages you cited. But now how am I supposed to feel about the missionaries? They are my heroes." He was visibly shaken.

"I am not fit to carry the shoes of those missionaries," I assured him. "They packed their coffins in the ships that brought them to Africa, and many of them were martyred for the sake of the gospel. They are worthy of your highest admiration. But like all of us, they had some weaknesses."

Unfortunately, this man's experience was not unique. The Great Reversal has shaped the North American church's mission strategies since the late nineteenth century. Often lacking an appreciation of the comprehensive implications of the kingdom of God, many missionaries have focused on evangelism to save people's souls but have sometimes neglected to "make disciples of all nations." Converts need to be trained in a biblical worldview that understands the implications of Christ's lordship for all of life and that seeks to answer the question: If Christ is Lord of all, how do we do farming, business, government, family, art, etc., to the glory of God?

Failure to include this "all of life" element in the gospel has been devastating in the Majority World. There is perhaps no better example of this than Rwanda. Despite the fact that 80 percent of Rwandans claimed to be Christians, a bloody civil war erupted in 1994 in which the Hutu majority conducted a brutal genocide against the Tutsi minority and Hutu moderates. Over a three-month period, an estimated 800,000 people were slaughtered, the vast majority of them Tutsis.

How could this happen? In their book *Changing the Mind of Missions: Where Have We Gone Wrong?* missiologists James Engle and William Dyrness explain that the answer lies in the Rwandan church's failure to apply a biblical world-view, a kingdom perspective, to all of life. For most Rwandans, Christianity was "little more than a superficial, privatized veneer on a secular lifestyle characterized by animistic values and longstanding tribal hatred and warfare. . . . The church was silent on such critical life-and-death issues as the dignity and worth of each person made in the image of God."[16] In other words, the church in Rwanda lacked a Christ-centered, fully orbed kingdom perspective and hence was not equipped to fulfill the Great Commission by "discipling the nation."

So what do Laurel, Mississippi and Kigali, Rwanda have in common? Two things.

First, they both had churches that did not fully understand the implications of why Jesus came to earth. As a result, what was taught from the pulpit on Sunday morning didn't have the impact that the gospel should have had on people's lives from Monday through Saturday.

Second, despite the failures of His people, King Jesus brought His healing to the churches in both places. Over time, Reverend Marsh came to a fuller understanding of the implications of the gospel, eventually preaching a sermon entitled "Amazing Grace for Every Race" and taking a public stand against racism. And today, churches in Rwanda are helping the Hutus and the Tutsis to reconcile with one another. The healing of the kingdom cannot be stopped. And announcing this good news—this gospel of the kingdom—is the reason that Jesus Christ came to earth.

REFLECTION QUESTIONS AND EXERCISES

Please write responses to the following:

1. Reflect on your answer to the question at the start of this chapter: why did Jesus come to earth? How has your answer to this question shaped the way you live your life? How might you live a life that more fully reflects a Christ-centered, kingdom perspective? Be specific.

2. Did you know before reading this chapter that one of the reasons Israel was sent into captivity was her failure to care for the poor? If not, why not? What does the North American church's ignorance about the cause of the captivity suggest about the way it is reading Scripture?

3. Reflect on how your church answers the question: what is the primary task of the church? Your church's answer to this question might not be explicit. Hence, you might have to discern your church's implicit answer to this question by thinking about the messages from the pulpit, the types of ministries pursued, and the way those ministries are conducted. How might your church more fully reflect a Christ-centered, kingdom theology in its ministries? Be specific.

4. When poor people look at your church, in what ways do they see the embodiment of Jesus Christ and the comprehensive healing of His kingdom? What else could your church be doing?

5. List three specific things you will try to do as a result of this chapter. Pray for God to give you the strength to be faithful in doing these things.

WHAT'S THE **PROBLEM?**

THE POOR SPEAK OUT ON POVERTY

At the end of World War II, the Allies established the World Bank to finance the rebuilding of war-torn Europe. The World Bank's efforts were remarkably successful, and the European economies experienced the fastest growth in their history. Given this success, the World Bank tried a similar approach to assisting low-income countries: lending them money on generous terms to promote economic growth and poverty reduction. The results were less than stellar. Pouring in capital had worked to rebuild countries like France, but it did little to help in places like India. On the surface the problems in both places looked the same—poverty and starvation, refugees, lack of infrastructure, inadequate social services, and anemic economies—but something was different about the Majority World.

Solving the problem of poverty continues to perplex the World Bank, which remains the premier public-sector institution trying to alleviate poverty in low-income countries. Hence, during the 1990s, after decades of very mixed results, the World Bank tried a new approach. It consulted with "the true poverty experts, the poor themselves,"[1] by asking more than sixty thousand poor people from sixty low-income countries the basic question: what is poverty? The results of this study have been published in a three-volume series of books called *Voices of the Poor*. Below is a small sample of the words that the poor used to describe their own situation:

> For a poor person everything is terrible—illness, humiliation, shame. We are cripples; we are afraid of everything; we depend on everyone. No one needs us. We are like garbage that everyone wants to get rid of.[2]
> — MOLDOVA

> When I don't have any [food to bring my family], I borrow, mainly from neighbors and friends. I feel ashamed standing before my children when I have nothing to help feed the family. I'm not well when I'm unemployed. It's terrible.[3]
> — GUINEA-BISSAU

> During the past two years we have not celebrated any holidays with others. We cannot afford to invite anyone to our house and we feel uncomfortable visiting others without bringing a present. The lack of contact leaves one depressed, creates a constant feeling of unhappiness, and a sense of low self-esteem.[4]
> — LATVIA

> When one is poor, she has no say in public, she feels inferior. She has no food, so there is famine in her house; no clothing, and no progress in her family.[5]
> — UGANDA

> [The poor have] a feeling of powerlessness and an inability to make them-selves heard.[6]
> — CAMEROON

> Your hunger is never satisfied, your thirst is never quenched; you can never sleep until you are no longer tired.[7]
> — SENEGAL

> If you are hungry, you will always be hungry; if you are poor, you will always be poor.[8]
> — VIETNAM

> What determines poverty or well-being? The indigenous people's destiny is to be poor.[9]
> — ECUADOR

What one shouldn't lack is the sheep, what one cannot live without is food.[10]
— CHINA

Please take a few minutes to list some key words or phrases that you see in the quotes listed above. Do you see any differences between how you described poverty at the start of this chapter and how the poor describe their own poverty? Is there anything that surprises you?

We have conducted the previous exercise in dozens of middle-to-upper-class, predominantly Caucasian, North American churches. In the vast majority of cases, these audiences describe poverty differently than the poor in low-income countries do. While poor people mention having a lack of material things, they tend to describe their condition in far more psychological and social terms than our North American audiences. Poor people typically talk in terms of shame, inferiority, powerlessness, humiliation, fear, hopelessness, depression, social isolation, and voicelessness. North American audiences tend to emphasize a lack of material things such as food, money, clean water, medicine, housing, etc. As will be discussed further below, this mismatch between many outsiders' perceptions of poverty and the perceptions of poor people themselves can have devastating consequences for poverty-alleviation efforts.

How do the poor in North America describe their own poverty? While there do not appear to be any comparable studies to the World Bank's survey, many observers have noted similar features of poverty in the North American context. For example, consider Cornel West, an African-American scholar, as he summarizes what many are now saying about ghetto poverty[11] in America:

> The most basic issue now facing black America [is]: *the nihilistic threat to its very existence.* This threat is not simply a matter of relative economic deprivation and political powerlessness—though economic well-being and political clout are requisites for meaningful progress. It is primarily a question of speaking to the profound sense of psychological depression, personal worthlessness, and social despair so widespread in black America.[12]

Similar to the Majority World, while there is a material dimension to poverty in the African-American ghetto, there is also a loss of meaning, purpose, and hope that plays a major role in the poverty in North America. The problem goes well beyond the material dimension, so the solutions must go beyond the material as well.

THE DISTINCTION IS MORE THAN ACADEMIC

Defining poverty is not simply an academic exercise, for the way we define poverty—either implicitly or explicitly—plays a major role in determining the solutions we use in our attempts to alleviate that poverty.

When a sick person goes to the doctor, the doctor could make two crucial mistakes: (1) Treating symptoms instead of the underlying illness; (2) Misdiagnosing the underlying illness and prescribing the wrong medicine. Either one of these mistakes will result in the patient not getting better and possibly getting worse. The same is true when we work with poor people. If we treat only the symptoms or if we misdiagnose the underlying problem, we will not improve their situation, and we might actually make their lives worse. And as we shall see later, we might hurt ourselves in the process.

Table 2.1 illustrates how different diagnoses of the causes of poverty lead to different poverty-alleviation strategies. For example, during the initial decade following World War II, the World Bank believed the cause of poverty was primarily a lack of material resources—the last row of table 2.1—so it poured money into Europe and the Majority World. The strategy worked in the former but not in the latter. Why? The fundamental problem in the Majority World was not a lack of material resources. The World Bank misdiagnosed the disease, and it applied the wrong medicine.

If We Believe the Primary Cause of Poverty Is . . .	Then We Will Primarily Try to . . .
A Lack of Knowledge	Educate the Poor
Oppression by Powerful People	Work for Social Justice
The Personal Sins of the Poor	Evangelize and Disciple the Poor
A Lack of Material Resources	Give Material Resources to the Poor

TABLE 2.1

Similarly, consider the familiar case of the person who comes to your church asking for help with paying an electric bill. On the surface, it appears that this person's problem is the last row of table 2.1, a lack of material resources, and many churches respond by giving this person enough money to pay the electric bill. But what if this person's fundamental problem is not having the self-discipline to keep a stable job? Simply giving this person money is treating the symptoms rather than the underlying disease and will enable him to continue with his lack of self-discipline. In this case, the gift of the money does more harm than good, and it would be better not to do anything at all than to give this handout. Really! Instead, a better—and far more costly—solution would be for your church to develop a relationship with this person, a relationship that says, "We are here to walk with you and to help you use your gifts and abilities to avoid being in this situation in the future. Let us into your life and let us work with you to determine the reason you are in this predicament."

Unfortunately, the symptoms of poor people largely look the same around the world: they do not have "sufficient" material things.[13] However, the underlying diseases behind those symptoms are not always very apparent and can differ from person to person. A trial-and-error process may be necessary before a proper diagnosis can be reached. Like all of us, poor people are not fully aware of all that is affecting their lives, and like all of us, poor people are not always completely honest with themselves or with others. And even after a sound diagnosis is made, it may take years to help people to overcome their problems. There will likely be lots of ups and downs in the relationship. It all sounds very time-consuming, and it is. "If you *spend yourselves* in behalf of the hungry and satisfy the needs of the oppressed, then your light will rise in the darkness, and your night will become like the noonday" (Isa. 58:10, italics added). "Spending yourself" often involves more than giving a handout to a poor person, a handout that may very well do more harm than good.

A sound diagnosis is absolutely critical for helping poor people without hurting them. But how can we diagnose such a complex disease? Divine wisdom is necessary. Although the Bible is not a textbook on poverty alleviation, it does give us valuable insights into the nature of human beings, of history, of culture, and of God to point us in the right direction. Hence, in the remainder of this chapter and the next, we root our understanding of poverty and its alleviation in the Bible's grand narrative: creation, the fall, and redemption. We recognize that some of the material in these two chapters is a bit abstract. Hang in there! It won't hurt too much. By design, the book moves from the theoretical to the applied. We need to establish a solid theoretical foundation if we want to build successful poverty-alleviation efforts.

POVERTY: A BIBLICAL FRAMEWORK

In the Beginning

Bryant Myers, a leading Christian development thinker, argues that in order to diagnose the disease of poverty correctly, we must consider the fundamental nature of reality, starting with the Creator of that reality. Myers notes that the triune God is inherently a relational being, existing as three-in-one from all eternity. Being made in God's image, human beings are inherently relational as well. Myers explains that before the fall, God established four foundational relationships for each person: a relationship with God, with self, with others, and with the rest of creation (see figure 2.1).[14] These relationships are the

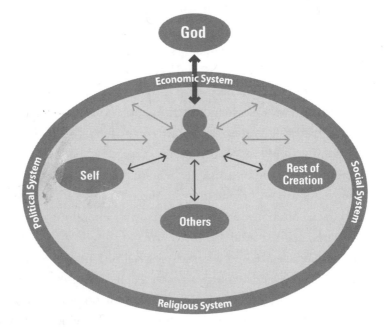

FIGURE 2.1

Adapted from Bryant L. Myers, *Walking with the Poor: Principles and Practices of Transformational Development* (Maryknoll, N.Y.: Orbis Books, 1999), 27.

building blocks for all of life. When they are functioning properly, humans experience the fullness of life that God intended, because we are being what God created us to be. *In particular for our purposes, when these relationships are functioning properly, people are able to fulfill their callings of glorifying God by working and supporting themselves and their families with the fruit of that work.*

Note that human life is not all up for grabs! God designed humans to be a certain thing and to operate in a certain way in all of these relationships:

- **RELATIONSHIP WITH GOD:** This is our primary relationship, the other three relationships flowing out of this one. The Westminster Shorter Catechism teaches that human beings' primary purpose is "to glorify God and to enjoy Him forever." This is our *calling*, the ultimate reason for which we were created. We were created to serve and give praise to our Creator through our thoughts, words, and actions. When we do this, we experience the presence of God as our heavenly Father and live in a joyful, intimate relationship with Him as His children.

- **RELATIONSHIP WITH SELF:** People are uniquely created in the image of God and thus have inherent worth and dignity. While we must remember that we are not God, we have the high *calling* of reflecting God's being, making us superior to the rest of creation.

- **RELATIONSHIP WITH OTHERS:** God created us to live in loving relationship with one another. We are not islands! We are made to know one another, to love one another, and to encourage one another to use the gifts God has given to each of us to fulfill our *callings*.

- **RELATIONSHIP WITH THE REST OF CREATION:** The "cultural mandate" of Genesis 1:28–30 teaches that God created us to be stewards, people who understand, protect, subdue, and manage the world that God has created in order to preserve it and to produce bounty. Note that while God made the world "perfect," He left it "incomplete." This means that while the world was created to be without defect, God *called* humans to interact with creation, to make possibilities into realities, and to be able to sustain ourselves via the fruits of our stewardship.

The arrows pointing from human beings to the surrounding ovals in figure 2.1 highlight that these foundational relationships are the building blocks for all of life. The way that humans create culture—including economic, social, political, and religious systems—reflect our basic commitments to God, self, others, and the rest of creation. For example, because William Wilberforce viewed "others" as being created in the image of God, he devoted his life as a politician to banning the slave trade in England at the start of the nineteenth century. Wilberforce shaped the political system in a way that reflected his fundamental commitment to love other human beings, including Africans. And the same is true of all other aspects of culture. The systems that humans create, including both formal institutions (governments, schools, businesses, churches, etc.) and cultural norms (gender roles, attitudes toward time and work, understandings of authority, etc.), reflect the nature of our foundational relationships to God, self, others, and the rest of creation.

But culture reflects more than just the expression of human effort. Consider again Colossians 1:16–17: "For by him [Jesus] *all things* were created; things in heaven and on earth, visible and invisible, whether thrones or powers or rulers or authorities; *all things* were created by him and for him. He is before all things, and in him all things hold together" (italics added). Note in this passage that Christ is the Creator and Sustainer of more than just the material world. His creative and sustaining hand extends to "all things." This sustenance is continuing, even in a fallen world. Hence, Christ is actively engaged in sustaining the economic, social, political, and religious systems in which humans live. There is certainly real mystery here, but the central point of Scripture is clear: as humans engage in cultural activity, they are unpacking a creation that Christ created, sustains, and as we shall see later, redeems.

As figure 2.1 illustrates, the arrows connecting the individual to the systems point both ways. *People affect systems, and systems affect people.* For example, much of our lives are spent working in organizations that play a huge role in shaping our self-images, our relationships to coworkers, the means by which we steward creation, and the setting in which we respond to God and in which He responds to us. And these organizations operate in the context of local, national, and global systems characterized by rapid flows of information, capital, and technology, which greatly impact the scope and nature of their operations.

More than ever before, the organizations in which we work are shaped by events on the other side of the world. For example, as China's economic policies emerge, the entire global economy is affected. Hence, the context in which we relate to God, self, others, and the rest of creation is influenced by actions of the Chinese government!

What's This Stuff Good for Anyway?

The importance of the doctrine of creation will become more evident as the book proceeds, but let's look at a few implications right away:

- The four key relationships highlight the fact that human beings are multi-faceted, implying that poverty-alleviation efforts should be multifaceted as well. If we reduce human beings to being simply physical—as Western thought is prone to do—our poverty-alleviation efforts will tend to focus on material solutions. But if we remember that humans are spiritual, social, psychological, and physical beings, our poverty-alleviation efforts will be more holistic in their design and execution.

- Dirt matters, as do giraffes, wells, families, schools, music, crops, governments, and businesses. We must engage with the entire creation, including culture, for our Creator is deeply engaged with it.

- Our basic predisposition toward poor communities—including their people, organizations, institutions, and culture—should include the notion that they are part of the good world that Christ created and is sustaining. They are not *just* filth and rubble. (If you are wondering about the effects of sin, hang on until the next section.)

- We are not bringing Christ to poor communities. He has been active in these communities since the creation of the world, sustaining them "by his powerful word" (Heb. 1:3). Hence, a significant part of working in poor communities involves discovering and appreciating what God has been doing there for a long time! This should give us a sense of humility and awe as we enter poor communities, for part of what we see there reflects the very hand of God. Of course, the residents of these communities may not recognize that God has been at work. In fact, they might not even know who God is. So part of our task may include introducing the community to who God is and to helping them to appreciate all that He has been doing for them since the creation of the world. We will return to this issue in chapter 6.

The Fall Really Happened

Of course, the grand story of Scripture does not end with creation. Adam and Eve disobeyed God, and their hearts were darkened. The Genesis account records that all four of Adam and Eve's relationships immediately became distorted: their relationship with God was damaged, as their intimacy with Him was replaced with fear; their relationship with self was marred, as Adam and Eve developed a sense of shame; their relationship with others was broken, as Adam quickly blamed Eve for their sin; and their relationship with the rest of creation became distorted, as God cursed the ground and the childbearing process.

Furthermore, as figure 2.2 illustrates, because the four relationships are the building blocks for all human activity, the effects of the fall are manifested in the economic, social, religious, and political systems that humans have created throughout history. For example, not loving "others" as they should have, politicians have passed laws institutionalizing slavery and racial discrimination. And not caring for "the rest of creation," at times shareholders have allowed their companies to pollute the environment. The systems are broken,

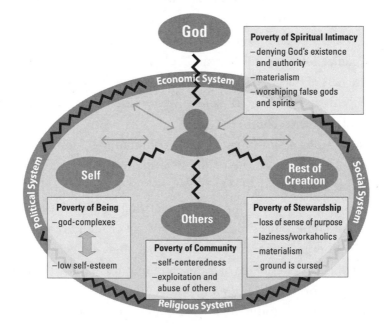

FIGURE 2.2

Adapted from Bryant L. Myers, *Walking with the Poor: Principles and Practices of Transformational Development* (Maryknoll, N.Y.: Orbis Books, 1999), 27.

reflecting humans' broken relationships. Moreover, in addition to sinful human natures and behaviors, Satan and his legions are at work, wreaking havoc
in both the individuals and systems.

These considerations lead to Myers's description of the fundamental nature of poverty:[15]

> **Poverty is the result of relationships that do not work, that are
> not just, that are not for life, that are not harmonious or enjoyable.
> Poverty is the absence of shalom in all its meanings.**

Although Myers's definition correctly points to the all-encompassing effects
of the fall, it is important to remember that neither humans nor the systems
they create are as bad as they could possibly be. Christ continues to "hold all
things together" and to "sustain all things by his powerful word." Hence, while
the good creation—including both individuals and the systems they create—
is deeply distorted, it retains some of its inherent goodness. Flowers are still
pretty. A baby's smile brings joy to all who see it. People are often kind to one
another. Governments build roads that enable us to get around better. Companies often pay their workers decent wages. And both poor individuals and
communities continue to exhibit God-given gifts and assets.

WHO ARE THE POOR?

Stop and think: If poverty is rooted in the brokenness of the foundational
relationships, then who are the poor?

Due to the comprehensive nature of the fall, every human being is poor in
the sense of not experiencing these four relationships in the way that God intended. As figure 2.2 illustrates, every human being is suffering from a poverty
of spiritual intimacy, a poverty of being, a poverty of community, and a poverty
of stewardship. We are all simply incapable of being what God created us to be
and are unable to experience the fullness of joy that God designed for these
relationships. Every minute since the fall, each human being is the proverbial
"square peg in a round hole." We don't fit right because we were shaped for
something else.

For some people the brokenness in these foundational relationships results in material poverty, that is their not having sufficient money to provide for the basic physical needs of themselves and their families. For example, consider Mary, who lives in a slum in western Kenya. As a female in a male-dominated society, Mary has been subjected to polygamy, to regular physical and verbal abuse from her husband, to fewer years of schooling than males, and to an entire cultural system that tells her that she is inferior. As a result, Mary has a poverty of being and lacks the confidence to look for a job, leading her into material poverty.

Desperate, Mary decides to be self-employed, but needs a loan to get her business started. Unfortunately, her poverty of community rears its ugly head, as the local loan shark exploits Mary, demanding an interest rate of 300 percent on her loan of twenty-five dollars, contributing to Mary's material poverty. Having no other options, Mary borrows from the loan shark and starts a business of selling homemade charcoal in the local market, along with hundreds of others just like her. The market is glutted with charcoal sellers, which keeps the prices very low. But it never even occurs to Mary to sell something else, because she does not understand that she has been given the creativity and capacity to have dominion over creation. In other words, her poverty of stewardship locks her into an unprofitable business, further contributing to her material poverty. Frustrated by her entire situation, Mary goes to the traditional healer (witch doctor) for help, a manifestation of her poverty of spiritual intimacy with the true God. The healer tells Mary that her difficult life is a result of angry ancestral spirits that need to be appeased through the sacrificing of a bull, a sacrifice that costs Mary a substantial amount of money and further contributes to her material poverty. Mary is suffering from not having sufficient income, but her problems cannot be solved by giving her more money or other material resources, for such things are insufficient to heal the brokenness of her four foundational relationships.

Mary's brokenness manifested itself in material poverty, but for other people the effects of these broken relationships are manifested in different ways. For example, for most of my life I have struggled with workaholic tendencies, reflecting a poverty of stewardship, a broken relationship with the rest of creation. Instead of seeing work as simply one of the arenas in which I am to glorify God, there are times in which I have made my work my god and have tried to find all of my meaning, purpose, and worth through being productive. This is not how God designed humans' relationship with the rest of creation to be. Of course, I am unlikely to experience material poverty, as my high level of productivity will usually put food on my table; however, at times my poverty of stewardship has had serious consequences, including strained relationships with family and friends, physical and emotional ailments resulting from stress, and spiritual weakness from inadequate time for a meaningful devotional life.

The fall really happened, and it is wreaking havoc in all of our lives. We are all broken, just in different ways.

WHEN HELPING HURTS

One of the major premises of this book is that *until we embrace our mutual brokenness, our work with low-income people is likely to do far more harm than good.* As discussed earlier, research from around the world has found that shame—a "poverty of being"—is a major part of the brokenness that low-income people experience in their relationship with themselves. Instead of seeing themselves as being created in the image of God, low-income people often feel they are inferior to others. This can paralyze the poor from taking initiative and from seizing opportunities to improve their situation, thereby locking them into material poverty.

At the same time, the economically rich—including most of the readers of this book—also suffer from a poverty of being. In particular, development practitioner Jayakumar Christian argues that the economically rich often have "god-complexes," a subtle and unconscious sense of superiority in which they believe that they have achieved their wealth through their own efforts and that they have been anointed to decide what is best for low-income people, whom they view as inferior to themselves.[16]

Few of us are conscious of having a god-complex, which is part of the problem. We are often deceived by Satan and by our sinful natures. For example, consider this: why do you want to help the poor? Really think about it. What truly motivates you? Do you really love poor people and want to serve them? Or do you have other motives? I confess to you that part of what motivates me to help the poor is my felt need to accomplish something worthwhile with my life, to be a person of significance, to feel like I have pursued a noble cause . . .

to be a bit like God. It makes me feel good to use my training in economics to "save" poor people. And in the process, I sometimes unintentionally reduce poor people to objects that I use to fulfill my own need to accomplish something. It is a very ugly truth, and it pains me to admit it, but "when I want to do good, evil is right there with me" (Rom. 7:21).

And now we have come to a very central point: *one of the biggest problems in many poverty-alleviation efforts is that their design and implementation exacerbates the poverty of being of the economically rich—their god-complexes—and the poverty of being of the economically poor—their feelings of inferiority and shame.* The way that we act toward the economically poor often communicates—albeit unintentionally—that we are superior and they are inferior. In the process we hurt the poor and ourselves. And here is the clincher: this dynamic is likely to be particularly strong whenever middle-to-upper-class, North American Christians try to help the poor, given these Christians' tendency toward a Western, materialistic perspective of the nature of poverty.

This point can be illustrated with the story of Creekside Community Church, a predominantly Caucasian congregation made up of young urban professionals in the downtown area of an American city. Being in the Christmas spirit, Creekside Community Church decided to reach out to the African-American residents of a nearby housing project, which was characterized by high rates of unemployment, domestic violence, drug and alcohol abuse, and teenage pregnancy. A number of the members of Creekside expressed some disdain for the project residents, and all of the members were fearful of venturing inside. But Pastor Johnson insisted that Jesus cared for the residents of this housing project and that Christmas was the perfect time to show His compassion.

But what could they do to help? Believing that poverty is primarily a lack of material resources—the last row in table 2.1—the members of Creekside Community Church decided to address this poverty by buying Christmas presents for the children in the housing project. Church members went door to door, singing Christmas carols and delivering wrapped toys to the children in each apartment. Although it was awkward at first, the members of Creekside were moved by the big smiles on the children's faces and were encouraged by the warm reception of the mothers. In fact, the congregation felt so good about the joy they had brought that they decided to expand this ministry, delivering baskets of candy at Easter and turkeys at Thanksgiving.

Unfortunately, after several years, Pastor Johnson noticed that he was struggling to find enough volunteers to deliver the gifts to the housing project. At the congregational meeting, he asked the members why their enthusiasm was waning, but it was difficult to get a clear answer. Finally, one member spoke up: "Pastor, we are tired of trying to help these people out. We have been bringing them things for several years now, but their situation never improves. They just sit there in the same situation year in and year out. Have you ever noticed that there are no men in the apartments when we deliver the toys? The residents are all unwed mothers who just keep having babies in order to collect bigger and bigger welfare checks. They don't deserve our help."

In reality, there was a different reason that there were few men in the apartments when the toys were delivered. Oftentimes, when the fathers of the children heard the Christmas carols outside their front doors and saw the presents for their kids through the peepholes, they were embarrassed and ran out the back doors of their apartments. For a host of reasons, low-income African-American males sometimes struggle to find and keep jobs. This often contributes to a deep sense of shame and inadequacy, both of which make it even more difficult to apply for jobs. The last thing these fathers needed was a group of middle-to-upper-class Caucasians providing Christmas presents for their children, presents that they themselves could not afford to buy. In trying to alleviate material poverty through the giving of these presents, Creekside Community Church increased these fathers' poverty of being. Ironically, this likely made the fathers even less able to apply for a job, thereby exacerbating the very material poverty that Creekside was trying to solve!

In addition to hurting the residents of the housing project, the members of Creekside Community Church hurt themselves. At first the members developed a subtle sense of pride that they were helping the project residents through their acts of kindness. Later, when they observed the residents' failure to improve their situations, the members' disdain for them increased. What is often called "compassion fatigue" then set in as the members became less willing to help the low-income residents. As a result, the poverty of being increased for the church members. Furthermore, the poverty of community increased for everyone involved, as the gulf between the church members and the housing project residents actually increased as a result of this project.

Our efforts to help the poor can hurt both them and ourselves. In fact, as this story illustrates, very often the North American church finds itself locked into the following equation:

Material Definition of Poverty	+	God-complexes of Materially Non-Poor	+	Feelings of Inferiority of Materially Poor	=	Harm to Both Materially Poor and Non-Poor

What can be done to break out of this equation? Changing the first term in this equation requires a revised understanding of the nature of poverty. North American Christians need to overcome the materialism of Western culture and see poverty in more relational terms. Changing the second term in this equation requires ongoing repentance. It requires North American Christians to understand our brokenness and to embrace the message of the cross in deep and profound ways, saying to ourselves every day: "I am not okay; and you are not okay; but Jesus can fix us both." And as we do this, God can use us to change the third term in this equation. By showing low-income people through our words, our actions, and most importantly our ears that they are people with unique gifts and abilities, we can be part of helping them to recover their sense of dignity, even as we recover from our sense of pride.

Repenting of the Health-and-Wealth Gospel

One Sunday I was walking with a staff member through one of Africa's largest slums, the massive Kibera slum of Nairobi, Kenya. The conditions were simply inhumane. People lived in shacks constructed out of cardboard boxes. Foul smells gushed out of open ditches carrying human and animal excrement. I had a hard time keeping my balance as I continually slipped on oozy brown substances that I hoped were mud but feared were something else. Children picked through garbage dumps looking for anything of value. As we walked deeper and deeper into the slum, my sense of despair increased. *This place is completely God-forsaken,* I thought to myself.

Then to my amazement, right there among the dung, I heard the sound of a familiar hymn. *There must be Western missionaries conducting an open-air ser-*

vice in here, I thought to myself. As we turned the corner, my eyes landed on the shack from which the music bellowed. Every Sunday, thirty slum dwellers crammed into this ten-by-twenty foot "sanctuary" to worship the God of Abraham, Isaac, and Jacob. The church was made out of cardboard boxes that had been opened up and stapled to studs. It wasn't pretty, but it was a church, a church made up of some of the poorest people on earth.

When we arrived at the church, I was immediately asked to preach the sermon. As a good Presbyterian, I quickly jotted down some notes about the sovereignty of God and was looking forward to teaching this congregation the historic doctrines of the Reformation. But before the sermon began, the service included a time of sharing and prayer. I listened as some of the poorest people on the planet cried out to God: "Jehovah Jireh, please heal my son, as he is going blind." "Merciful Lord, please protect me when I go home today, for my husband always beats me." "Sovereign King, please provide my children with enough food today, as they are hungry."

As I listened to these people praying to be able to live another day, I thought about my ample salary, my life insurance policy, my health insurance policy, my two cars, my house, etc. I realized that I do not really trust in God's sovereignty on a daily basis, as I have sufficient buffers in place to shield me from most economic shocks. I realized that when these folks pray the fourth petition of the Lord's prayer—*Give us this day our daily bread*—their minds do not wander as mine so often does. I realized that while I have sufficient education and training to deliver a sermon on God's sovereignty with no forewarning, these slum dwellers were trusting in God's sovereignty just to get them through the day. And I realized that these people had a far deeper intimacy with God than I probably will ever have in my entire life.

* * *

Surprisingly, as this story illustrates, for many of us North Americans the first step in overcoming our god-complexes is to repent of the health-and-wealth gospel. At its core, the health-and-wealth gospel teaches that God rewards increasing levels of faith with greater amounts of wealth. When stated this way, the health-and-wealth gospel is easy to reject on a host of biblical grounds. Take the case of the apostle Paul, for example. He had enormous faith and lived a godly life, but he was shipwrecked, beaten, stoned, naked, and poor.

Think about it. If anybody dares suggest to me that the poor are poor because they are less spiritual than the rest of us—which is what the health-and- wealth gospel teaches—I am quick to rebuke them. I immediately point out that the poor could be poor due to injustices committed against them. Yet, all of this notwithstanding, I was still amazed to see people in this Kenyan slum who were simultaneously so spiritually strong and so devastatingly poor. Right down there in the bowels of hell was this Kenyan church, filled with spiritual giants who were struggling just to eat every day. This shocked me. At some level I had implicitly assumed that my economic superiority goes hand in hand with my spiritual superiority. This is none other than the lie of the health-and-wealth gospel: spiritual maturity leads to financial prosperity.

The health-and-wealth gospel is just one aspect of my "god-complex," for there are all sorts of areas in which I need to embrace the message of the cross: "I stink, but God loves me anyway!" And without such repentance, my own arrogance is likely to increase the poverty of the materially poor people I encounter by confirming their feelings of shame and inferiority.

That day in the Kibera slum, God used the materially poor, people more visibly broken than I, to teach me about my own brokenness. They blessed me, even while I was trying to bless them.

One of These Things Is Not Like the Other

Although all human beings are poor in the sense that all are suffering from the effects of the fall on the four foundational relationships, it is not legitimate to conclude that there is nothing uniquely devastating about material poverty. Low-income people daily face a struggle to survive that creates feelings of helplessness, anxiety, suffocation, and desperation that are simply unparalleled in the lives of the rest of humanity.

Development expert Robert Chambers argues that the materially poor are trapped by multiple, interconnected factors—insufficient assets, vulnerability, powerlessness, isolation, and physical weakness—that ensnare them like bugs caught in a spider's web.[17] Imagine being caught in such a web. Every time you try to move, you just get more hung up on another strand. You think to yourself, *Maybe this time will be different,* so you try to make a change in your life. But immediately you find yourself even more entangled than before. After a while you come to believe that it is better to just lie still. This is miserable, but any further movement only brings even greater misery. You hate your situation, but you have no choice.

Most of the readers of this book do not lead this type of life. We believe that we have choices and that we can make changes, and in our situations, this is a correct assumption. According to Nobel Laureate Amartya Sen, it is this lack of freedom to be able to make meaningful choices—to have an ability to affect one's situation—that is the distinguishing feature of poverty.[18]

Similarly, while "material poverty" is rooted in the brokenness of the four foundational relationships—a brokenness we all experience in different ways—this does *not* mean that there is nothing unique about "the poor" in Scripture. Although there are places in the Bible in which the term "poor" is used generically to describe the general plight of humanity, there are a host of texts (see chapter 1) in which the term is referring very specifically to those who are economically destitute. We cannot let ourselves off the hook by saying to ourselves, "I am fulfilling the Bible's commands to help the poor by loving the wealthy lady next door with the troubled marriage." Yes, this lady is experiencing a "poverty of community," and it is good to help her. But this is not the type of person referred to in such passages as 1 John 3:17.

The economically poor are singled out in Scripture as being in a particularly desperate category and as needing very specific attention (Acts 6:1–7). The fact that all of humanity has some things in common with the materially poor does not negate their unique and overwhelming suffering nor the special place that they have in God's heart, as emphasized throughout the Old and New Testaments.

REFLECTION QUESTIONS AND EXERCISES

Please write responses to the following:

1. Reflect on your relationships with God, self, others, and the rest of creation. List specific things that you would like to see improved in your four key relationships.

2. Read Romans 5:6–11. To what extent do you embrace the message of the cross: God Almighty died for you while you were still His "enemy"? How worthy are you of God's love expressed through Jesus Christ?

3. In what ways do you suffer from a "god-complex," the belief that you are superior to others and are well-positioned to determine what is best for them? If you have this problem, what specific steps can you take to change this?

4. What really motivates you to want to help materially poor people?

5. Think about the approach of your church or your ministry to materially poor people. Is there any evidence of a god-complex?

6. Think back to a situation in which you have tried to minister to others. In what ways did your approach help both you and them to overcome a poverty of spiritual intimacy, a poverty of being, a poverty of community, and a poverty of stewardship? In what ways did your approach actually contribute to greater "poverty" in the four relationships for both you and them?

7. Now answer question 6 for your church by reflecting on the type of ministries that your church pursues and the manner in which it pursues them.

8. Think back to your answers to the question at the start of this chapter: *What is poverty?* Compare your answers to the answers that the poor themselves give. What differences do you see?

9. Do you have a "material definition of poverty"? If so, how has this influenced the way that you have approached ministry to the poor? What harm might this have done?

10. Are you or your church locked into the equation mentioned in this chapter (see p. 64)? If so, what steps can you take to break out of it?

INITIAL THOUGHTS

Please take a few minutes to write short answers to
the following questions:

1. What is poverty alleviation?

2. How do you define "success" in ministering to the materially poor?

CHAPTER

ARE WE **THERE** YET?

W e need to have a clear concept of "success" if we want to have any hope of getting there. Just as our diagnosis of the causes of poverty shapes the remedies we pursue, so too does our conception of the ultimate goal. Building on the concept of poverty as being rooted in the brokenness of human beings' four foundational relationships, this chapter explores what successful poverty alleviation entails and paves the way for the principles, applications, and methods to be discussed in the remainder of this book.

THE ENTRAPMENT OF ALISA COLLINS

During the 1990s, Alisa Collins and her children lived in one of America's most dangerous public housing projects in inner-city Chicago.[1] Alisa had become pregnant at the age of sixteen, had dropped out of high school, and had started collecting welfare checks. She had five children from three different fathers, none of whom helped with child rearing. With few skills, no husband, and limited social networks, Alisa struggled to raise her family in an environment characterized by widespread substance abuse, failing schools, high rates of unemployment, rampant violence, teenage pregnancy, and an absence of role models.

From time to time, Alisa tried to get a job, but a number of obstacles prevented her from finding and keeping regular work. First, there were simply not a lot of decent-paying jobs for high school dropouts living in ghettos. Second, the welfare system penalized Alisa for earning money, taking away benefits for every dollar she earned and for every asset she acquired. Third, Alisa found government vocational training and jobs assistance programs to be confusing and staffed by condescending bureaucrats. Fourth, Alisa had child-care issues that made it difficult to keep a job. Finally, Alisa felt inferior and inadequate. When she tried to get vocational training or a job and faced some obstacle, she quickly lost confidence and rapidly retreated into her comfort zone of public housing and welfare checks. Alisa felt trapped, and she and her family often talked about how they couldn't "get out" of the ghetto.

How can your church or ministry help to alleviate poverty for people like Alisa? What does success look like? There are no easy answers to these questions, but moving in the right direction involves exploring the rest of the grand narrative of the Bible. In the previous chapter we diagnosed the problem of poverty by examining the first two acts of the biblical drama: "creation" and "fall." We saw that humans were created to live in right relationship with God, self, others, and the rest of creation, and that the fall has broken these relationships for each of us. But there is good news, for the drama is not over. We still need to consider the remaining act in the story: "redemption."

THE KINGDOM THAT IS BOTH HERE AND STILL COMING

We saw in the previous chapter that poverty consists of broken relationships. Furthermore, we saw that the brokenness in these relationships is expressed not just at a personal level but also in the economic, political, social, and religious systems that humans create.

In this light, how can we alleviate Alisa's poverty? Consider again Colossians 1:19–20:

> For God was pleased to have all his fullness dwell in him [Jesus], and through him to reconcile to himself *all things*, whether things on earth or things in heaven, by making peace through his blood, shed on the cross. (italics added)

Reverend Marsh was wrong. Jesus is not just "beaming up" our souls out of planet Earth in Star Trek fashion; rather, Jesus is bringing reconciliation to every last speck of the universe, including both our foundational relationships and the systems that emanate from them. *Poverty is rooted in broken relationships, so the solution to poverty is rooted in the power of Jesus' death and resurrection to put all things into right relationship again.*

Of course, the full reconciliation of all things will not happen until the final coming of the kingdom, when there will be a new heaven and a new earth. Only then will every tear be wiped from our eyes (Rev. 21:4). There is real mystery concerning how much progress we can expect to see before Jesus comes again, and good people can disagree. Fortunately, what we are to do every day does not hinge on resolving this issue, for the task at hand is quite clear. The King of kings is ushering in a kingdom that will bring healing to every last speck of the cosmos. As His body, bride, and fullness, the church is to do what Jesus did: bear witness to the reality of that coming kingdom using both words and anticipatory deeds. We can then trust God to "establish the work of our hands" as He chooses (Ps. 90:17).

HOW SHOULD WE THEN ALLEVIATE?

Jesus' work focuses on "reconciliation," which means putting things back into right relationship again. The church must pursue reconciliation as well:

> All this is from God, who reconciled us to himself through Christ and gave us the ministry of reconciliation: that God was reconciling the world to himself in Christ, not counting men's sins against them. And he has committed to us the message of reconciliation. We are therefore Christ's ambassadors, as though God were making his appeal through us. We implore you on Christ's behalf: Be reconciled to God. *(2 Cor. 5:18–20)*

We are not the reconciler; Jesus is. However, we are His ambassadors, representing His kingdom and all that it entails to a broken world, which leads to the following definition of poverty alleviation:

> ### POVERTY ALLEVIATION
> Poverty alleviation is the ministry of reconciliation: moving people
> closer to glorifying God by living in right relationship with God,
> with self, with others, and with the rest of creation.

Reconciliation of relationships is the guiding compass for our poverty-alleviation efforts, profoundly shaping both the goals that we pursue and the methods we use.

The goal is *not* to make the materially poor all over the world into middle-to-upper-class North Americans, a group characterized by high rates of divorce, sexual addiction, substance abuse, and mental illness. Nor is the goal to make sure that the materially poor have enough money. Indeed, America's welfare system ensured that Alisa Collins and her family had more than enough money to survive, but they felt trapped. Rather, the goal is to restore people to a full expression of humanness, to being what God created us all to be, people who glorify God by living in right relationship with God, with self, with others, and with the rest of creation. One of the many manifestations of these relationships being reconciled is material poverty alleviation:

> ### MATERIAL POVERTY ALLEVIATION
> Material poverty alleviation is working to reconcile the four
> foundational relationships so that people can fulfill their callings
> of glorifying God by working and supporting themselves and
> their families with the fruit of that work.

There are two key things to note in this definition. First, material poverty alleviation involves more than ensuring that people have sufficient material things; rather, it involves the much harder task of empowering people to *earn* sufficient material things through their own labor, for in so doing we move people closer to being what God created them to be. (Of course, we recognize that this is impossible for some people because of disability or other factors.) Second, work is an act of worship. When people seek to fulfill their callings by glorifying God in their work, praising Him for their gifts and abilities, and seeing both their efforts and its products as an offering to Him, then work is an act of worship to God. On the other hand, when work is done to glorify oneself or merely to achieve more wealth, it becomes worship of false gods. How we work and for whom we work really matters.

Defining poverty alleviation as the reconciliation of relationships also shapes the methods our churches or ministries should use to achieve that goal. As we shall see later in this book, a reconciliation perspective has major implications for how we choose, design, implement, and evaluate our efforts. But before getting into those specifics, the remainder of this chapter lays out some initial implications of the reconciliation perspective for our methods of poverty alleviation.

Praying for Transformation Together

Because every one of us is suffering from brokenness in our foundational relationships, all of us need "poverty alleviation," just in different ways. Our relationship to the materially poor should be one in which we recognize that both of us are broken and that both of us need the blessing of reconciliation. Our perspective should be less about how we are going to fix the materially poor and more about how we can walk together, asking God to fix both of us.

Think about it. If poverty alleviation is about reconciling relationships, then we do not have the power to alleviate poverty in either the materially poor or in ourselves. It is not something that we can manufacture through better techniques, improved methods, or better planning, for reconciliation is ultimately an act of God. Poverty alleviation occurs when the power of Christ's resurrection reconciles our key relationships through the transformation of both individual lives and local, national, and international systems.

Do we strive for such reconciliation? Of course, for we are "ministers of reconciliation"! We must do our best to preach the gospel, to find cures for malaria, and to foster affordable housing. But part of our striving is also to fall on our knees every day and pray, "Lord, be merciful to me and to my friend here, because we are both sinners." And part of our striving means praying every day, "Thy kingdom come, Thy will be done in earth, as it is in heaven, for without You we cannot fix our communities, our nations, and our world."

Faith Comes from Hearing

Ultimately, the profound reconciliation of the key relationships that comprise poverty alleviation cannot be done without people accepting Jesus Christ as Lord and Savior. Yes, people can experience some degree of healing in their relationships without becoming Christians. For example, although it is typically more difficult, unbelievers can often stop drinking, become more loving spouses, and improve as employees without becoming Christians. And as these things happen for unbelievers, they are more likely to earn sufficient material things. However, none of the foundational relationships can experience fundamental and lasting change without a person becoming a new creature in Christ Jesus. Furthermore, simply having sufficient material things is not the same as "poverty alleviation" as we defined it above. We want people to fulfill their calling "to glorify God and to enjoy Him forever" in their work and in all that they do. Again, this requires that people accept and experience Jesus Christ as Lord and Savior.

While the biblical model is that the gospel is to be communicated in both word and deed, the Bible indicates that without the verbal proclamation of the gospel, one cannot be saved: "How, then, can they call on the one they have not believed in? And how can they believe in the one of whom they have not heard? And how can they hear without someone preaching to them?" (Rom. 10:14).

A host of contextual issues determine the best manner and the appropriate time to present the gospel verbally, particularly in militant Muslim or Hindu settings. But without such a presentation, it is not possible for people to be personally transformed in all their relationships, which is what poverty alleviation is all about.

This implies that the local church, as an institution, has a key role to play in poverty alleviation, because the gospel has been committed by God to the church. This does *not* mean that the local church must own, operate, and manage all ministries. Parachurch ministries and individuals have a role to play as well. However, it does mean that we cannot hope for the transformation of people without the involvement of the local church and the verbal proclamation of the gospel that has been entrusted to it.

People and Processes, Not Projects and Products

The goal is to see people restored to being what God created them to be: people who understand that they are created in the image of God with the gifts, abilities, and capacity to make decisions and to effect change in the world around them; and people who steward their lives, communities, resources, and relationships in order to bring glory to God. These things tend to happen in highly relational, process-focused ministries more than in impersonal, product-focused ministries.

This point can be illustrated with the story of Sandtown, a seventy-two-block area in Baltimore, Maryland, that embodies the typical characteristics of a North American, inner-city ghetto; high rates of drug abuse, out-of-wedlock pregnancy, violence, dilapidated houses, and unemployment. But in the midst of Sandtown's carnage is New Song Urban Ministries and Community Church, which has created a fifteen-block beacon of hope in the darkness. Now in its twentieth year, New Song employs more that eighty staff members and manages a multimillion-dollar annual budget to run its programs for housing, job placement, health care, education, and arts. More than two hundred homes have been rehabilitated, and there is hope in the eyes of the residents for the first time in decades. Deservedly, New Song has received national attention as one of the premier models of church-based community development in North America.

I visited New Song for the first time in 1996, hoping to understand their formula for success. Impressed with all the houses they had rehabilitated and the numerous ministries they had started, my questions focused on how to start and operate all their programs: "How do you manage your ministry? What are the costs of each program? How do you raise the money? Who is on your board? Where can I read the operations manuals? How did you find the housing contractors?"

The cofounders of New Song, Mark Gornik and Allan and Susan Tibbels, patiently answered my questions, but they kept trying to redirect my thoughts away from money and programs toward something else, which is captured in the following passage from Mark Gornik's powerful book:

> We [Mark, Allan, and Susan] decided to relocate to an inner-city neighborhood—not to change it or save it, but to be neighbors and to learn the

agenda of the community and to live on the terms set by our neighbors. . . .
We held tightly to a commitment of God's *shalom* for Sandtown, but we had
no plans or programs. Instead of imposing our own agendas, we sought to
place our lives in service to the community. . . . For over two years we weren't
working to renovate houses, we were out and around in the community,
"hanging out." . . . During this time the foundational relationships of the
church were formed. . . . Everything revolved around building community
together. So during the summer, for example, at least once a month all of
us would pile into a couple of vans and go to a park for a picnic. We would
go downtown and sometimes take trips to other cities. Community came
through having fun together, sharing our lives, and learning to be followers
of Christ together.[2]

Imagine going to a donor and asking for funds to transform a city through
"hanging out"! Yes, buildings, programs, budgets, and boards would eventually come to New Song, but all of those were established upon a process that
was intentionally highly *relational* from its inception. As Mark, Allan, and Susan developed friendships with the long-standing residents, they all began to
dream together about what could be done to improve the community. The
community members identified a need for improved housing as their priority,
and with only one dollar and no housing expertise, decided to form a chapter
of Habitat for Humanity in order to renovate vacant homes for community
residents. Gornik explains:

> This was a community-based strategy that would enable the people of the
> community—who had always been left out of the process and the benefits of
> urban development—to own, manage, and be stewards of their architectural
> and economic environments. We didn't start planning by considering the
> funding or even what funds we thought could be raised. Instead, we began
> with what was right for Sandtown and faithful to the gospel.[3]

In 1990, four years after Mark, Allan, and Susan moved into the neighborhood, Sandtown Habitat for Humanity completed its first housing renovation.
Four years to produce a single house? If the goal was to build a house, this was
not a very impressive program. But as Gornik explains, the goal was a *process*,
not a *product*:

Is such a housing process too slow? Why not let professional developers do it? Questions like these indicated a misperception of our undertaking. New Song and Sandtown Habitat were building people, leaders, community, an economic base, and capacity, not a product for profit.[4]

One of the hallmarks of Mark, Allan, and Susan's success is that they no longer direct New Song. Instead, New Song continues to thrive under the leadership of community members, low-income *people* who were empowered by a relational *process* that focused on reconciling their foundational relationships instead of on implementing *projects* to produce *products*.

EVERYTHING I REALLY NEEDED TO KNOW I LEARNED IN SUNDAY SCHOOL (WELL, ALMOST!)

A long-standing debate in the political arena concerns the extent to which people are materially poor due to their personal failures or to the effects of broken systems on their lives. Political conservatives tend to stress the former, while political liberals tend to emphasize the latter. Which view is correct?

Many of us learned as children in Sunday school that Adam and Eve's sin messed up absolutely everything, implying that *both* individuals and systems are broken. Hence, Christians should be open to the idea that individuals and/or systems could be the problem as we try to diagnose the causes of poverty in any particular context. This much we learned in Sunday school.

Unfortunately, what few of us seem to have learned in Sunday school is that Jesus' redemption is cosmic in scope, bringing reconciliation to both individuals and systems. And as ministers of reconciliation, His people need to be concerned with both as well, the subject to which we now turn.

Working at the Individual Level: Worldview Matters

When working at the level of individual poor people, it is imperative that they and we have a correct understanding of the nature of God, self, others, and creation *and* the way that God intends for human beings to relate to each of them. Another way of stating this is that the correct functioning of these foundational relationships requires a proper *worldview*, which may be defined as the "total set of beliefs or assumptions that comprise the mind-set of an individual and determine what they believe and how they behave."[5] Our worldview is the spectacles through which we see and interpret reality, shaping the way we relate to God, self, others, and creation on both the personal and systemic levels. As the following examples illustrate, faulty worldviews can be a major cause of material poverty.

Distorted Worldview Concerning God

A Christian relief and development agency attempted to improve crop yields for poor farmers in Bolivia's Alto Plano. Although successful in increasing output, the impact on the farmers' incomes was far less than hoped because of the farmers' deep reverence for Pachamama, the mother earth goddess who presides over planting and harvesting. Seeking Pachamama's favor, farmers purchased llama fetuses, a symbol of life and abundance, to bury in their fields before planting. At the time of the harvest, the farmers held a festival to thank Pachamama. The larger the harvest, the larger the celebration was. In fact, a large percentage of the farmers' income was being spent on the fetuses and on the harvest festival, thereby contributing to the farmers' material poverty. Furthermore, by increasing agricultural output without worldview transformation, the development agency realized it was actually adding to these farmers' idolatry, as the farmers were giving increasing levels of praise to Pachamama for her benevolence.

Distorted Worldview Concerning Self

Alisa Collins's daughter Nickcole described the economic impact of Alisa's broken worldview: "Every once in a while, Mom tried to get off public aid, but it was like she was trapped there. Finding and keeping a job was a struggle, because with kids, no high school diploma and little confidence, I know she had it in her mind that she couldn't succeed."[6]

In addition to preventing her from looking for work, Alisa's feelings of inferiority likely contributed to her material poverty in more subtle ways. David Hilfiker, an inner-city medical doctor, explains, "For many young women (young girls, really), having a child may be the only way of finding someone to love and be loved by. Sex and childbirth among teenagers in the ghetto . . . [is] about personal affirmation."[7] Getting pregnant as a teenager caused Alisa to drop out of high school. Without a diploma and with nobody to watch her children, Alisa's teenage pregnancy led to economic ruin for her and her family.

Distorted Worldview Concerning Others

One day, "Johnny" and "Tyrone," two boys aged ten and eleven respectively, killed Eric Morse, a five-year old, by dropping him out of the fourteenth-floor window of a low-income housing project in a Chicago ghetto. Eric had refused to steal candy for Johnny and Tyrone from the neighborhood store. LeAlan and Lloyd, teenagers who have lived their entire lives in that same neighborhood, reflect upon the incident:

> **LeAlan:** If you took the time to think about all the death that goes on around here, you'd go crazy! But that shows you how life is valued now when ten-year-old kids kill for a piece of candy. Life has the value of a quarter now—not even that! It's funny, if you think about it, but it's sad. I mean, killing over a piece of candy!
>
> **Lloyd:** They were raised like that, I guess. They were just following footsteps. That's how it all began.
>
> **LeAlan:** No one around them appreciates life, so why should they? Look at the building [where the crime happened]—you walk in and it smells like urine, you walk up the stairs and it's dark, broken lights. When you live in filth, your mind takes in filth and you feel nothing.[8]

Carl Ellis, a scholar who has studied "ghetto nihilism" extensively, notes that incidents like this emanate from a worldview of "predatory gratification" that is embraced by some members of the criminal subset of ghetto populations. This worldview sees other human beings simply as "prey" that may be destroyed if it fills the hunter's belly.[9] Crimes emanating from such a worldview obviously contribute directly to the material poverty of their victims, but the total impact on ghetto residents' material poverty is more subtle and far more comprehensive. Living in the context of violence, some ghetto children correctly assume that they will not live very long. This can make them very present-oriented[10] and give them little incentive to invest in their futures through such things as being diligent in school. And of course, a failure to get a good education contributes to their long-run material poverty.

Distorted Worldview Concerning the Rest of Creation

A common feature of animism, the worldview that dominates in many regions of the Majority World, is that unpredictable spirits control the rest of creation, implying that the creation is chaotic and uncontrollable by humans. This can lead to a fatalism that prevents animistic people from exercising dominion and improving their material well-being.

For example, the Pokomchi Indians are some of the poorest people in Guatemala. Through the efforts of missionaries, many of the Pokomchi converted to Christianity. Unfortunately, the missionaries failed to communicate a biblical worldview concerning human stewardship over the rest of creation; hence, the Pokomchi continued in their fatalism, literally just waiting to die in order to be delivered from the horrors of this life. Over the years, a number of development organizations tried to help the Pokomchi by building schools and latrines for them, but these largely went unused.

Arturo Cuba, a pastor and community development worker, decided to confront the worldview lies that lay at the foundation of the Pokomchi culture. Arturo noticed that the Pokomchi failed to use adequate crop storage facilities, allowing rats to eat the harvest and contributing to widespread malnutrition. Arturo asked the Pokomchi farmers, "Who is smarter, you or the rats? Do you have dominion over the rats, or do the rats have dominion over your lives?"[11] The farmers admitted that they were allowing the rats to get the best of them. Arturo then explained the biblical worldview that humans are created to have dominion over the rest of creation. As the Pokomchi began to embrace the biblical worldview, dramatic changes took place: better food storage facilities were created, children went to school, women learned to read, and the men adopted improved agricultural techniques.

As these examples illustrate, faulty worldviews can be key obstacles, implying that worldview transformation must often play a central role in poverty-alleviation efforts. In fact, in some cases people's worldviews are so distorted that it is difficult to bring about any progress at all until the people undergo a major paradigm shift. This has huge implications for the design of our programs and ministries and for the funding sources that we choose. Governments are not usually good donors for biblical worldview transformation! In this regard, consider the insightful comments of LeAlan and Lloyd, the teenagers from the Chicago housing project mentioned above, concerning the need for a worldview change—not just more money or resources—to solve their community's problems:

> Now they're talking about tearing down all the high-rises and putting everyone in low-rise buildings as the solution [to children dropping other children out of high-rise windows]. True, it's a start. But "Tyrone" and "Johnny" could have thrown Eric out of a vacant apartment in the low-rises and he could have fallen and broken his neck. So what are you going to do—make the low-rise homes lower? It's more than just the buildings. You don't know how it is to take a life until you value life itself. Those boys didn't value life. Those boys didn't have too much reason *to* value life. Now they killed someone and a part of them is dead too.[12]

Of course, we must always remember that our own worldviews need transformation as well. North Americans Christians have been deeply affected by modernist and now postmodernist worldviews resulting in secularism, materialism, and relativism, all of which have contributed to addictions, mental illnesses, and broken families in our own culture. For example, in pursuit of more material possessions as the source of our happiness, many American couples are running themselves ragged, with both parents working long hours in high-stress jobs. In the process, children and marriages are often neglected, tearing families apart and leading to a host of long-range psychological and social problems. Like some of the materially poor, our own worldviews need transformation.

Although worldview transformation is often necessary for material poverty alleviation, such transformation is often insufficient to alleviate poverty for several reasons. First, having the right concept about how a relationship is supposed to work does not automatically make the relationship work well. For example, I know I am supposed to love my wife, but knowing this is not sufficient to make me get off the couch to help her with the dishes! Healthy relationships require transformed hearts, not just transformed brains. Second, Satan and his legions are at work in the world and have the capacity and desire to damage our relationships. Even if all humans had the correct worldview, Satan would still be on the prowl, attacking us and the rest of creation, thereby causing "poverty" in many manifestations (Eph. 6:12).

Third, one of the results of the fall is that the entire creation is cursed (Gen. 3:17–19), meaning that crops fail and tsunamis happen even when our worldviews are not faulty. Fourth, other people sometimes actively work against or undermine the efforts of an individual poor person to change his situation. Finally, most of the systems in which the materially poor live—systems that contribute to their poverty—are outside of their control. Transforming the worldview of the materially poor will not transform these systems, a point that will be elaborated on in the next section.

BROKEN SYSTEMS CONTRIBUTE TO POVERTY TOO

During the 1970s, OPEC restricted output and drove up oil prices around the world. Members of OPEC earned huge dollar revenues, many of which they deposited into US banks, which then lent these "petrodollars" to countries across the Majority World in dollar-denominated, variable-interest rate loans. The oil price rises caused rampant inflation in the United States, prompting the US Federal Reserve Board to lower the money supply, which caused interest rates to skyrocket and the dollar to appreciate. Faced with rising interest rates and an appreciating dollar, the borrowers in the Majority World could no longer repay their loans. Needing assistance, these countries turned for help to the International Monetary Fund, which responded by rescheduling the loans as long as the borrowers cut their federal expenditures, devalued their currencies, slashed trade barriers, abolished inflation indexing for wages, and moved toward free market economies.

Did you catch all of that? It sounds pretty complicated, doesn't it? The farmers in Bolivia's Alto Plano and the Pokomchi Indians in Guatemala did not understand these events either, and they had absolutely nothing to do with causing any of them to happen. Still, these events had a tremendous impact on their entire economic situation.

Look back at figure 2.2 on page 58. The vast majority of the economic, social, religious, and political systems in which a particular individual lives are not created or even influenced by that individual. Rather, most of these systems are the result of thousands of years of human activity operating on a local, national, and international scale. Yes, these systems have been and continue to be shaped by human beings, but most individuals, particularly the materially poor, have very little control over them. Nevertheless, these systems can play a huge role in contributing to their material poverty.

The systems are particularly tricky because they tend to be invisible when we are working with individual poor people. For example, the events initiated by OPEC's actions impacted all the prices that matter to farmers in Bolivia—prices of fertilizer, seed, credit, land, labor, petroleum, output, etc.—and thus played a major role in these farmers' economic well-being. But if one is working at the community level, one does not easily observe this entire global story and the role it plays in the farmers' poverty. All one sees are materially poor people who waste their money worshiping the Pachamama. It is easy to conclude that the majority of the problem lies with the people themselves—their worldviews, behaviors, and values—because the people's faults are far more obvious than the fallen systems in which they live.

The Broken American System

Take the case of Alisa Collins. While her worldview, values, and behaviors clearly contributed to her material poverty, as an African-American woman growing up in a ghetto, she is also a victim of powerful systemic forces that have dealt her a different set of cards than those received by most North Americans. The ghetto into which Alisa was born, through no choice of her own, originated in the massive migration of African Americans from the rural South to northern cities from 1910 to 1960 as a result of the increased mechanization of Southern agriculture.[13] Centuries of slavery and racial discrimination contributed to the relatively low levels of education of these migrants, who fled north looking for blue-collar manufacturing jobs. Upon their arrival in the North, a combination of economic forces, public policy, and housing discrimination caused the migrants to concentrate in inner cities.

Despite the crowded conditions, in the early 1950s the African-American sections of America's inner cities were largely viable, stable communities; however, the subsequent three decades were quite destabilizing. Federal urban renewal and highway programs required land in inner cities, and African-American neighborhoods were often razed. Low-income African Americans were then relocated into publicly funded housing projects, while middle- and upper-class African Americans were forced to relocate elsewhere. Using a set of policies that both explicitly and implicitly discriminated against African Americans, the Federal Housing Administration (FHA) then began to offer subsidized mortgages that enabled millions of Caucasians to purchase homes in the suburbs and flee the cities. Ironically, advances in the civil rights movement later reduced suburban housing discrimination, allowing middle- and upper-class African Americans to relocate to the suburbs as well. As a result of this suburban flight, the remaining inner-city, African-American communities lost leaders, role models, working families, and a solid economic base.

And then the jobs left. America transitioned from a predominantly manufacturing economy to a service economy. From 1970 to 1985, millions of high-paying, blue-collar jobs simply disappeared from inner cities, moving to other parts of the country or overseas. Unemployment in the inner cities skyrocketed, and many African-American inner-city residents joined the welfare rolls, a system that penalized them for working by taking away benefits for every dollar they earned.

Which Came First, the Broken Individual or the Broken System?

What happens when society crams historically oppressed, uneducated, unemployed, and relatively young human beings into high-rise buildings; takes away their leaders; provides them with inferior education, health care, and employment systems; and then pays them not to work? Is it really that surprising that we see out-of-wedlock pregnancies, broken families, violent crimes, and drug trafficking? Worse yet, we end up with nihilism, because these broken systems do serious damage to people's worldviews. *Worldviews affect the systems, and the systems affect the worldviews.* The arrows in figure 2.2 point both ways.

For example, as Gornik explains, high rates of unemployment caused by a broken economic system can be devastating to one's view of self:

> In our capitalist society, where identity is measured by economic and individual success, the absence of work brings shame and discouragement. Since our society also defines identity by individual success, the absence of meaningful employment corrodes a sense of self and, by extension, family and community. To feel unable to support a family and the wider community—which is what occurs with the structural absence of work in the inner

city—can severely constrain the manner in which one thinks, feels, and acts with respect to the future. The effects of this in Sandtown have been severe.[14]

Again, worldviews affect the systems, and the systems affect the worldviews.

These considerations ought to give us some pause before deciding that we know what the fundamental problem is with people like Alisa Collins. The fall really happened, affecting both Alisa *and* the systems into which she was born. Unfortunately, as recent research has demonstrated, Caucasian evangelicals in the United States, for whom the systems have worked well, are particularly blind to the systemic causes of poverty and are quick to blame the poor for their plight.[15] Evangelicals tend to believe that systemic arguments for poverty amount to shifting the blame for personal sin and excusing moral failure.

Evangelicals are certainly correct that the Bible never allows one's circumstances to be an excuse for one's sin. Period. Yes, Alisa sinned by having extramarital sex, and this was a major contributor to her poverty. But many people commit the same sin without plunging into decades of poverty. Why? Part of the answer is that for a variety of historic and contemporary reasons, ghetto residents are embedded in systems that are distinctly different from that of mainstream society. Some of these systems are of their own making, but many of them are not.

Our being cognizant of this background makes all the difference when Alisa walks into our church asking for assistance. Does Alisa have personal sins and behaviors that are contributing to her material poverty? Yes! But to reduce her problem to this ignores the comprehensive impact of the fall on both individuals and systems and blinds us to our need to bring the reality of Christ's redemption to bear on both.

WHEN WORLDVIEWS COLLIDE

We Are Not Neutral

As we work with materially poor people, it is crucial that we realize that we are not coming to them as blank slates. Rather, the way that we act toward the materially poor expresses our own worldview, painting a picture for them of our understanding about the nature of God, self, others, and the rest of creation. Unfortunately, our own worldviews are broken, causing us to communicate a perspective, a way of understanding reality, that is often deeply at odds with a biblical perspective.

Development thinker Darrow Miller summarizes the situation in figure 3.1.[16]

DIFFERENT VIEWS OF REALITY

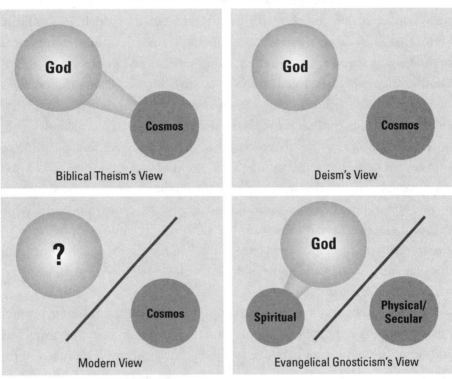

FIGURE 3.1
Adapted from Darrow L. Miller with Stan Guthrie, *Discipling the Nations: The Power of Truth to Transform Cultures* (Seattle, WA: YWAM, 2001), figures 1.7–1.10, pp. 43–4.

The worldview of biblical theism describes a God who is distinct from His creation but connected to it, a reality in which the spiritual and material realms touch each other. Indeed, Colossians 1 describes God, in the person of Jesus Christ, as the Creator, Sustainer, and Reconciler of all things, including the material world. He holds the universe in the palm of His hand, and He is actively working on it to bring the blessings of His kingdom "as far as the curse is found."

Unfortunately, Enlightenment thinking of the seventeenth century introduced the worldview of deism, a perspective in which God is separated from His world. Although deism sees God as the creator of the universe, He is irrelevant to its daily functioning. The God of deism created the world to operate on its own, winding it up like a clock and letting it run according to natural laws without any need for His sustaining hand. In this worldview, humans are largely independent from God and are able to use their own reason to understand the world that He created.

The modern worldview, sometimes called "Western secularism," took deism one step further, removing the need for God altogether. In the modern worldview, not only do the spiritual and material realms not touch, the spiritual realm does not even exist! In the modern worldview, the universe is fundamentally a machine whose origins and operations are rooted in natural processes that humans can master through their own reason.

And therein lies the root cause of the first two terms in the equation on page 64:

- The material definition of poverty emanates from the modern worldview's belief that all problems—including poverty—are fundamentally material in nature and can be solved by using human reason (science and technology) to manipulate the material world in order to solve those problems. Indeed, from the World Bank, to short-term missions teams, to handing a quarter to the homeless person on the street corner, the Western approach to poverty alleviation is to provide material resources and the technology we have developed to master those material resources.

- The god-complexes of the materially non-poor are also a direct extension of the modern worldview. In a universe without God, the heroes are those who are best able to use their reason to master the material world. In other words, the materially non-poor are the victors in the modern worldview, the gods who have mastered the universe and who can use their superior intelligence and the material possessions they have produced to save mere mortals, namely the materially poor.

In this light, repenting of the first two terms in the equation requires us to go even deeper: repenting of the modern worldview that underlies these terms. Repentance never sounds like much fun, but in this case it is the key to discovering a God who is connected to His world, a God who is relevant to every facet of our everyday lives, and a God who can actually respond to our prayers.

Although Christians reject modernism's denial of God, like many others, Darrow Miller argues that North American Christians have engaged in syncretism, combining biblical theism with the modern worldview into a hybrid he calls "evangelical gnosticism," a sacred-secular divide in which God is lord of the spiritual realm—Sunday worship, devotions, evangelism, discipleship, etc.—but is largely irrelevant to the "physical" or "secular" realms—business, the arts, politics, science, and poverty alleviation. This sacred-secular divide severely cripples Christianity in North America, making it irrelevant to the day-to-day functioning of our individual lives and culture. And as discussed in chapter 1, too often the North American missions movement has exported this sacred-secular divide to other cultures, failing to communicate the full implications of Christ's kingdom for all aspects of life.

Moreover, evangelical gnosticism often permeates the poverty alleviation efforts of North American Christians. Too often we drill wells, dispense medicine, and provide food without narrating that Jesus Christ is the Creator and Provider of these material things. Then later we offer a Bible study in which we explain that Jesus can save our souls. This approach communicates evangelical gnosticism: material things solve material poverty, and Jesus solves spiritual poverty. In other words, we communicate "Star Trek Jesus" rather than "Colossians 1 Jesus." As a result, we fail to introduce materially poor people to the only one who can truly reconcile the broken relationships that underlie their material poverty.

When faulty worldviews—whether modernism or evangelical gnosticism—collide with the worldviews of the materially poor themselves, the results can be devastating . . .

Pachamama and Penicillin

For example, as we saw earlier with the Bolivian farmers who worshiped the Pachamama, many of the materially poor in the Majority World have an animistic worldview; they believe that the world is controlled by powerful and unpredictable spirits. When North Americans introduce new technology or material resources into such settings—whether agricultural methods, Western medicine, or money—they often prove more powerful than the spirits. Seeing this, the Bolivian farmers may very well go from worshiping the Pachamama to worshiping the penicillin! In other words, we may inadvertently replace the traditional worldview with a secular, "modern" worldview, which puts its faith in science, technology, and material things.[17] Or alternatively, the farmers may engage in syncretism, simply enfolding the new technology into their worship of Pachamama, thanking her for providing them with the power in the penicillin.

A similar dynamic can be present when working with the materially poor in North America, particularly in the context of the US government's "Faith-Based Initiative," which allows Christian organizations to receive federal funds for the "nonspiritual" components of their ministries. For example, I once served on the board of an inner-city ministry that serves an African-American population. We applied for federal funds to pay for part of our jobs preparedness training program for unemployed people. As part of this program, our ministry was very committed to using a curriculum that communicated a biblical worldview concerning work, including the need for Jesus Christ to restore us to being productive workers.

The government's grant administrator, who happened to be a Christian, informed us that the law prohibited us from using the government's money to cover the costs of such an explicitly gospel-focused curriculum. He was doing his job in informing us of this law. No problem with that. However, he then said, "Brian, just remove the explicitly Christian material from the lessons. You can teach the same values that you want to teach—responsibility, punctuality, respect, hard work, discipline, etc.—without articulating their biblical basis. These values work whether people see them as coming from God or not." In essence, the grant administrator was encouraging us to apply evangelical gnosticism, separating Christ from His world, encouraging us to use Christ's techniques without recognizing Him as the Creator of the techniques and without calling on Him to give people the power to employ those techniques.

We decided not to use the federal funds to pay for the curriculum. Teaching the values of a "Protestant work ethic" without teaching about the Creator of those values and about the transforming power of Jesus Christ is like giving out penicillin without ever explaining the source of the penicillin's power. Yes, like penicillin, these values work. But how sad it would have been if we had ended up communicating to the program participants: "You can pull yourselves up by your own bootstraps. Become more disciplined, hardworking, and responsible, and you too can achieve the American dream of material prosperity." Even if the participants had then managed to change their behaviors without the biblical teaching, the result might have been people who put their faith in middle-class values and in their ability to adopt those values. We would have replaced their own worldview with that of the modern worldview, which believes that humans can achieve progress through their own strength.

It is interesting to consider that in this case, many of the participants in the jobs program already embraced, at least at an intellectual level, most of the elements of a Christian worldview. The prominence of churches in the life of the African-American community ensured this. Ironically, had we simply communicated middle-class American values in our curriculum, our "ministry" might have replaced those elements of a biblical worldview that the participants already embraced with a modern or an evangelical gnostic worldview! Failing to root the curriculum in an explicitly biblical worldview could have been devastating, even if the program participants successfully obtained jobs and increased their incomes as a result of the program. Remember, the goal is for everyone involved to glorify God, not just to increase people's incomes.

The dynamics just described are particularly dangerous for North American Christians in the twenty-first century. On the one hand, all of us have been heavily influenced by the modern worldview, which believes that human reason and effort are able to understand and control the material world without a need for understanding or relying upon God. As a result, we are very prone to putting our trust in ourselves and in technology to improve our lives, forgetting that it is God who is the Creator and Sustainer of us and of the laws that make the technology work.

On the other hand, many of us are now being influenced by a postmodern worldview, which argues that absolute truth is not knowable: "What is true for me might not be true for you. What this Bible passage says to me, it might not say to you." The influence of postmodernism is making many

North American Christians fearful of engaging in evangelism and discipleship activities, lest they be imposing their culturally bound interpretation of Scripture onto other cultures. "Who are we to tell them what the Bible says?"

While postmodernism has provided some helpful corrections to modernism's overconfidence, shackling people from communicating the transcendent truth of the Scriptures is not one of them. Yes, we are finite, frail, and sinful creatures who are deeply influenced by our own cultural settings in ways that we cannot even identify. We really do need to be careful that we are not imposing our culturally bound interpretations and applications of Scripture's transcendent truths onto other people. But while these cautions are in order, the Bible never suggests that these realities should prevent us from studying, applying, and communicating the gospel and its implications to others (Ps. 119:105, 130; Matt. 28:18–20; 2 Tim. 3:16–4:5). Yes, we must be humble and must constantly reexamine ourselves in the light of Scripture. But we must not shy away from declaring biblical truth, for our confidence rests in the power of the Word of God and in the active presence of the Holy Spirit to overcome our inadequacies.

In summary, at the end of the day, people need to move from worshiping Pachamama to worshiping the Creator of the penicillin. Such a move requires a verbal articulation of biblical theism: the penicillin works because the Creator makes it work. Fall down and worship Him.

Material Poverty Alleviation for Alisa Collins

After decades of living on welfare checks, Alisa Collins suddenly started finishing her high school degree, working full-time as a kindergarten teacher, and getting up at 4:00 a.m. to wash her family's clothes before she was due at work. What happened? Alisa's worldview changed *and* the system in which she lived changed.

It all began when Miss Miller, the principal of the local school, hired Alisa to work part-time as a teacher's aide. Miss Miller soon observed that Alisa had natural teaching gifts and took the time to encourage her to get the education and certification required to pursue a teaching career. With Miss Miller's relational and nurturing approach, Alisa began to gain confidence. And while her worldview was changing, two important changes also occurred in Alisa's economic environment. First, Congress passed welfare-reform legislation, making welfare more "pro-work" and placing limits on the length of time people could stay on it. Alisa knew her days on welfare were coming to an end and that she simply had to find a full-time job. Second, Miss Miller offered Alisa a job as a full-time teacher, thereby making the economic system finally work for Alisa.

Churches are uniquely positioned to provide the relational ministries on an individual level that people like Alisa need. While making major changes to national and international economic systems is more difficult, churches can often make just enough changes in local systems to allow people like Alisa to move out of material poverty. Such systemic change can take on the form of political advocacy, but more often it simply means changing the economic options for the materially poor so that they have an opportunity to support themselves. For example, business owners in your church could provide jobs for poor people, giving them a rare opportunity to make a fresh start. Or your church might hire poor people part-time, giving them practical experience and an opportunity to develop strong work habits that can lead to full-time employment elsewhere.

Of course, churches can also offer Alisa something that Miss Miller could not: a clear articulation of the gospel of the kingdom so that Alisa can experience the profound and lasting change required to achieve material poverty alleviation in its fullest sense: *the ability to fulfill her calling of glorifying God through her work and life.*

Parts 2, 3, and 4 of this book will elaborate further on ways the church can address both individuals and the systems in which they live in order to be ministers of reconciliation.

REFLECTION QUESTIONS AND EXERCISES

Please write responses to the following:

1. Reflect on your answers to the questions at the start of this chapter. Have your views changed at all? If so, how? Be specific.

2. Have you ever felt trapped by life's circumstances to the point where you believed that you could not do anything to change the situation? If so, describe the emotions and behaviors that this produced in you. Did you ever feel like just giving up?

3. When you get sick, what do you do? Now read 2 Chronicles 16:7–9, 12 and Psalm 20:7. What was Asa's sin? One of the features of the modern worldview is an unbiblical separation between the spiritual and the physical realms. Like Asa, we tend to rely on science—medicine, technology, machines, power, etc.—to solve our problems and forget to call on the one who created and upholds the universe. Are you like Asa? How does your worldview need to be transformed?

4. Think about your church's ministries and missions efforts. Do they include a clear, verbal articulation of the gospel? If not, what are some specific things that could be done to improve this?

5. Again, think about your church's ministries and mission efforts. Are they about *people* and *processes* or about *projects* and *products*? List some specific things that you could do to improve these initiatives.

6. Answer questions 4 and 5 for any parachurch ministries with which you are involved.

7. Consider your community, city, or region. How might the economic, social, religious, and political systems be unjust and oppressive to some people? If you are able, ask several materially poor people or people who are ethnic minorities (e.g., Native Americans, African Americans, Hispanics in the Southwestern part of the United States) to share their perspective on this with you. Spend some time really listening to them and considering what they have to say. Then ask: is there anything you or your church could do to make these systems more just?

8. Do the ministries to the poor with which you are involved narrate that God is the Creator, Sustainer, and Redeemer of the technology, resources, and methods that you are bringing? Or are you inadvertently communicating that the power is in the technology, resources, and methods?

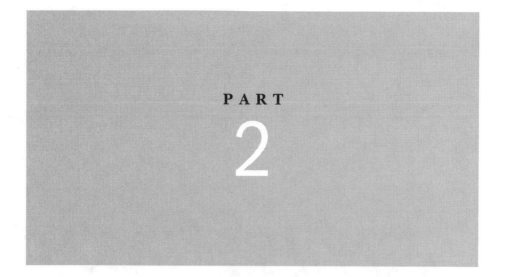

PART
2

GENERAL PRINCIPLES
for HELPING
WITHOUT HURTING

Please write short answers to the following questions:

1. *Think about materially poor people in North America who have asked you or your church for immediate financial assistance. Under what conditions do you believe it would be appropriate to give things or money to these people? Be specific.*

2. *Think about any ministry to the poor that you or your church has conducted in the Majority World; for example, a short-term mission trip. Under what conditions do you believe it would be appropriate for you or your church to give things or money to these people? Be specific.*

3. *Are your answers to the previous two questions the same or different? Why?*

NOT ALL **POVERTY**
IS CREATED EQUAL

You turn on the evening news and see that a tsunami has devastated Indonesia, leaving millions without food, adequate clothing, or shelter. Following a commercial break, the news returns and features a story about the growing number of homeless men in your city, who are also without food, adequate clothing, or shelter. At first glance the appropriate responses to each of these crises might seem to be very similar. The people in both situations need food, clothing, and housing, and providing these things to both groups seems to be the obvious solution. But there is something nagging in us as we reflect on these two news stories. Deep down it seems like the people in these two crises are in very different situations and require different types of help.

How should we think about these scenarios? Are there principles to guide us to the appropriate response in each case?

PICK A NUMBER BETWEEN 1 AND 3

A helpful first step in thinking about working with the poor in any context is to discern whether the situation calls for relief, rehabilitation, or development. In fact, the failure to distinguish among these situations is one of the most common reasons that poverty-alleviation efforts often do harm.

"Relief" can be defined as the urgent and temporary provision of emergency aid to reduce immediate suffering from a natural or man-made crisis. As pictured in figure 4.1, when a crisis such as the Indonesian tsunami strikes at point 1, people are nearly or even completely helpless and experience plummeting economic conditions. There is a need to halt the free fall, to "stop the bleeding," and this is what relief attempts to do. The key feature of relief is a provider-receiver dynamic in which the provider gives assistance—often material—to the receiver, who is largely incapable of helping himself at that time. The Good Samaritan's bandaging of the helpless man who lay bleeding along the roadside is an excellent example of relief applied appropriately.

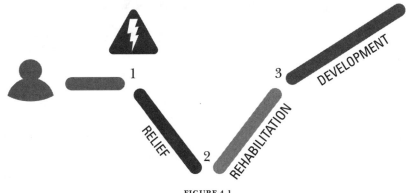

FIGURE 4.1

"Rehabilitation" begins as soon as the bleeding stops; it seeks to restore people and their communities to the positive elements of their precrisis conditions. The key feature of rehabilitation is a dynamic of working *with* the tsunami victims as they participate in their own recovery, moving from point 2 to point 3.

"Development" is a process of ongoing change that moves all the people involved—both the "helpers" and the "helped"—closer to being in right relationship with God, self, others, and the rest of creation. In particular, as the materially poor develop, they are better able to fulfill their calling of glorifying God by working and supporting themselves and their families with the fruits of that work. Development is not done *to* people or *for* people but *with* people. The key dynamic in development is promoting an empowering process in which all the people involved—both the "helpers" and the "helped"—become more of what God created them to be, moving beyond point 3 to levels of reconciliation that they have not experienced before.

It is absolutely crucial that we determine whether relief, rehabilitation, or development is the appropriate intervention:

> **One of the biggest mistakes that North American churches make— by far—is in applying relief in situations in which rehabilitation or development is the appropriate intervention.**

The Good Samaritan's handouts were appropriate for the person at point 1, a victim who needed material assistance to stop the bleeding and even prevent death; however, the person at point 3 is not facing an emergency, and handouts of material assistance to such people do not help to restore them to being the productive stewards that they were created to be. In fact, as we saw in chapter 2, applying a material solution to the person at point 3, whose underlying problem—like ours—is relational, is likely to do harm to this person and to the provider of the material assistance, exacerbating the brokenness in the four key relationships for both of them.

The remainder of this chapter uses the relief-rehabilitation-development paradigm to flesh out some principles as we seek the goal of poverty alleviation—low-income people and ourselves increasingly glorifying God through reconciling relationships with God, self, others, and the rest of creation.

Who's #1?

Many of the people coming to your church for help will state that they are in a crisis, needing emergency financial help for utility bills, rent, food, or transportation. In other words, they will state that they are at point 1 in figure 4.1. Is relief the appropriate intervention for such a person? Maybe, but maybe not. There are several things to consider.

First, is there really a crisis at hand? If you fail to provide immediate help, will there really be serious, negative consequences? If not, then relief is not the appropriate intervention, for there is time for the person to take actions on his own behalf.

Second, to what degree was the individual personally responsible for the crisis? Of course, compassion and understanding are in order here, especially when one remembers the systemic factors that can play a role in poverty. But it is still important to consider the person's own culpability in the situation, as allowing people to feel some of the pain resulting from any irresponsible behavior on their part can be part of the "tough love" needed to facilitate the reconciliation of poverty alleviation. The point is not to punish the person for any mistakes or sins he has committed but to ensure that the appropriate lessons are being learned in the situation.

Third, can the person help himself? If so, then a pure handout is almost never appropriate, as it undermines the person's capacity to be a steward of his own resources and abilities.

Fourth, to what extent has this person already been receiving relief from you or others in the past? How likely is he to be receiving such help in the future? As special as your church is, it might not be the first stop on the train! This person may be obtaining "emergency" assistance from one church or organization after another, so that your "just-this-one-time gift" might be the tenth such gift the person has recently received.

My family experienced this situation two months ago when a young woman knocked on the door of our house asking for some food. We complied, but we later found out that she had received similar assistance from other members of our community for many weeks, and we still see her going door-to-door asking for food. When neighbors have sought to provide her with long-term solutions, she has refused such help. The loving thing to do for this woman is for the entire community to withhold further relief, to explain our reason for doing so, and to offer her wide-open arms should she choose a path of walking together with us in finding long-term solutions.

While many of these rules of thumb strike an intuitive chord when working with the materially poor in North America, many of us ignore these principles when working with the materially poor in the Majority World. Compared to our own situation, the levels of poverty in the Majority World seem so devastating, and the people seem so helpless. In such contexts, many of us are quick to hand out money and other forms of relief assistance in ways that we would never even consider when ministering to the poor in North America.

To illustrate, consider the savings and credit association affiliated with Jehovah Jireh Church, a congregation located in a slum in Manila, the Philippines. Each of the members of this savings and credit association lives on approximately one to five dollars per day. Each member of the association deposits into the group just twenty cents per week, which the association uses to make very small, interest-bearing loans to the members. In addition, each member contributes five cents per week to the association's emergency fund, which can be used to provide relief to members facing an emergency crisis.

From a North American perspective, these people are extremely poor. In this light, it is instructive to consider the policies that the savings and credit association developed for its emergency fund. Money from the fund is lent—not given—at a 0 percent interest rate to group members whose family members get sick. No assistance is available for people who have had their electricity or water cut off for not paying their utility bills. According to the group, such a situation does not constitute an emergency, since electric and water bills are regular household expenditures for which they should all be prepared. The group will not even give emergency loans for hospitalization for giving birth, because the family had nine months to prepare for the delivery of the baby. Finally, the amount of the loan from the emergency fund is limited to the amount of the savings contributions of the member getting the loan. The members of this savings and credit association are tough cookies!

Now what happens when a North American church encounters the members of Jehovah Jireh Church's savings and credit association? We often project our own ideas of what is an acceptable standard of living onto the situation and are quick to take a relief approach, doling out money in ways that the local people would consider unwise and dependence-creating. And in the process, we can undermine local judgment, discipline, accountability, stewardship, savings, and institutions. In fact, research has shown that the injection of outside funds into these savings and credit groups typically dooms them to collapse.[1] The point here is not that the policies of Jehovah Jireh's savings and credit association are normative for all churches and all contexts. The point is that, in deciding if relief is the appropriate intervention, we must be careful lest we impose our own cultural assumptions into contexts that we do not understand very well.

As discussed further in chapter 11, assessment tools can help you to discern the nature of a person's situation. These tools can range from an informal set of questions used in an initial conversation to a more formal and detailed written form. Such assessment tools help to identify the type of assistance that would be most beneficial and can also help to determine if the need for help is real. Furthermore, these tools can reveal the willingness of the person to address larger life issues that may have contributed to the present situation.

In particular, it is helpful for your church or ministry to have a set of benevolence policies in place to guide decision making when working with materially poor people. These policies should flow from your mission and vision and be consistent with a biblical perspective on the nature of poverty and its alleviation.

Who is #1? It is unlikely that you know many people in this category, for the reality is that only a small percentage of the poor in your community or around the world require relief. These would include the severely disabled; some of the elderly; very young, orphaned children; the mentally ill homeless population; and victims of a natural disaster. People in these categories are often unable to do anything to help themselves and need the handouts of relief. However, for most people, the bleeding has stopped, and they are not destitute. Acting as though they are destitute does more harm than good, both to them and to ourselves. This does not mean that we should do nothing to help those who are not destitute. It just means that rehabilitation or development—not relief—is the appropriate way of helping such people. This help could very well include providing them with financial assistance, but such assistance would be conditional upon and supportive of their being productive. Chapters 8 and 9 provide examples of interventions that do this by complementing people's work and thrift with additional resources.

How Do You Spell "Effective Relief"?

If you do determine that relief is the appropriate response in a given situation, there are some principles that can help to make your relief efforts more effective.

First, relief needs to be immediate. If a person is in the midst of a crisis and cannot help himself, a timely response is crucial. For example, when a large-scale natural disaster hits, the victims cannot wait weeks while churches try to think of what they should do and secure funding. What is true for large-scale disasters is true for the battered woman who has bravely come to the church office seeking safe shelter. Sending her back home to wait while the church tries to find her some alternative shelter is not a good relief response.

In order to provide timely relief, it is important to engage in disaster preparedness. This simply means looking ahead and forecasting the types of relief situations that the church or ministry may encounter. Financial, material, and human resources can be identified and secured to be ready to be put into play at the right time. For example, the deacons can ensure that the church either obtains or creates a directory of services that are available in the community to address relief needs. The deacons can also line up people within the congregation who would be ready to give of themselves to help someone who is in the midst of a crisis. Such help could include opening their home for a few nights, providing transportation to an agency, taking a person out to eat, or working in the church's clothing closet to ensure it is well organized.

Second, relief is also temporary, provided only during the time that people are unable to help themselves. Unfortunately, determining when to stop relief is never easy. On the one hand, we can make the mistake of ending our assistance too early. An uninsured family facing ongoing medical bills due to a health emergency may need more than a single gift of one hundred dollars from the church's benevolence fund. On the other hand, if relief is given for too long, it can do harm by creating dependence. Again, your church needs to have benevolence policies in place that define the degree, frequency, and length of relief efforts. While there may be occasions that call for working outside of these policies, having such policies can greatly aid in providing relief appropriately.

How do you spell "effective relief"? S-e-l-d-o-m, I-m-m-e-d-i-a-t-e, and T-e-m-p-o-r-a-r-y.

Doing Relief and Rehabilitation, Developmentally

Once relief efforts have stopped the bleeding, it is time to move quickly into rehabilitation, working *with*, not *for*, people to help them return to the positive elements of their precrisis conditions. Again, rehabilitation must be done in a way consistent with the long-run goal of poverty alleviation: low-income people and ourselves increasingly glorifying God through reconciling relationships with God, self, others, and the rest of creation.

About twenty years ago, my wife and I helped to mobilize our church to volunteer at a Christian homeless shelter. Most of the men living in the shelter had experienced some sort of trauma such as a divorce, a death in the family, or the loss of a job. Turning to drugs or alcohol to ease the pain, these men had lost everything and needed emergency help to survive in the frigid conditions of the Connecticut winter. By providing food and warm beds, the shelter had stopped the downward plunge for these men and was now trying to help them to rehabilitate through a range of counseling services.

Once a month the members of our church graciously bought food, prepared a meal, served it to the shelter residents, and cleaned up afterward. We did everything short of spoon-feeding the men, never asking them to lift a finger in the entire process. A more developmental approach would have sought greater participation of these men in their own rehabilitation, asking them to exercise stewardship as part of the process of beginning to reconcile their key relationships. We could have involved the men every step along the way, from planning the meal, to shopping for the food, to helping with serving and clean-up. We could have done supper *with* the men, working and eating side by side, rather than giving supper *to* the men, engaging in a provider-recipient dynamic that likely confirmed our sense of superiority and their sense of inferiority.

Doing rehabilitation and even relief using a more developmental approach is now considered the "best practice" in the field. For example, the *Minimum Standards of Disaster and Rehabilitation Assistance* includes the following guidelines, to which we've added some comments.[2]

• *Ensure participation of the affected population in the assessment, design, implementation, monitoring, and evaluation of the assistance program.* This is the equivalent of saying that the men in the homeless shelter need to be involved in every aspect of not just preparing supper, but in the design, implementation, and evaluation of the entire homeless shelter's programs! Does this sound crazy? Clearly, judgment is necessary to determine the capacity of the target population to make wise decisions and to shoulder responsibilities. But it is important to work from a perspective that we are all created in the image of God, that we are all broken, and that we all can experience Christ's reconciliation. As much as possible, we need to treat people as the responsible stewards that we want them to be, even asking their opinions once in a while! Homeless men might actually know something about, well, being homeless.

- *Conduct an initial assessment to provide an understanding of the disaster situation and to determine the nature of the response.* This is a little different from loading up a truck of volunteers from your church and running down to New Orleans the day after the levies break. It requires you to know the local context and situation or to be working under the auspices and coordination of those who do.

- *Respond when needs of an affected population are unmet by local people or organizations due to their inability or unwillingness to help.* Note how cautious this approach is. If local people and organizations are able and willing to help those in the crisis, then stay away! The local people will typically have a better understanding of the best way to get the job done. Moreover, the entire goal of development work is for local people to take charge of their individual lives and communities. Rushing in with all sorts of outside knowledge and resources can undermine the four key relationships in that community, one of which is being a steward of "the rest of creation." If they need help, give it; but if they do not, your giving may do harm.

From a biblical perspective, we need to qualify this "best practice" guideline a bit. Whenever possible, the first responders to a crisis should be the victims' family members, whether those family members are geographically local or not (1 Tim. 5:3–4). However, in many relief situations there is not sufficient time to involve the family members, particularly if they live far away from the crisis. In such situations, the geographically local people should become the first responders.

- *Target assistance based on vulnerability and need, and provide it equitably and impartially.* Note the concern here with precision, making sure that the people who get the assistance are truly vulnerable and needy. Flinging resources around undermines the development of individual and communal stewardship, responsibility, and capacity. The women in the savings and credit association of Jehovah Jireh Church understood this quite well.

- *Aid workers must possess appropriate qualifications, attitudes, and experience to plan and effectively implement appropriate assistance programs.* Note the concern here is with both ability and attitude. There are complex disaster situations in which untrained volunteers are more of a hindrance than a help, particularly when they are not working under the auspices of an experienced organization. Again, jumping in a truck and heading down to New Orleans during a major disaster might do more harm than good. And an attitude of humility and brokenness is everything. The provider-receiver dynamic in the relief situation lends itself to all of the problems we have discussed concerning the god-complexes of the providers interacting with the recipients' feeling of inferiority. And the dangers are even greater in rehabilitation contexts in which the recipients have the capacity to participate in their own recovery. In such settings, top-down, "I-am-here-to-save-you" attitudes can seriously undermine the development of the recipients' initiative and stewardship.

Bad Relief Undermines Worship

The sprawling Kibera slum of Nairobi, Kenya, is believed to be the largest slum in Africa. Development workers commonly refer to Kibera as "scorched earth," because decades of well-meaning outside organizations have made it nearly impossible to do long-lasting development work there. Failing to recognize that the appropriate intervention in Kibera is neither relief nor rehabilitation, outside organizations have poured in financial and human resources, crippling local initiative in the process. Alvin Mbola, a Kenyan community development worker who tries to build up the indigenous churches in Kibera, describes the situation as follows:

> To many people, the Kibera slum in Nairobi, Kenya is a place with no equals. It is filthy, congested, degraded, and unfit for human habitation. Like the proverbial scriptural reference to the birthplace of Jesus Christ, many people believe that "nothing good can come out of Kibera." Therefore, most remedies directed toward Kibera are motivated by the sympathy of outsiders, who often give handouts in an attempt to cushion the residents against their perceived, gigantic problems.

In reality, many of the problems of Kibera stem from chronic issues that can only be solved through a consistent and long-term relationship between the change agent and the residents. Changes within individuals and communities are not instantaneous; long-term relationships are needed to bring out the best of "what is" and of "what could be." The people in Kibera have capacities, skills, and resources that need to be tapped if genuine development is to be realized, but the process of identifying and mobilizing these gifts and assets takes time. Unfortunately, for many years nongovernment organizations working in Kibera have tended to operate on the basis of "quick fixes." Frustrations set in because changes in individuals are not forthcoming as quickly as anticipated. Many of these organizations then either close down or move to other parts of the country, leaving people in a worse situation than they were before. In the process, individual and community lives have been devastated. It appears that many donors are willing to give to any venture as long as they see pictures of "dilapidated" Kibera....

Of course, there are some occasions in which there is a need for relief work in Kibera. For example, often times there are fire breakouts where houses and business premises are gutted down. It might be necessary to bring in outside resources to provide relief and to rehabilitate these homes and businesses. But even in these situations, caution should be taken so that the relief efforts are not prolonged to the point in which they undermine local people's stewardship of their own lives and communities.

The root issue in all of these considerations is that God, who is a worker, ordained work so that humans could worship Him through their work. Relief efforts applied inappropriately often cause the beneficiaries to abstain from work, thereby limiting their relationship with God through distorted worship or through no worship at all.[3]

THE POISON OF PATERNALISM

Are you feeling overwhelmed yet? Poverty alleviation is more complex than it appears at first glance. However, there is a good rule of thumb that is extremely useful in cutting through a lot of the complexity: Avoid Paternalism.[4]

Avoid Paternalism.
Do not do things for people that they can do for themselves.

Memorize this, recite it under your breath all day long, and wear it like a garland around your neck. Every time you are engaged in poverty-alleviation ministry, keep this at the forefront of your mind, for it can keep you from doing all sorts of harm.

Paternalism comes in a variety of forms:

Resource Paternalism

Resource paternalism has been discussed in this book at some length already. Being from a materialistic culture, North Americans often view the solution to poverty in material terms and tend to pour financial and other material resources into situations in which the real need is for the local people to steward their own resources. In addition, legitimate local businesses can be undermined when outsiders bring in such things as free clothes or building supplies, undercutting the price that these local businesses need to survive.

Spiritual Paternalism

Spiritual paternalism has also been discussed earlier. Many of us assume that we have a lot to teach the materially poor about God and that we should be the ones preaching from the pulpit, teaching the Sunday school class, or leading the vacation Bible school. We do have much to share out of our knowledge and experiences, but oftentimes the materially poor have an even deeper walk with God and have insights and experiences that they can share with us, if we would just stop talking and listen.

Knowledge Paternalism

Knowledge paternalism occurs when we assume that we have all the best ideas about how to do things. As a result, the materially poor need us to think for them concerning the best way to plant crops, to operate their businesses, or to cure diseases. Handling knowledge is a very tricky area in poverty alleviation, because the truth is that we often do have knowledge that can help the materially poor. But we must recognize that the materially poor also have unique insights into their own cultural contexts and are facing circumstances that we do not understand very well.

For example, during the first several decades after World War II, the leading Western economists and agriculturalists concluded that peasant farmers in the Majority World were irrational and culturally backward because the farmers failed to adopt new varieties of crops that had higher average yields. Subsequent research discovered that the farmers were, indeed, acting very rationally. While the new crop varieties had higher average yields, these new crops also had much greater variation in their yields from year to year than the farmers' traditional varieties. For farmers living in highly vulnerable situations in which a bad crop could result in starvation for their children, it was better to choose the low-risk-low-return traditional varieties than the high-risk-high-return new varieties, particularly in a setting in which landlords and loan sharks tended to reap the majority of any increase in profits.[5] The failure of the outside "experts" to understand the realities of life on the ground led them to give life-threatening advice to the materially poor and then to demean the poor when they failed to listen to this "expert" advice.

All of us need to remember that the materially poor really are created in the image of God and have the ability to think and to understand the world around them. They actually know something about their situation, and we need to listen to them! This does not need to degenerate into some sort of new-age, "the-truth-is-within-you" quagmire. Like all of us, the materially poor are often wrong about how the world works and can benefit from the knowledge of others. In fact, a key trigger point for change in a community is often being exposed to a new way of understanding or of doing something. But it is reflective of a god-complex to assume that we have all the knowledge and that we always know what is best.

Knowledge paternalism may be a particular temptation for Christian businesspeople from North America, many of whom are showing considerable passion for using their God-given abilities to train low-income entrepreneurs in the Majority World. This passion is a wonderful development and has enormous potential to advance Christ's kingdom around the world. But the fact that a person successfully operates a software company in Boston does not ensure that this person has the best business advice for a highly vulnerable cassava farmer living on one dollar per day in the semi-feudal institutional setting of rural Guatemala. Humility, caution, and an open ear are in order.

Similarly, pastors of middle-to-upper-class North American churches may be susceptible to knowledge paternalism, making the mistake of thinking that their own ministry styles are normative for all cultural settings. Churches of different socioeconomic classes even within North America differ dramatically in terms of the ways that they handle money, prayer, sermons, staffing, music, membership, counseling, etc. For example, in a lower-class church, prayers tend to be participatory, with individual members praying for God to heal specific problems that they are having. In contrast, in middle-class churches the pastor tends to offer the prayers, asking God more generally to "help those who are sick." Finally, in wealthy churches, prayers are often done through highly stylized liturgy.[6]

Wherever the Bible speaks specifically about church life, it must be heeded. But where the Bible is silent, North American pastors must be careful not to impose their own culturally determined ministry styles into settings in which the local pastors might know more about the most effective way to minister.

Labor Paternalism

Labor paternalism occurs when we do work for people that they can do for themselves. I remember going on a spring break mission trip to Mississippi while I was in college. I will never forget the sick feeling I had as I stood on a ladder painting a house while the young, able-bodied men living in the house sat on their front porch and watched. I did so much harm that day. Yes, the house got painted, but in the process I undermined these people's calling to be stewards of their own time and talents. It might have been better if I had stayed home for spring break, rather than to have gone and done harm.

Managerial Paternalism

Managerial paternalism is perhaps the hardest nut to crack. We middle-to-upper-class North Americans love to see things get done as quickly and efficiently as possible. Relative to many other cultures, including many low-income communities in North America, we are prone to take charge, particularly when it appears that nobody else is moving fast enough. As a result, we often plan, manage, and direct initiatives in low-income communities when people in those communities could do these things quite well already. The structure and pace might be different if the low-income communities undertook the projects themselves, but they could do a good job nonetheless.

You might be asking, "Then why don't they take charge and manage these projects if they are so gifted?" There are lots of reasons that the people, churches, and organizations in low-income communities might not take charge, but here are several common ones that should give us some pause before rushing into a low-income community and grabbing the reins in any project:

- They do not need to take charge because they know that we will take charge if they wait long enough.
- They lack the confidence to take charge, particularly when the "superior," middle-to-upper-class North Americans are involved.
- They, like we, have internalized the messages of centuries of colonialism, slavery, and racism: Caucasians run things and everyone else follows.
- They do not want the project to happen as much as we do. For example, they might know the project will accomplish little in their context but are afraid to tell us for fear of offending us.
- They know that by letting us run the show it is more likely that we will bring in money and other material resources to give to them.

There are situations in which a lack of local leadership and managerial ability may require the outsiders to perform these functions, but we should be very, very cognizant of our tendencies as middle-to-upper-class North Americans to take charge and run things. Remember, the goal is not to *produce* houses or other material goods but to pursue a *process* of walking with the materially poor so that they are better stewards of their lives and communities, including their own material needs.

Of course, there are exceptions to every rule! There are times when the Holy Spirit might move us to do something for the materially poor that they can do for themselves. But just remember that these situations are the exception, not the rule. Avoid paternalism.

FINDING YOUR NICHE

It is extremely difficult for the same person or organization to provide relief, rehabilitation, *and* development, for the relational dynamics in each of these types of ministry are quite different. For example, if your church is known as the place to go for free food (relief), it might have difficulty convincing people that they need to start working to earn their daily bread (development). In addition, each of these ministries is demanding. If a church tries to do all of them, it runs the risk of being spread too thin. Hence, it might be better for your church to focus on relief, rehabilitation, *or* development.

How do you decide? Determine the sorts of services that are already being provided by organizations in the community in which you want to serve. Next, find out both the assets and the needs of the materially poor in your community. Are the people destitute, or can they contribute to their own improvement? In many if not most instances, you will find that the materially poor in your community are not in a free fall; that is, they are not in need of relief.

Ironically, you will also typically find that most existing organizations in your community are focusing on providing relief. Why? There are at least three reasons. First, many service organizations have a material definition of poverty; hence, they believe that handouts of material things are the solution to that poverty. As a result, they often provide relief to people who really need development. Second, relief is easier to do than development. It is much simpler to drop food out of airplanes or to ladle soup out of bowls than it is to develop long-lasting, time-consuming relationships with poor people, which may be emotionally exhausting. Third, it is easier to get donor money for relief than for development. "We fed a thousand people today" sounds better to donors than "We hung out and developed relationships with a dozen people today."

In this light, your church might decide to find a niche in development, choosing to focus on ministering intensely over time to a few people rather than superficially and quickly to many people. Indeed, many churches are well-placed in terms of mission, programmatic focus, financial resources, relational skills, and basic giftedness for the long and sometimes grinding haul required for development work. After all, the church is designed by Christ Himself to be all about developing and growing people through long-term discipleship![7]

If your church chooses a development niche, it might want to put in its benevolence policies that no more than, say, 10 percent of the benevolence fund will normally be used for relief work, with the other 90 percent going toward development. Your church should also keep a list of organizations that do offer relief and rehabilitation in your community in case you encounter people who actually need it. In compiling such a list, you might try to discern which organizations do relief and rehabilitation "developmentally" so that you can feel confident about referring people to them.

Not all poverty is created equal; hence, there is not a "one-size-fits-all" approach. Take the time to find the niche that is right for your church and your community.

REFLECTION QUESTIONS AND EXERCISES

Please write responses to the following:

1. Reflect back on your answers to the "Initial Thoughts" questions at the start of this chapter. Is there anything you would now like to change about those answers? Be specific.

2. Think about the materially poor people in North America whom your church or ministry is trying to help. Do these people need relief, rehabilitation, or development? Is your church or ministry pursuing the right strategy for these people? If not, what harm might you be doing to these people and to yourselves? What changes could you make to improve your approach?

3. Think about the materially poor people in the Majority World whom your church or ministry is trying to help. Do these people need relief, rehabilitation, or development? Is your church or ministry pursuing the right strategy for these people? If not, what harm might you be doing to these people and to yourselves? What changes could you make to improve your approach?

4. Are you, your church, or your ministry being paternalistic in any of your poverty-alleviation efforts? If so, what could you do to change this?

5. Think about the organizations to which you are donating money. Are they pursuing relief, rehabilitation, or development appropriately? If you do not know, then try to find out by examining their literature, exploring their website, or asking them some questions.

6. Make a list of all the organizations that minister to the materially poor in your community. Determine the exact services that they provide and whether they are doing relief, rehabilitation, or development. To which organizations would you feel comfortable referring people? Keep this information handy for your church or ministry to use.

7. If you have relationships with the materially poor in your target community, conduct a focus group discussion to determine their assets and needs. Try to discern if relief, rehabilitation, or development is most needed in this community. What specific services are lacking?

8. Reflect on the information you have gathered in questions 6 and 7. What seems to be the best niche for your church or ministry?

INITIAL THOUGHTS

Please write short answers to the following questions:

1. Once you have determined whether relief, rehabilitation, or development is the correct intervention for your context, what do you think you should do next? What are the next steps? Be specific.

2. List some of your own gifts and abilities.

GIVE ME YOUR TIRED, YOUR POOR, AND THEIR **ASSETS**

Now that you have determined whether relief, rehabilitation, or development is the correct intervention, what do you do next? It seems like the next step would be to ascertain the needs of the individual or community in order to determine the best way to help. In fact, many ministries do begin this way, conducting a "needs assessment" by using an interview or a survey to determine what is wrong and the best way to provide assistance. This "needs-based" approach has merit, for diagnosing the underlying problems is essential to formulating the proper solutions. However, starting with a focus on needs amounts to starting a relationship with low-income people by asking them, "What is wrong with you? How can I fix you?" Given the nature of most poverty, it is difficult to imagine more harmful questions to both low-income people and to ourselves! Starting with such questions initiates the very dynamic that we need to avoid, a dynamic that confirms the feelings that we are superior, that they are inferior, and that they need us to fix them.

BEGINNING WITH ASSETS, NOT NEEDS

For these reasons, many Christian community-development experts have discovered the benefits of using "asset-based community development" (ABCD) as they seek to foster reconciliation of people's relationships with

God, self, others, and creation. ABCD is consistent with the perspective that God has blessed every individual and community with a host of gifts, including such diverse things as land, social networks, knowledge, animals, savings, intelligence, schools, creativity, production equipment, etc. ABCD puts the emphasis on what materially poor people already have and asks them to consider from the outset, "What is right with you? What gifts has God given you that you can use to improve your life and that of your neighbors? How can the individuals and organizations in your community work together to improve your community?" Instead of looking outside the low-income individual or community for resources and solutions, ABCD starts by asking the materially poor how they can be stewards of their own gifts and resources, seeking to restore individuals and communities to being what God has created them to be from the very start of the relationship. Indeed, the very nature of the question—What gifts do you have?—affirms people's dignity and contributes to the process of overcoming their poverty of being. And as they tell us of their gifts and abilities, we can start to see them as God does, helping us to overcome our sense of superiority; that is, our own poverty of being.

In contrast, needs-based development focuses on what is lacking in the life of a community or a person. The assumption in this approach is that the solutions to poverty are dependent upon outside human and financial resources. Churches and ministries using a needs-based approach are often quick to provide food, clothes, shelter, and money to meet the perceived, immediate needs of low-income people, who are often viewed as "clients" or "beneficiaries" of the program. Pouring in outside resources is not sustainable and only exacerbates the feelings of helplessness and inferiority that limits low-income people from being better stewards of their God-given talents and resources. When the church or ministry stops the flow of resources, it can leave behind individuals and communities that are more disempowered than ever before.

Asset-based approaches to poverty alleviation should not be seen as denying the fact that low-income people—like all of us—have glaring needs. Some of these needs emanate from their personal sins; some result from unjust social, economic, political, and religious systems; and some come from natural disasters resulting from Adam and Eve's sin. Indeed, the fall has tainted every last speck of the cosmos. The point of ABCD is not to deny those needs or the deep-seated brokenness that undergirds them. On the contrary, the point of ABCD is to recognize—from the very start—that poverty is rooted in the brokenness of the foundational relationships and to start the process of restoring both low-income people and ourselves to living in right relationship with God, self, others, and the rest of creation. What is wrong will come out soon enough; but by starting with what is right, we can change the dynamics that have marred the self-image of low-income people and that have created a sense of superiority in ourselves.

Once the assets have been identified, it is appropriate to then ask the poor individual or community the questions: "What needs can you identify that must be addressed? What problems do you see that must be solved? How can you use your assets to address those needs and to solve those problems?"

Of course, as the process proceeds, it may become clear that the individual or community does not have sufficient assets to address all of the needs. If and when such needs become pressing, it is then appropriate to bring in outside resources to augment local assets. But gauging the appropriate magnitude and timing of these outside resources takes an enormous amount of wisdom. It is crucial that such outside resources do not undermine the willingness or the ability of the poor individual or community to be stewards of their own gifts and resources. When considering bringing in outside resources, we must always ask two questions: (1) Is it too much? (2) Is it too early? It would be far better to let a nonemergency need go unmet than to meet that need with outside resources and cripple local initiative in the process. Again, poverty alleviation is about reconciling people's relationships, not about putting bandages over particular manifestations of the underlying brokenness.

One of the most difficult dynamics in all of this is that even the belief that outside resources may soon be forthcoming can mask people's true motivations for their behaviors. For example, the introduction to this book discussed a small-business class that I helped to initiate in a slum in Kampala. Why did people come to this class? Was it because they really valued the training, or was it because they believed that jumping through this hoop would increase their likelihood of getting some sort of financial assistance from me? I believe some people sincerely valued the training, but I also know that a number of the participants stopped coming when they became convinced that I was not going to give them any money. Their initial, enthusiastic attendance at the classes masked their true motivation: they wanted money, not training. All of us—myself included—do strange things in the presence of money and power. And in poor communities, the outsiders usually represent both, whether they realize it or not.

In summary, ABCD has four key elements:

- Identify and mobilize the capabilities, skills, and resources of the individual or community. See poor people and communities as full of possibilities, given to them by God.
- As much as possible, look for resources and solutions to come from within the individual or community, not from the outside.
- Seek to build and rebuild the relationships among local individuals, associations, churches, businesses, schools, government, etc. God intended for the various individuals and institutions in communities to be interconnected and complementary.
- Only bring in outside resources when local resources are insufficient to solve pressing needs. Be careful about bringing in resources that are too much or too early. Do this in a manner that does not undermine local capacity or initiative.

BACK TO THE BIBLE

The creation-fall-redemption motif outlined in chapters 2 and 3 provides a biblical foundation for thinking about both the nature and relationship of assets and needs in poor individuals and communities. As we discussed, Colossians 1:16–17 indicates that the goodness of God's creation includes "all things," extending beyond the natural world into culture as a whole. Our basic predisposition should be to see poor communities—including their natural resources, people, families, neighborhood associations, schools, businesses, governments, culture, etc.—as being created by Jesus Christ and reflective of His goodness. Hence, as we enter a poor community, there is a sense in which we are walking on holy ground, because Christ has been actively at work in that community since the creation of the world! This should give us an attitude of respect and a desire to help the community residents to discover, celebrate, and further develop

God's gifts to them. And that is exactly what ABCD is all about.

Of course, the fall has distorted the inherent goodness of the creation design, damaging the assets. As a result, communities do have pressing and urgent needs: individual lives are broken; organizations, associations, businesses, churches, and governments often pursue power more than the public interest; and even local customs or cultures often glorify the profane. But all is not lost. Colossians 1:16–17 teaches that Christ is holding all things together. He does not allow the effects of sin to completely destroy the inherent goodness of the assets that He created. In the midst of the decay, the assets persist—albeit in distorted fashion—because the Creator of the universe makes them persist. We do not need to despair. There is plenty of goodness to discover and to celebrate—plenty of ABCD to do—even in a fallen world!

And finally, the good news of the gospel of the kingdom is that Christ is not just sustaining all things, but He is reconciling all things. One day all of the assets—natural resources, individuals, neighborhood associations, schools, businesses, governments, etc.—will be liberated from their "bondage to decay" (Rom. 8:21). Jesus Christ created, sustains, and is redeeming assets in poor communities. As the body of Christ, the church should seek to do the same.

MZUNGU MISTAKES

We have covered a lot of ground since the introductory chapter to this book. Recall from that chapter that I gave eight dollars to Elizabeth, a Ugandan church leader, so that she could buy penicillin to save the life of Grace, the ex–witch doctor. I later realized that I might have done an enormous amount of harm to St. Luke's Church and its pastor, to the refugees in the small-business class, and even to Grace herself. Consider now all that we have discussed thus far. Why might it have been a mistake for me to pay for the penicillin? How might I have done harm in the process of trying to help? What would have been a more effective strategy for assisting Grace? As you consider these questions, never lose sight of the goal: reconciling relationships is the essence of poverty alleviation.

Grace was clearly in need of relief. Lying in agony on the floor of her shack, she was unable to help herself and needed somebody to provide assistance to her. But was I the best person to provide such relief? Remember a key relief principle we learned in chapter 4: *Respond when needs of the affected population are unmet by local people or organizations (or family members) due to their inability or unwillingness to help.* I never even considered this principle when reaching into my pocket for the eight dollars to pay for the penicillin. Relief was the right intervention, but I was not the right person to offer it.

I failed to consider the local assets that already existed in this slum, assets that included small amounts of money, a church, a pastor, and the social bonds of the one hundred refugees attending the small-business class. The truth is that there was more than enough time to walk back to the church, where the small-business class was still assembled, and ask the participants what they could do to help Grace. While the refugees were extremely poor, they could have mustered the eight cents per person to pay for the penicillin. In short, by providing the eight dollars, I violated the four key elements of ABCD mentioned above.

Of course, handing over the money was so much easier and so much faster than asking the refugees to assist Grace; and therein resides the problem of many poverty-alleviation efforts: the North American need for speed undermines the slow process needed for lasting and effective long-run development.

Why does all of this matter? Grace desperately needed relationships in the community in general and in St. Luke's Church in particular. Her former way of life had created many enemies, and, being infected with HIV, Grace was going to need solid support structures as time wore on. In fact, Grace needed to have her poverty of community alleviated if she was going to have any chance for long-term survival. Neither Elizabeth nor I could provide this for Grace over the long haul. I was soon leaving the country, and Elizabeth did not live in this slum. Grace needed the members of the community and of St. Luke's Church to embrace her and to consider her as one of their own. By giving the eight dollars myself, I missed an opportunity to facilitate such relationships between Grace and the local support structures that were crucial to her long-term survival.

But I may have done harm to more than just Grace. My failure to identify and mobilize local assets may have hindered the development of those assets. For example, St. Luke's was a poor church struggling to minister in a poor community. My eight dollars removed a chance for St. Luke's to be what the

Bible calls it to be: the body, bride, and fullness of Jesus Christ in this slum. I denied St. Luke's the chance to declare the good news of the kingdom of God in word and in deed to "the least of these." Instead of helping St. Luke's to be "salt and light," I joined decades of North American evangelicals in communicating that the mzungu—the powerful, rich, educated white person—was the "salt and light."

And what about the pastor of St. Luke's Church? Imagine being this pastor, preaching faithfully week in and week out to small crowds and earning a highly uncertain salary. And then one day the circus comes to town in the form of a 6'10" mzungu with a compelling small-business-training curriculum. The small-business classes draw bigger crowds than your Sunday morning worship services, and news is traveling that demons are even being cast out in these classes. And then when the newest member of your church, an ex–witch doctor, gets sick, the mzungu ringleader of the circus pays for her to get the medicine she needs. In fact, by the time you learn that Grace was sick, she has already recovered! And then the mzungu ringleader gets on an airplane, leaving you in the dust as you pursue the day in and day out grind of ministry. I may have undermined the pastor of St. Luke's Church. I did not realize it at the time, and I did not intend to do this. But I may have done so nonetheless.

Finally, there were the refugees themselves. Their eyes had grown wide and their faces had brightened throughout the small-business course. The message of the gospel was so freeing and empowering to them. For the first time they understood that they were created in the image of God and had inherent value and worth. Even if others saw them as being from an inferior tribe, the Creator of heaven and earth did not see them this way. They had gifts and abilities and could be stewards over their lives and communities, and in doing so they could glorify God Himself! Except, of course, that the first time a problem arose—how to minister to Grace—the mzungu took it upon himself to solve the problem, undermining every message that had been taught in the course.

Oh to have that eight dollars back. I wish I had encouraged Elizabeth to go back to St. Luke's to ask the refugees to assist Grace. Elizabeth could have brought the pastor in as part of the problem-solving process. While they were doing this, I should have gotten in the taxi and gotten out of there as fast as possible. Why? My entire presence in this situation, given all that it means to be a mzungu, was completely debilitating of local assets, be they human, financial, social, or spiritual.

But what if the refugees or the pastor had failed to respond while I was driving away? What then would have become of Grace? I highly doubt this would have happened, but if it had, Elizabeth had eight dollars from her own ministry to spend. I am absolutely sure Elizabeth would have stepped in with her own money if she had needed to do so—and she was less of an outsider than I. My jumping in the taxi without providing financial help would not have put Grace at immediate risk. In contrast, my giving the eight dollars, bringing in outside resources too quickly, missed opportunities for greater impact and may have done harm.

The point here is not that outside resources are always a bad idea. Indeed, North American Christians need to be giving more, not less, money to help the poor. But how that money is given and to whom it is given is crucial. We need to look for ways to give money that builds up local organizations and that truly empowers the poor. My eight-dollar gift failed to meet this standard.

COMMON APPROACHES TO ABCD

The remainder of this chapter reviews three common approaches to ABCD.

Asset Mapping

Made popular by John Kretzmann and John McKnight of the Asset-Based Community Development Institute at Northwestern University, Asset Mapping has become a common approach to community development work in the United States.[1] A better term for this approach might be "asset inventorying," since the strategy primarily uses individual or group-based interviews to catalogue the assets in a particular community. Prepared worksheets are used to document the assets in various categories, such as the abilities and resources of local individuals, businesses, associations, and institutions. Once local assets are "mapped"—that is, an inventory has been prepared—community residents and facilitators can identify strengths, make linkages between existing individuals and groups, and determine the best ways to leverage these assets to improve the community and to solve problems.

Although this all sounds rather mechanical, this approach has potential power as a starting point for developing empowering relationships. I learned this firsthand when I participated in an asset-mapping exercise as part of a Sunday school class on community development at my church. During the Sunday school hour, our class visited a low-income housing project with which we wanted to develop a relationship. Each member of the class individually went door-to-door, saying to people, "Hello, I am from Community Presbyterian Church, the church just around the corner. We are conducting a survey today to find out what gifts God has placed in this community. What skills and abilities do you have?"

The truth is that I wanted to die. Racial tensions are still very present in our city, so I knew there would be at least some social discomfort for both the African-American residents of this housing project and for me. Furthermore, my height can be quite startling and intimidating, adding awkwardness to virtually all first encounters. And finally, the words I was supposed to repeat sounded totally hokey to me. "Hello, I am from Community Presbyterian Church, the church just . . ." Yuck! I would rather be selling Girl Scout cookies. I had a bad attitude about this exercise and wished I had chosen to attend the Sunday school class that was examining the finer points of Presbyterianism. But alas, I had chosen this class, so off I dutifully marched and knocked on the first door.

The thirty something African-American woman who cracked open the door slightly was about 5′2″, giving her a wonderful view of my belly. She looked up at me the way one would look at one's first sight of a Martian. I tried not to flinch and launched into my sales pitch, "Hello, I am from Community Presbyterian Church, the church . . ."

She said, "What?!" looking even more incredulous than before. I knew she was thinking to herself, *The Martian can talk, but he sure says weird things.*

I swallowed hard and repeated, "What skills do you have? What are you good at doing?"

She repeated, "What?!" And then I repeated my questions again, asking God to add jewels to my crown for going through all of this.

Getting past her incredulousness at the entire situation, the lady said sheepishly, "Well, I guess I can cook."

Suddenly, a voice from the dark unknown behind the lady shouted out,

"She can cook chitlins like there is no tomorrow!"

Another voice yelled, "Yeah, ain't nobody can cook as good as she can!"

Slowly a smile spread across her face and she said, "Yes, I think I can cook."

Next thing I knew, I found myself sitting in the living room with about six African Americans gathered around. I live in the South. This does not happen easily. Not sure what to do, I reverted to script, "Hello, I am from Community Presbyterian Church . . ." They took it from there.

"This is Joe, he can fix bikes. Whenever one of the kids in the project has a bike that needs fixing, Joe is the man." A smile spread across Joe's face. "And this here is Mac. How is your car running? If you ever have trouble with your car, bring it right here to Mac." I noticed that Mac started to sit up a little straighter in his chair. They went on and on, bragging about one another to me. All I had to do was sit there and write it all down.

Yes, we got an inventory of people's assets that day, an inventory that we later used to help the residents dream about how to solve some of their problems. But more importantly, we started a process of empowerment by asking a simple question: what gifts do you have? When one is feeling marginalized, such a question can be nothing short of revolutionary.

Participatory Learning and Action

Participatory Learning and Action (PLA) is a mind-set and an associated set of tools developed by community development workers in the Majority World during the 1990s.[2] PLA uses a variety of group-based exercises to engage and energize community members in thinking about their community's history, assets, survival strategies, and goals. The processes are designed to affirm the community members' knowledge and skills in order to empower them to take greater ownership of their futures. There are a wide range of PLA exercises including time lines, seasonal calendars, community mapping, matrix rankings, etc. Although originally designed for use in rural communities in the Majority World, PLA exercises can be adapted to the North American context and may be particularly effective with populations accustomed to community-based decision making, such as immigrants, native Americans, African Americans, and Hispanics.

Appreciative Inquiry

Similar to Asset Mapping and PLA, Appreciative Inquiry (AI) focuses on what is right and good in a community's past as a means of creating a more positive future.[3] Based on a postmodern perspective that says that humans construct their own reality, AI argues that we should facilitate a process in which poor communities narrate what has worked well for them in the past. Once the community has constructed this positive understanding of its history, it can then use this narration to imagine how life can be even better in the future. Central to AI is the belief that people have more confidence to face an unknown future if they are bringing forward positive elements of their past.

Christians need to reject a fundamental assumption of AI. Truth is not socially constructed; it is divinely constructed. However, the tools of AI can be useful, particularly when viewed from the creation-fall-redemption perspective. God has indeed placed good gifts into every community. While sin has brought enormous brokenness, Christ has been sustaining all of creation—including culture—since the dawn of time and is in the process of reconciling all of it. Hence, all communities are a mix of good and bad. Christians can use AI to identify the good gifts that God has placed in a community and to dream about how to use those gifts to fix what is wrong, thereby bringing about a greater witness to the realities of the coming kingdom.

The AI approach to ABCD asks poor individuals and communities to consider the questions in the four-part process highlighted in the following figure:

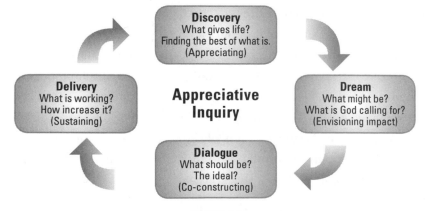

FIGURE 5.1

Adapted from Scott Johnson and James D., Ludema, *Partnering to Build and Measure Organizational Capacity: Lessons from NGOs around the World* (Grand Rapids, Mich.: Christian Reformed World Relief Committee, 1997), 75.

Some Christian, nongovernment organizations (NGOs) working in the Majority World have experienced outstanding results from using AI. For example, Bryant Myers reports that a Christian NGO in Tanzania wanted to stop the dynamic of poor communities presenting the NGO with a laundry list of things they expected the NGO's staff to do for them. Wanting the communities to take greater responsibility for their own improvement, the NGO has been using AI with remarkable results:

> The laundry list of problems the community would like the NGO to fix is lost in the enthusiasm of describing what is already working. The community comes to view its past and itself in a new light. We do know things. We do have resources. We have a lot to be proud of. We are already on the journey. God has been good to us. We can do something. We are not god-forsaken. This is a major step toward recovering the community's true identity and discovering its true vocation. With these discoveries a major transformational frontier has been crossed.[4]

It may be difficult for readers to understand how AI can unleash such a powerful process, but that is because most of us do not understand the profound sense of despair and shame that envelops many poor communities around the world. AI can help shift the focus from all that has gone wrong to all that has gone right.

AI can also work in the North American context. A church in Florida operated a monthly food pantry in which it handed out boxes of food to needy people, who were required before they could get their food to listen to a devotional delivered by a person with whom they had no relationship. The church's community ministries director realized the church was simply enabling the recipients to persist in poverty by providing relief when development was the correct intervention; hence, she decided to use AI to move to a more empowering dynamic. Rather than talking at the recipients of the food, they broke into small groups consisting of a mix of the recipients and the church members. The small groups then used AI to discover the gifts and abilities of the recipients. The community ministries director reports on the effects:

> Rather than trying to "fix" them, we are engaging in relationships with them. In the process "we" are finding out how impoverished we are and how

much we need "them" in order to see our own spiritual poverty. There is a real spirit of authentic community growing, and more participants are beginning to come to worship. Members are picking people up and bringing them to church and are working with them on budgeting and finding jobs and best of all, just enjoying one another as friends. I believe it is ever so slowly changing the culture of our church. We are beginning to look more broken but beautiful. . . . I guess the words of some of [the food pantry] participants have been my biggest encouragement that we are heading in the right direction. One lady said, "I no longer feel like I'm just a number in the crowd. Now I have a face." Another said, "Even if I don't need groceries next month, can I still come?" We have begun using participants who come regularly as volunteers, and they are delighted to serve. Last month one man said, "I feel like we're sort of a church within a church." A volunteer told me that a person he did an exit interview with said that what set our ministry apart from other food pantries was that we treated them with respect and as though we actually enjoyed them.[5]

ABCD is not a recipe for success in poverty alleviation. Nothing is. But getting off on the right foot can make a huge difference in unleashing the empowering dynamics that are crucial for fostering reconciliation—poverty alleviation—both in the materially poor and in ourselves.

REFLECTION QUESTIONS AND EXERCISES

Please write responses to the following:

1. Consider your answer to the first question in the "Initial Thoughts" at the start of this chapter. What implicit assumptions do you see about yourself and about poor people in your answers?

2. Describe how you felt after listing your gifts and abilities in the second question at the start of this chapter.

3. What light do Philippians 4:8 and 1 Thessalonians 5:11 shed on the perspective and tools of ABCD?

4. Consider using asset mapping, PLA, or AI with the individuals or communities with which you want to minister. Learn more about the available tools you can use to implement these approaches.

INITIAL THOUGHTS

Imagine that your church or ministry wants to help
an individual poor person or a poor community.
Whom would you ask for advice? Write down a list of the
people you might consult to design your approach.

McDEVELOPMENT:
OVER 2.5 BILLION PEOPLE
NOT SERVED

Wanting to assist a village in Colombia with its rice production, a non-profit organization gathered the villagers into a cooperative and bought them a thresher, a motorized huller, a generator, and a tractor. Rice production boomed, and the cooperative sold the rice at the highest price the farmers had ever received. The project appeared to be a tremendous success. The nonprofit organization then left the village, but several years later one of its staff members returned to find that the cooperative had completely disbanded and that all of the equipment was broken down and rusting away in the fields. In fact, some of the equipment had never been used at all. Yet, as the staff member walked through the village, the people pleaded with him, "If [your organization] would just come help us again, we could do so much!"[1]

The sad truth is that this story is extremely common. All around the world one can find donated equipment that is rusting away, latrines that have never been used, community associations that have disbanded, and projects that disintegrated soon after the nonprofit organization left town. Despite an estimated $2.3 trillion in foreign aid dispensed from Western nations during the post–World War II era,[2] more than 2.5 billion people, approximately 40 percent of the world's population, still live on less than two dollars per day.[3] And the story in many North American communities is similar, with one initiative after another failing to meet its intended objectives. Indeed, forty-five years after President Johnson launched the War on Poverty, the poverty rate in America stubbornly hovers around 12 percent, decade after decade, year after year.

Yes, there has been progress in the global fight against poverty, but the "bang for the buck" has been appallingly low. There are a lot of machines rusting away in fields. Why?

LEARNING PROCESS VERSUS BLUEPRINT APPROACHES

This book has already explained a number of reasons for the slow progress in poverty alleviation, but another reason needs to be highlighted: *inadequate participation of poor people in the process.* Researchers and practitioners have found that meaningful inclusion of poor people in the selection, design, implementation, and evaluation of an intervention increases the likelihood of that intervention's success. Unfortunately, the majority of post–World War II approaches to poverty alleviation have been highly nonparticipatory, using a "blueprint approach" in which the economically non-poor make all the decisions about the project and then do the project *to* the economically poor. The ultimate goal of the blueprint approach is often to develop a standardized product and then to roll out that product in cookie-cutter fashion on a massive scale. It's "McDevelopment," the fast-food-franchise approach to poverty alleviation, and it has resulted in more than 2.5 billion poor people not being well served.

Although the blueprint approach *appears* to be very efficient, it often fails because it imposes solutions on poor communities that are inconsistent with local culture, that are not embraced and "owned" by the community members, or that cannot work in that particular setting. The fact that the equipment worked well in Kansas simply does not mean it will work well in the cultural, economic, and institutional context of sub-Saharan Africa. "We're not in Kansas anymore!"

For example, the staff worker of a nonprofit organization working in a Latin American country describes how the nonparticipatory approach of a short-term mission team resulted in a house being built that may soon go unused:

One team came here to build the house of a low-income pastor of a local church. In the design of the house, the team put the bathroom in the middle of the house, which runs counter to local culture in which bathrooms are located in the back of the house. The pastor had not seen the plans of the house in advance. When he discovered this mistake while the team was building the house, he objected to the team leaders to no avail. The short-term team felt happy that they gave the pastor a much needed house, but the pastor is ashamed of his house and is not sure he wants to live in it.[4]

And the cultural barriers are there on our own soil in places we might not even anticipate. Consider the Farmers Home Administration (FmHA) program that attempted to provide housing loans for poor people in the rural southern United States. The FmHA specified that every house in the program would be standardized, having carpets on the floors and small kitchens that included washing machines. Research on the program's efficacy found the following:

> [The FmHa's] specifications for how houses may be built . . . actually defy community wisdom and experience. Many applicants [for housing loans] consider it unsanitary to cook and wash laundry in the same room. They know that overflowing, secondhand washing machines are best located in a storage or utility room outside the house. They know that there are other advantages to putting the washers outside. You can take off your work clothes before you go into the house, and your clean laundry is closer to the clothesline. People who live on dirt roads, who work the land, or who are employed in poultry processing plants or in lint-filled mills often prefer vinyl floors that can be swept. But they can't have them [in this program].[5]

Because of these types of pitfalls, many practitioners have abandoned the blueprint model in favor of a "learning process" approach to development, an approach that seeks to facilitate an action-reflection cycle in which poor people participate in all aspects of the project: proposing the best course of action, implementing the chosen strategy, evaluating how well things are working, and determining the appropriate modifications. The role of the outsider in this approach is not to do something *to* or *for* the economically poor individual or community but to seek solutions together *with* them.

A learning process approach increases the likelihood that the project will work well, for two main reasons. First, like all human beings, poor people are more likely to have a sense of enthusiasm for and ownership of a project if they have been *full* participants in it from the very beginning. When the project is "theirs," they are more likely to sacrifice to make it work well and to sustain it over the long haul. Second, poor individuals and communities are highly complex and not well understood by the materially non-poor. Hence, the knowledge and skills of the insiders—the materially poor themselves—are vital to getting things done and to making things work well. People living in North American ghettos, in Appalachia, in slums in Mexico City, and in rural India really do know a lot of things about those contexts that outsiders will never understand. It is simply foolish to ignore their insights.

Ironically, while a learning process approach typically takes more time to produce tangible results than a blueprint approach, the learning process approach is often more efficient in the long run because it is more likely to result in workable and sustainable interventions. Put another way, participation can reduce the likelihood of unused equipment rusting away in the fields.

Not Just a Means but an End

While it is good when the equipment is used and the rice output increases, viewing participation solely as a means of achieving those ends misses the fundamental reason that participation is so vital to poverty alleviation:

Participation is not just the means to an end but rather a legitimate end in its own right.

Why? It all goes back to the definition of poverty alleviation. Remember, the goal is to restore people to experiencing humanness in the way that God intended. The crucial thing is to help people to understand their identity as image bearers, to love their neighbors as themselves, to be stewards over God's creation, and to bring glory to God in all things. One of the many manifestations of such holistic reconciliation is that people exercise dominion over their individual lives and communities, constantly seeking better ways to use their gifts and resources to solve problems and to create bounty in service to God and others. Thus, the goal is not just that the equipment gets used and that rice output goes up, but rather that poor people are empowered to make decisions about the best way to farm, to act upon their decisions, to evaluate the results of their decisions, and then to start the decision-making process all over again. Hence, participation in its fullest sense is not just a means to an end but the most important end!

It is impossible to accomplish such reconciliation of relationships in a blueprint approach in which the outsiders are the ones deciding what to do, how to do it, and how well it worked. Such an approach undermines the action-reflection cycle for poor people, denying them the opportunity to be what God created them to be: image bearers who, through trial and error, unpack and unfold the wonders of God's creation.

Furthermore, the blueprint approach implicitly communicates, "I, the outsider, am superior; you are inferior; I am here to fix you." A participatory approach, in contrast, asks the poor at each step in the process, "What do you think?" and then really values the answers that are given. The very fact that the question is being asked is a powerful statement that says, "I believe you have value, knowledge, and insights. You know things about your situation that I do not know. Please share some of your insights with me. Let us learn together."

We saw an excellent example of a ministry using a learning process approach—both as a means and an end—in developing an entire community. Recall from chapter 3 that Mark Gornik and Allan and Susan Tibbels moved into inner-city Baltimore and then worked *with* the community residents using a participatory process that took four years to produce a single house. This participatory process created the energy and ownership that eventually led to the rehabilitation of hundreds of homes in the subsequent years, but these homes were the by-product of the central goal: *getting community members to participate more fully in all that it means to be human.*

A learning process can also be used when ministering to individuals one-on-one. For example, the director of a home and ministry for single mothers in Knoxville, Tennessee, describes his ministry's approach as follows:

> Instead of having a one-size-fits-all blueprint for each family, [our ministry] tries to journey alongside a single mother and her children, believing that the family's unique strengths, history, and future goals need to be understood and appreciated. The mother meets weekly with a Family Advocate,

who helps her begin to explore the areas of her family's life that are in need of restoration. While the Family Advocate facilitates the process, each single mother participates in the process by working to envision the family's future and setting goals and initiating the action steps necessary to achieve them. The Family Advocate is then able to help hold the mother accountable, as well as contribute to the family's long-term plan through resource development.[6]

The single mothers in this program desire to someday purchase their own homes and be self-sufficient, but the very fact that these mothers are dreaming, planning, and striving toward that end is a major success in its own right.

A Cautionary Word

A word of caution is in order. Secular arguments for participation often rest on two faulty assumptions. First, given the postmodern belief that truth is relative, some argue that poor people must participate in the process because they need to construct their own reality. Who are we outsiders to impose our ideas on poor people? they say. Second, a humanist faith in the inherent goodness of human beings leads some to believe that participation, like democracy, will necessarily produce positive results. Both of these assumptions are wrong from a biblical perspective. The Bible clearly teaches that there is absolute truth and that—to the extent that we know it—we are to speak such truth in love (Eph. 4:15). Moreover, all of us, including poor people, are sinful; participation does not have the capacity to overcome the basic corruption in the human condition. Individuals and groups make bad decisions all the time!

However, a participatory approach is consistent with a biblical perspective concerning poverty and its alleviation. The scriptural truths that all of us are broken and that all of us retain the image of God are affirmed by a process that solicits and values the positive contributions of everyone, both insiders and outsiders. Furthermore, the fact that participatory approaches enable the materially poor to "teach" the materially non-poor helps to overcome the inferior-superior dynamic that typically characterizes the interactions between them. As a result, the dignity of the materially poor is affirmed, and the god-complexes of the materially non-poor are dispelled.

Types of Participation

Table 6.1 summarizes a continuum of different levels of participation that are observed in practice. Reading the table from top to bottom, the approaches move from doing things *to* poor people (a blueprint approach), toward doing things *with* poor people (a learning process approach). When the poor have been completely empowered, they are in the "community initiated" category in which the projects are being directed by the poor themselves, and they determine the role of any outsiders in their initiatives. Unfortunately, the top-down, blueprint methods that are typically used in poverty alleviation make the community-initiated mode of participation a rarity, but both the existing literature and our own experiences demonstrate that achieving this mode is not impossible.[7]

There is a not a "one-size-fits-all" level of participation that is best for all churches, missionaries, and ministries in all settings. The appropriate nature and degree of participation depends on a host of contextual factors, including the mission of the organization, the type of intervention being considered, and the capacity and culture of the poor people involved. It takes wisdom to discern the best type and level of participation in each setting. That having been said, outsiders should normally seek to foster the "cooperation" or, better yet, "co-learning" modes of participation in hopes of achieving the "community initiated" level, the point at which the outsiders are no longer the key players.

Christians rightly understand that the church is the "pillar and foundation of the truth" (1 Tim. 3:15) and that unbelievers are people who "suppress the truth by their wickedness" (Rom. 1:18). By the grace of God alone, we really do have knowledge that unbelievers do not have. Unfortunately, this reality can create not just an unwarranted sense of pride in spiritual matters but also a sense of condescension toward unbelievers in all matters. We are often "know-it-alls" in situations in which we really do not know more. Naturally, it would be ludicrous to let an unbeliever determine the best way to administer the sacraments just because we want to use participatory methods! We really do know more about the right way to do this than they do. At the same time, it would be equally ludicrous to assume that we know more than an unbeliever in Thailand about the best way to plant rice in his country. As image bearers, unbelievers often have a lot of good ideas. To deny this is an affront to the One whose image they bear. And many times, those we seek to help are fellow believers who have important spiritual insights to teach us.

Seek the highest level of participation possible in each situation.

A Participatory Continuum

Mode of Participation	Type of Involvement of Local People	Relationship of Outsiders to Local People
Coercion	Local people submit to predetermined plans developed by outsiders.	DOING TO
Compliance	Local people are assigned to tasks, often with incentives, by outsiders; the outsiders decide the agenda and direct the process.	DOING FOR
Consultation	Local people's opinions are asked; outsiders analyze and decide on a course of action.	DOING FOR
Cooperation	Local people work together with outsiders to determine priorities; responsibility remains with outsiders for directing the process.	DOING WITH
Co-Learning	Local people and outsiders share their knowledge to create appropriate goals and plans, to execute those plans, and to evaluate the results.	DOING WITH
Community Initiated	Local people set their own agenda and mobilize to carry it out without outside initiators and facilitators.	RESPONDING TO

TABLE 6.1

Adapted from B. de Negri, E. Thomas, A. Ilinigumugabo, I. Muvandi, and G. Lewis, *Empowering Communities: Participatory Techniques for Community-Based Programme Development. Volume 1(2): Trainer's Manual (Participant's Handbook)* (Nairobi, Kenya: Centre for African Family Studies, 1998), 4.

GIVING VOICE TO THE VOICELESS

In many poor communities, there is considerable diversity in terms of ethnicity, race, gender, age, religion, and socioeconomic status. Hence, it is important to make sure that each group has meaningful participation both because each group may bring a unique perspective and because participation is an important goal in its own right. In particular, it is vital to give a "voice to the voiceless" by looking for ways to make it safe for those on the margins to express their views throughout the process.

As mentioned in chapter 5, one of the central methods that can be used to engage a community is Participatory Learning and Action (PLA), a mind-set and associated set of tools that enable an outsider to facilitate a learning process in poor communities. PLA engages people, creating a safe and fun way for them to share their knowledge and to construct their own solutions to the problems they are facing.

The importance of engaging a diversity of perspectives in PLA is illustrated in figure 6.1, which shows the result of a PLA exercise conducted in a rural Paraguayan village. Men and women from the *same* village were separately asked to draw maps of that village and to note on the maps the frequency with which they visited each spot. Clearly, the men and women had quite different perceptions of their community! It appears that "men are from Mars and women are from Venus" in Paraguay too. A failure to include multiple voices in the PLA process would have caused everyone involved to have a distorted view of how the community as a whole viewed itself.

DONOR ALERT!

It has become commonplace in charitable giving to ask, What is the most highly leveraged way to invest money in order to have the greatest impact for the kingdom? The question is legitimate, and it often reflects a godly desire to steward the Lord's resources faithfully. However, donors need to remember that reconciling people's relationships with God, self, others, and the rest of creation is simply not the same as producing and selling widgets. Deep and lasting change takes time. In fact, fully engaging the poor in a participatory process takes lots of time. But if donors do not want the equipment to rust in the fields, they are going to have to accept a slower process, a process in which the poor are empowered to decide whether or not they even want the equipment in the first place. It might help donors if they remembered that creating decision-making capacity on the part of the poor is a return—arguably the chief return—on their investment.

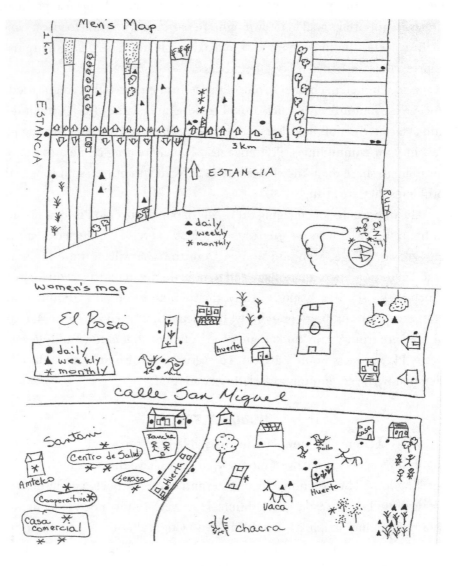

FIGURE 6.1

Peace Corps, *Gender and Development Training: Booklet 5* (Washington, D.C.: Peace Corps Information and Collection Exchange, 1998), 14–15.

REFLECTION QUESTIONS AND EXERCISES

Please write responses to the following:

Review your answer to the question in the "Initial Thoughts" at the start of this chapter.

(a) Whom did you ask for advice?

(b) Whom did you not ask for advice?

(c) What, if anything, does this reveal about your views of the poor and of yourself?

Extended Exercise: Indonesia Reconsidered

In the "Opening Exercise" at the start of this book, you were asked to design a project for your church to help with the restarting of small businesses in Indonesia, four months after the 2004 tsunami. We have covered a lot of ground since then, and it is now time for you to examine the plan you wrote. Please discuss the following questions with the group of people with whom you originally designed the project for Indonesia. If you are reading this book individually, then consider these questions on your own.

1. What implicit assumptions about the nature of poverty and its alleviation are reflected in your plan?

2. In chapter 2 we discussed an equation that captures a common dynamic that is often present when the materially non-poor interact with the materially poor:

$$\text{Material Definition of Poverty} + \text{God-Complexes of Materially Non-Poor} + \text{Feelings of Inferiority of Materially Poor} = \text{Harm to Both Materially Poor and Non-Poor}$$

(a) Were you aware that the materially poor often have feelings of shame and inferiority when you designed your project?

(b) If not, how might such an awareness have modified your plans?

(c) Do you see any evidence of a god-complex in the way you designed your project?

3. In chapter 4 we discussed some of the implications of a relational under-standing of poverty and its alleviation. How might this framework alter the approach that you took? Specifically:

   (a) Did you focus on "people and processes" or just on "projects and products"?

   (b) Did you address the brokenness in both individuals and systems?

4. Review the distinction between relief, rehabilitation, and development and consider the following:

   (a) Did the design of your trip reflect an accurate assessment as to which of these three approaches was appropriate for the context?

   (b) Did you provide relief in the context in which rehabilitation or devel-opment was the appropriate intervention?

   (c) How might a more accurate assessment of the appropriate intervention alter the plans that you made?

   (d) How could you have approached your project from a more "develop-mental" perspective? (Review the material from chapter 4, "Doing Relief and Rehabilitation, Developmentally.")

   (e) Were you at all paternalistic in your approach to this project?

5. Did you use an asset-based or a needs-based approach to this project? In par-ticular, consider how well your project exhibited the four key elements of an asset-based approach:

   (a) Did you identify and mobilize the capabilities, skills, and resources of the people in Indonesia?

   (b) As much as possible, did you look for resources and solutions to come from within Indonesia and not from the outside?

   (c) Did you seek to build and rebuild the relationships among local indi-viduals, associations, churches, businesses, schools, government, etc.?

   (d) Did you only bring in outside resources when local resources were in-sufficient to solve pressing needs?

6. Consider the extent to which you used a participatory approach to your project:

   (a) With whom did you plan to speak in determining whether or not to do this project?

   (b) Does the design of your project reflect doing things *to, for,* or *with* the people of Indonesia?

   (c) Where would your approach fall in the categories of participation described in table 6.1?

   (d) How could you have selected, designed, executed, and evaluated your project in a more participatory manner?

7. Stop and reflect on your answers to the previous six questions:

   (a) What have you learned about yourself?

   (b) Are there any changes you would like to ask God to make in you?

   (c) What have you learned about your church's approach to ministry?

   (d) Are there any changes you would like to ask God to make in your church or ministry?

   (e) What specific things would you like to do to pursue any of the changes that you desire in yourself, your church, or your ministry?

The following section describes what really happened when the Chalmers Center for Economic Development, the research and training center for which Steve and I work, was asked to help with the tsunami recovery in Indonesia. Please read this section and then answer the questions at the end.

THE REST OF THE STORY

Four months after the tsunami hit, a Christian relief and development organization working in Indonesia asked the Chalmers Center for help in designing a small-business recovery program. We sent two young staff members to the region and provided technical backup support to them from our home office in the United States. We share this story not to show you how smart we are—our failures outnumber our successes!—but because we believe the story illustrates many of the principles presented in this book. At various points in what follows, we have included references to the relevant questions and principles in the learning task you just completed. For example, "4a" at the end of a sentence means that this sentence illustrates the principle discussed in question 4 point *a* in the extended exercise above.

In considering whether or not to accept this request to work in Indonesia, we were greatly influenced by the fact that a well-respected relief and development organization on the ground was requesting our help. This organization had an outstanding track record of soliciting input from the local people, so we knew from the outset that our presence was in response to the wishes of the community and not something we were forcing on them (6a-b). While such a participatory approach is always important, it was particularly crucial in this case because this militant Muslim region was notorious for its hostility to outsiders in general and to Christians in particular.

The region had been devastated, but the downward spiral had stopped for the most part. Hence, rehabilitation and development, not relief, were the appropriate next steps (4a). In an attempt to identify the relevant local assets and the most significant obstacles (5a), our staff interviewed and consulted with the local leaders of ten small-business associations, individual business owners, and the mayor (6), discovering the following:

- They had a strong history of people using their own savings for business capital.
- In contrast to most settings in the Majority World, a remarkable bank had a history of providing savings and loan services to very poor people and it was well-trusted. Unfortunately, the bank's offices had been severely damaged, and it was low on loan capital.
- Businesses in the region were organized into strong guilds organized by the type of business: a baker's guild, a carpenter's guild, a rickshaw guild, etc.
- The mayor had an attitude of wanting to work with these guilds and with the Christian relief and development organization.
- There was a strong sense of community spirit exhibited in Gotong Royong, a practice of coming together as a group to solve problems, not unlike an Amish barn raising.

- Local labor was in abundance, as many had lost their livelihoods.
- Local construction firms existed but had been damaged by the tsunami.
- A lack of capital was identified as the primary obstacle to restarting the small businesses.

The obvious solution in such a situation would be to bring in construction crews to rebuild the businesses' shops and to set up a microenterprise development program to lend money to these businesses. Right? Wrong. This approach might undermine the local construction firms, the culture of savings, the remarkable bank, local knowledge and authority, and community spirit (2, 3a, 4e, 5). While the level of devastation did require outside resources to restore the city and these businesses to their pre-tsunami conditions, the trick was to introduce such resources without undermining the assets that had been identified (5d) and the stewardship abilities of the Indonesian people (4e, 6b). In particular, how could business capital be introduced quickly without undermining the culture of savings and the local bank?

Toward that end, it was decided that Phase I of the program would involve giving minigrants of capital to small-business owners to enable them to restart their businesses. However, receiving such grants was conditional upon the business owners' presenting evidence of having had a small business before the tsunami, of opening a savings account with the local bank, and of participating in a Gotong Royong to clean up buildings and streets, including the office of the local bank (5a–c). The evidence presented was reviewed by a committee of leaders from the guilds and local government (4e, 6). By design, the first grants were given to the local construction firms so that they—not outsiders—could rebuild the devastated buildings and homes, thereby re-establishing their construction businesses (4e, 5c).

Phase I also included a short series of small-business training sessions for the low-income entrepreneurs. These lessons included important technical material and related biblical principles. Thus, Muslim small-business owners received an exposure to the Scriptures in a practical way (3b). As discussed in chapter 3, poverty-alleviation efforts often need to address both broken systems and individuals, including a clear articulation of the gospel and a biblical worldview.

Phase II began eight weeks after Phase I and consisted primarily of a matched savings program to provide additional business capital while encouraging local savings and the reestablishment of the bank (5). Recipients of the minigrants in Phase I again had to present evidence of a consistent pattern of savings over the eight weeks to the local review committee (6). Each individual's savings were then matched with outside funds at a two-to-one ratio, with the matching funds being placed into their savings accounts at the bank (5c). Another series of small-business training classes incorporating a Christian worldview was offered (3b).

As with any program there were ups and downs, but the overall success was significant. Hundreds of businesses received assistance, local institutions were strengthened, and the midterm project evaluations indicated improvements in people's relationships with God, self, others, and the rest of creation (3). Moreover, the highly participatory approach enabled the Christian relief and development organization to establish a great deal of trust with the normally suspicious Indonesians, resulting in the organization being able to expand the small-business recovery program to other parts of Indonesia. Even a major, secular, international humanitarian organization was impressed with the results and invited the Christian organization to submit a grant proposal for funding to scale up the program.

The principles outlined in this book are not a magic formula for success. But they are powerful, and they have been used by God in even extremely difficult settings that are quite hostile to the gospel.

8. Now that you know "The Rest of the Story," consider again the way that you designed your church's project for Indonesia at the start of the book:

(a) What is good about the way that you designed your project?

(b) What damage might your project have done?

(c) How might your approach have strengthened or weakened the four key relationships?

9. List any specific action steps you will take to improve your church's current poverty-alleviation efforts.

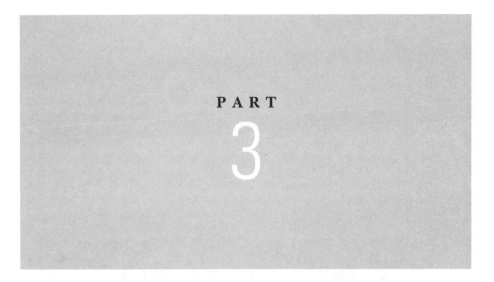

PART

3

PRACTICAL STRATEGIES
for HELPING
WITHOUT HURTING

Think about a short-term mission trip (one to two weeks) that you have been involved with in some capacity as a team member, planner, financial or prayer supporter, etc. If you have not been personally involved with such a trip, then think of a short-term trip with which you are familiar. If possible, think of a trip that was designed to minister to materially poor people. Write short answers to the following questions:

1. *What were some of the perceived benefits of the trip? Consider all the stakeholders involved, including the team members, the sending church or organization, the hosts, and the communities or individuals served.*

2. *Can you think of any negative impacts of this trip? Again, consider all the stakeholders.*

DOING SHORT-TERM
MISSIONS WITHOUT DOING
LONG-TERM HARM

There were 120,000 in 1989; 450,000 in 1998; 1,000,000 in 2003; and 2,200,000 in 2006. The numbers reflect a tsunami of epic proportions, a tidal wave of American short-term "missionaries" flooding the world. The cost? Americans spent $1.6 billion on short-term missions (STMs) in 2006 alone.[1]

The phenomenal growth of STMs over the past decade is accompanied, or fueled, by much positive press. Reports claim that STMs accomplish much in the host community and have a positive impact on those who go, especially in terms of their becoming further engaged in missions through giving and becoming long-term missionaries. While there may be some truth in these reports, a different story line is also emerging, one that is questioning whether STMs are as good as advertised.

For example, missions expert Miriam Adeney relates a story told to her by an African Christian friend:

Elephant and Mouse were best friends. One day Elephant said, "Mouse, let's have a party!" Animals gathered from far and near. They ate. They drank. They sang. And they danced. And nobody celebrated more and danced harder than Elephant. After the party was over, Elephant exclaimed, "Mouse, did you ever go to a better party? What a blast!" But Mouse did not answer. "Mouse, where are you?" Elephant called. He looked around for his friend, and then shrank back in horror. There at Elephant's feet lay Mouse. His little body was ground into the dirt. He had been smashed by the big feet of his exuberant friend, Elephant. "Sometimes, that is what it is like to do mission with you Americans," the African storyteller commented. "It is like dancing with an Elephant."[2]

Elephant did not mean to do harm, but he did not understand the effects he was having on Mouse. The same can be true for many STM trips, particularly those to poor communities.

The term "short-term missions" refers to trips ranging from one week to two years, either to other locations within North America or around the world. The focus of this chapter will be on trips of two weeks or less, the length experienced by more than 50 percent of the 2.2 million STM participants from the United States in 2006;[3] however, many of the issues discussed also apply to longer STMs. In addition, this chapter will pay particular attention to STMs that seek to minister to the physical needs of materially poor people, whether they are at home or abroad. We will then examine the wisdom of STMs from the perspective of stewardship and conclude the chapter with suggestions for improving the STM experience for everyone. However, we first lay the background for the entire discussion with a quick introduction to some important cross-cultural issues.

CROSS-CULTURAL ENGAGEMENT 101

One of the reasons that STM teams sometimes dance like Elephant is that the teams are unaware of what happens when cultures collide. The focus here is not on such cultural differences as dress, food, architecture, art, etc., but rather on the differences in the value systems that silently drive people to respond in predictable patterns. These value systems involve quite a range of things, including people's view of who or what is in control of their lives, of the nature of risk and uncertainty, of the organization and role of authority, of the nature of time, and of the role of individuals versus groups. Space only permits a discussion of the last two factors just mentioned.

Cultures around the world exhibit contrasting views of how time operates. The monochronic view sees time as a limited and valuable resource. Time can be lost or saved. Good stewardship of time means getting the most out of every minute. The favorite monochronic proverb is "Time is money." Day-timers are important tools for success. The biblical injunction to "redeem the time" brings visions of to-do lists being completed day after day.

A second perspective of time is the polychronic view. In this understanding time is a somewhat unlimited resource. There is always more time. Schedules and plans are mere guidelines that have little authority in shaping how one spends one's day. Tasks typically take a backseat to forming and deepening relationships. While fewer goods and services might get produced in a polychronic culture, people in such cultures often have a deeper sense of community and belonging.

Figure 7.1 shows where various countries fit on the monochronic-polychronic continuum. The United States is an extreme monochronic culture, whereas nations in the Majority World are strongly polychronic. Many low-income African-American and Hispanic communities in North America would also be more polychronic than middle-to-upper-class North American churches and people are.

Concept of Time

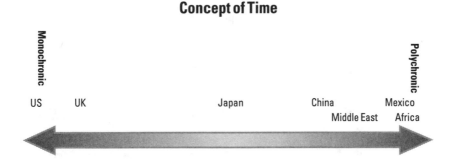

FIGURE 7.1

Adapted from Craig Storti, *Figuring Foreigners Out: A Practical Guide* (Yarmouth, Me.: Intercultural Press, 1999), 82.

Similarly, cultures differ in their understanding of the role of the individual and the group in shaping life. On the one hand there are individualistic cultures, which focus on the intrinsic value and uniqueness of each human being and exhibit the egalitarian perspective that all people should be treated equally as much as possible. People in individualistic cultures are taught to strive to be "all that they can be" in terms of personal achievement. Being "Employee of the Month" and "Most Valuable Player" on the team are seen as positive and motivating awards. Churches in such cultures stress one's personal calling and conduct inventories of spiritual gifts and personality tests.

Collectivist cultures, on the other hand, minimize individual identity and focus on the well-being of the group. Loyalty to and self-sacrifice for the sake of other group members are seen as virtuous. People in collectivist cultures have extremely deep bonds with the various groups of which they are a part, such as the extended family, tribe, employer/company, school, etc. For Christians in a collectivist culture, the importance of the local church body is much more deeply felt than is often found in individualistic cultures.

Where various countries fit on the individualistic-collectivist continuum is shown in figure 7.2. Again, the United States is at an extreme end, being far more individualistic than countries in the Majority World. Many low-income, African-American and Hispanic communities in North America would be less individualistic than middle-to-upper-class North American churches as well.

Concept of Self

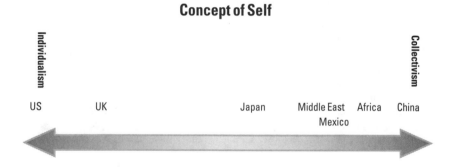

FIGURE 7.2

Adapted from Craig Storti, *Figuring Foreigners Out: A Practical Guide* (Yarmouth, Me.: Intercultural Press, 1999), 52.

The point here is neither to affirm nor to condemn different views of time or of self, although it is our belief that from a biblical perspective there are both pros and cons to each end of these continua. Rather, the point here is simply that there are major cultural differences that we North Americans do not always fully appreciate. It is crucial that North American STM teams move beyond ethnocentric thinking that either minimizes these cultural differences or that immediately assumes that middle-to-upper-class North American cultural norms are always superior to those of other cultures. Furthermore, it should give North American STMs some pause to realize that they are from an "extreme culture," that is, from the far end of these continua, creating the distinct possibility that the STM teams may have very different perceptions than the recipient communities about just how wonderful the STM dance really is.

THE EFFECTS OF STMS ON POOR COMMUNITIES

Most discussions of STMs have focused on their impacts on the teams and on the churches that send them. Less attention has been devoted to considering STMs' impacts on recipient, materially poor communities. This section explores these effects using the concepts developed earlier in the book.

The core problem with STMs to poor communities is that STMs tend to reflect the perspective of "poverty as deficit," the idea that poverty is due to the poor lacking something. North Americans often view the "something" as material resources, but a lack of knowledge or spirituality is also commonly cited.[4] This conception of poverty leads to poverty-alleviation strategies in which the materially non-poor are necessarily in the position of giving the "something" to the materially poor, since the non-poor have the "something" and the poor do not have it. Chapter 2 expressed some of this dynamic in the following equation:

This "poverty as deficit" perspective is especially problematic in the context of STMs, since all of the "giving" needs to get done within just two weeks!

In contrast, we have discussed how a more relational understanding of poverty sees both the materially poor and materially non-poor as suffering from broken relationships, albeit in different ways, and seeks to pursue processes that foster the reconciling work of Jesus Christ in the lives of both parties.

Against this backdrop, let us now consider STMs from the perspective of the material from the previous three chapters.

STMs and the Relief-Rehabilitation-Development Continuum

Very few STM trips are done in situations in which relief is the appropriate intervention. Even when a natural disaster has occurred, by the time the team arrives it may well be that the "bleeding has stopped" and that the rehabilitation phase has begun. Furthermore, most of the time, STMs to materially poor communities are not even done in postdisaster situations but rather in communities experiencing chronic problems that need long-term development. Unfortunately, STMs rarely diagnose the situation and often pursue a relief approach, even though this is seldom the appropriate intervention.

For example, after Hurricane Katrina wreaked havoc along parts of the Gulf Coast, tens of thousands of Christians rushed to assist. This aid took many diverse forms and in many ways it was a great testimony to the beauty of the body of Christ. One particular STM team made up of young people went to the New Orleans area very soon after Katrina hit and worked hard to clear roads and homes of debris. The same STM team returned about a year later to help with the rehabilitation of some of the damaged homes. By this time the residents were returning to the area. The STM team was asked to work on restoring the house owned by a family that included several young adult males. While the STM team worked hard every day tearing out Sheetrock, carpeting, and more, the young men living in the house sat back and watched the STM team all day long.

The first trip was an appropriate STM response, applying relief in a context in which it was needed. But the second STM trip, while well intentioned, was an incorrect response. The homeowner's family had the capacity to participate in the renovation of its house but was unwilling to do so. It would have been better for the STM team to go back to the local ministry and ask to be reassigned to work on another house whose owners were open to helping with their own recovery.

Even when relief is the appropriate intervention, the STM team might not be the best group to provide this relief. As discussed in chapter 4, when local organizations or ministries are willing and able to provide the necessary relief assistance, it is preferable to let them do so. They have the local knowledge about who really needs help and who does not, and they are the ones who will still be there conducting ministry long after the STM team has gone. At a minimum, the STM team needs to be seen as an extension of local organizations rather than as independent, outside agents.

Finally, consider the fact that most contexts require development—not relief or rehabilitation—in light of the cultural differences discussed earlier. STM teams are typically monochronic and are looking at the two-week trip as a chance to "do missions." The team wants to use its time "wisely," getting as much done as possible. The team's expectation is that many evangelistic meetings will take place, that the building project will be completed, or that health checkups will be given to hundreds or even thousands of people. But getting things done quickly is simply not what development is all about! Development is a lifelong *process*, not a two-week *product*.

And while the STM team is in monochronic high gear, the receiving culture is in polychronic mode, working at a slower pace. Getting the job done is less important than being together and getting to know one another. This can quickly cause frustrations for the STM team members, as they watch the seconds tick away while little is getting "done." It is not long before many of us start to look down on our polychronic brothers and sisters, quickly deciding that they are inept or even lazy. And then the paternalism kicks in. We take over and do everything because otherwise it just won't get done, at least not before the two weeks are over, which would be a disaster from the perspective of many STM teams.

Adeney summarizes the situation as follows:

> By definition, short-term missions have only a short time in which to "show a profit," to achieve pre-defined goals. This can accentuate our American idols of speed, quantification, compartmentalization, money, achievement, and success. Projects become more important than people. The wells dug. Fifty people converted. Got to give the church back home a good report. Got to prove the time and expense was well worth it. To get the job done (on our time scale), imported technology becomes more important than contextualized methods. Individual drive becomes more important than respect for elders, for old courtesies, for taking time. We end up dancing like elephants. We dance hard, and we have big feet.[5]

"But we formed such great relationships on our trip! Aren't such relationships consistent with the process of development?" While God through

His Spirit does create special bonds between believers from very different backgrounds, individualist North Americans are prone to underestimating how long this takes in a collectivist culture and to overinterpreting the depth of their relationships with their new "friends." North Americans often think it is easy to develop one-on-one, deep, personal relationships simply by hanging out with an individual from Thailand for a week. In reality, the Thai person is likely to perceive this relationship as very superficial compared to his deep allegiances to his "group."

STMs from the Perspective of Asset- and Needs-Based Approaches

Remember that initially focusing on the assets of a community is preferable to focusing on the community's needs. It is crucial to recognize and mobilize the natural, material, social, knowledge, and spiritual resources of individuals and communities before trying to determine what additional resources might be needed from the outside.

Unfortunately, STM teams are generally in "needs-based" mode, bringing their knowledge, skills, and material resources to poor communities in order to accomplish a task as fast as possible. Indeed, there is not even time for the STM team to identify existing resources in the recipient communities. As a result, paternalism rears its ugly head, and we undermine local assets and increase poverties of being, community, and stewardship.

For example, consider the following observation of an American staff member who works with an indigenous organization that is trying to bring development to poor communities in a Latin American country:

> The indigenous staff in my organization lead weekly Bible studies with children in low-income communities. These Bible studies are just one aspect of my organization's overall attempts to bring long-lasting development in these broken communities. After a short-term team conducts a Bible study in one of these communities, the children stop attending the Bible studies of my organization. Our indigenous staff tell me that the children stop coming because we do not have all the fancy materials and crafts that the short-term teams have, and we do not give away things like these teams do. The children have also come to believe that our staff are not as interesting or as creative as the Americans that come on these teams.[6]

Similarly, Rick Johnson writes from the perspective of one who has been engaged for decades with STMs in Mexico, the location of 30 percent of American STMs.[7] In speaking of the many STMs that come to do vacation Bible schools; conduct evangelistic campaigns; build church buildings, schools, houses, and medical clinics; and distribute goods to the poor, Johnson states:

> Few pastors will speak up or reject these offers of help even if inside they resent the paternalism and humiliation of being directed by a group which many times doesn't speak the language, know the congregation or understand the community in which they work. A congregation struggling to learn to depend on the Lord and be a light in their own community can find it easy to surrender their responsibilities and needs to a wealthy group which is more than anxious to assume these responsibilities. The initiative of the congregation to meet their God-given opportunities and duties can be squelched by well-meaning outsiders.[8]

And there are even more subtle forces at work. The individualistic cultural value of STM teams can undermine local knowledge in a collectivist context. For example, an STM team will tend to assume that treating every individual in the community the same way is obviously the right thing to do and may give out, say, food, in equal amounts to everyone. But some collectivist societies have found that giving a disproportionately large amount of food to particular individuals can increase the chances of financial success for those individuals, who will then share their earnings with the community as a whole. This community-based survival strategy reflects indigenous knowledge acquired over centuries of struggling against the elements. A failure to discover and appreciate this local knowledge can cause the STM team to do unintentional harm while trying to do good.

How can the STM team discover local assets—including knowledge about survival strategies—in the context of a two-week trip? The answer to this question is not obvious, but a good first step is for the STM trip to be done as part of a long-term, asset-based, development approach being implemented by local ministries. The STM team needs to understand how it fits within the overall strategy of this local ministry and take care not to undermine this ministry's effectiveness.

STMs from the Perspective of Participatory Development

Chapter 6 addressed the importance of people participating in their development. The need is to get beyond token or even forced participation to having poor communities, churches, and families participate in planning, implementing, and evaluating the interventions in their lives.

At a minimum, the principle of participation implies that the community, church, or organization that receives the STM team needs to be the primary entity deciding what should be done, as well as how it should be done. Even more importantly, they need to be the ones requesting the team. Too many field workers feel pressure to use STMs from their larger agency, supporting churches, or donors. Indeed, research is finding that most host organizations would rather have the sending organizations give them money instead of sending a team.[9]

I (Steve) know that if someone from Switzerland said to my small church of 130 people in rural Georgia, "You can choose between our sending thirteen people this summer to help with your VBS or our giving you the $25,000 it will cost to send the team," we would definitely take the money. We would use $20,000 to finish off the church addition we have been working five years to build debt free. And the remaining $5,000 would nearly double our normal VBS budget, so we could have a dynamic VBS as well. It is not that we would not appreciate the cultural exchange and fellowship, but we have more pressing priorities for the long-term well-being of our church. Now if we thought that hosting this Swiss team might lead to an ongoing relationship and more money in the long run, then we might be open to their coming after all!

The discussions about STMs need to include the potential calculations that may be going on in the minds of our materially poor brothers and sisters in Christ. If they really had the social, political, and economic power to speak their minds, we might be a bit surprised at what we might hear. But they really do not have this power. Middle-to-upper-class North American believers have to accept that their power has silenced their brethren at home and abroad more than we realize. People who have power seldom think about that power, while people who do not have it are very aware that they do not. This issue is much broader than STMs, but STMs are a big place where these tensions are silently played out. We dance hard, and we have big feet. We do not mean to crush Mouse, but Mouse gets crushed nonetheless.

Dollars and Sense

The primary questions concerning STMs to poor communities need to focus on the impacts of the trips on those communities. *It is not about us. It is about them!* The previous discussion should give us some pause concerning the positive impacts of STMs. But another issue also needs to be considered as we weigh the strengths and weaknesses of much of the current STM movement.

The North American church needs to more deeply appreciate the fact that Christians at home and abroad are ministering within their *own* nations, people groups, and communities at a large and growing rate, particularly in the Majority World where the church continues to expand and mature. God has blessed many of these indigenous Christian workers with amazing talents and strong passions for advancing His kingdom. They often minister long term in environments that would be a deep challenge for even the most impassioned outsider. Furthermore, these indigenous workers' understanding of local cultures and languages makes them far more effective than the outsiders could typically be, either in the short or long term. Moreover, these indigenous workers usually do this work at salaries that are far below mainstream North American standards.

The presence of these indigenous ministries raises some significant stewardship issues for North American STMs. For example, a highly respected organization equips and manages national evangelists across the continent of Africa. The total annual cost of these evangelists is $1,540 per year for salary ($1,200), mountain bike ($250), and backpack, team shirt, and bedroll ($90). Another outstanding Christian relief and development organization employs community-level workers doing holistic development work for $1,500 to $5,000 per year. Contrast these numbers with the expense of doing an STM trip. Spending $20,000 to $40,000 for ten to twenty people to be on location for two weeks or less is not uncommon. The money spent on a single STM team for a one- to two-week experience would be sufficient to support more than a dozen far more effective indigenous workers *for an entire year.* And we complain about wasteful government spending! The profound stewardship issues here should not be glossed over.

Some defenders of STMs argue that the money spent on STMs is new money for missions. Because the giver typically knows the person or team and the gift is seen as one time and without a deep commitment, money given for STMs is money that would not be given for other forms of missions such as supporting indigenous ministries. If this is an accurate description of the nature of giving to STMs, it is very sad. Why can't God's people be challenged—from the pulpit and beyond—to exercise better stewardship of kingdom resources with their missions giving? While higher impact strategies may provide less satisfaction than STMs for the giver in terms of "personal involvement or connection," isn't it a great modeling of the gospel to die to self so that others might benefit? Yes, this goes against the current cultural demand to touch, taste, and experience for myself. But the gospel has always called for challenging societal norms if they hinder the advancement of Christ's kingdom. *It is not about us. It is about Him!*

Other defenders of STMs argue that such trips should be seen as an investment that yields large returns for the kingdom by producing increased missions giving, more long-term missionaries, and profound, cross-cultural relationships. At first glance this argument seems plausible. Many returning STM team members declare: "My life has been changed, and I will become an active participant in God's mission movement!" Indeed, it is common to hear long-term missionaries report that an STM experience was part of what led them to pursue a longer commitment. And many STM teams report that the deep relationships they formed with people in the recipient communities were the most significant part of the trip. While no doubt these statements are sincerely made, there is growing evidence that these reports seriously overestimate the long-run impacts of the trips on those who go.

Kurt Ver Beek, an assistant professor of sociology at Calvin College with more than twenty years of experience in Honduras, has conducted research into the long-run impacts of the STM trips on team members, looking beyond their initial statements to their actual behaviors.[10] Ver Beek's data indicates that there simply is not a significant increase in long-term missions giving for either the team members or their sending churches. It is also hard to support the claim of increases in the number of long-term missionaries, given that the number of long-term missionaries is fairly stable despite the explosion of

STMs. And as for all those great relationships that get developed, the reality is that only a small percentage of STM team members ever have any contact—at all—with their new "friends" after the trip ends.

In summary, the returns do not seem to justify the investment.

SUGGESTIONS FOR IMPROVING THE IMPACT OF STMS

There is good news. There are many things that your church or ministry can do in designing, recruiting/screening, training, and funding its STM trips to increase the benefits and reduce the harm for everyone involved. In fact, a growing number of churches and ministries are pursuing these practices.

Designing the Field Experience

It is important to pay very careful attention to the overall design of the trip itself. Here are a few tips:

Make sure the host organization, i.e., the agency receiving the STM team, understands the nature of poverty and practices the basic principles of appropriate poverty alleviation.

Make sure the host organization *and* community members have requested a team as part of their plan to improve their ministry and lives. They should have the real option of asking the sending church or organization to do something other than send an STM team. Make sure the host organization and community members are the lead decision makers concerning what the STM team will and will not do.

Be sincerely open to not sending a team. STM teams have significant capacity to do harm to both the teams and the recipients. While your church might need to get itself moving, it is important not to trample the poor just so your church can get more engaged in ministry.

Design the trip to be about "being" and "learning" as much as about "doing." Stay in community members' homes and create time to talk and interact with them. Ask local believers to share their insights with team members about who God is and how He works in their lives; have team members share the weaknesses in their own lives and churches, and have the local believers pray for them. If the local believers are materially poor, this can be a powerful step in overcoming any implicit beliefs that team members may have in the "health-

and-wealth gospel" (see the discussion in chapter 2).

Ensure that the "doing" portion of the trip avoids paternalism. Remember, do not do for people what they can do for themselves. The goal is for the work to be done primarily by the community members with the team in a helping role. Thus, there should be explicit guidelines or policies as to roles and authority, including what to do if the community members don't carry out their responsibilities. We highly recommend that the STM team not step in and take up those responsibilities.

Keep the number of team members small. This will promote more learning and interaction with the host environment and will lessen the damage from Elephant's foot!

Recruiting and Screening the Team

The messages and procedures used to recruit STM teams are crucial, as recruitment sets the initial expectations for what to expect and influences the type of people who will join the team. Here are a few things to consider.

Stay away from the "go-help-and-save-them" message and use a "go-as-a-learner" message. We need no more STM brochure covers with sad, dirty faces of children and the words "Will you die to self and go and serve?" Such a message places too much focus on the sacrifice the STM team is making to change people's lives—a level of change that is simply not realistic in two weeks—and on how helpless the poor people are without the team's help.

Do not advertise or create STM trips that focus on the adventure and fun the team will have. Promises of tourist attractions and shopping excursions have found their way into the marketing literature for STMs. There is nothing wrong with enjoying such things; just don't label vacations as "missions" nor dare ask people to fund them with their tithes and offerings. Doing so is an outrageous insult to the thousands of indigenous and expatriate brothers and sisters who sacrifice in mighty ways in ministry and to the poor themselves.

Change the name from "Short-Term Mission Trip" to something like "Vision Trip" or "Go, Learn, Return, and Respond." Names such as these point to seeing the STM trip as a learning experience that is to be part of producing future engagement and might help focus the trips as a means to achieving a bigger end rather than as an end in themselves. In addition to giving people a more proper expectation of the experience, such titles might make everyone stop and ask a fundamental question: How much money do we really want to spend on achieving this type of experience for ourselves?

Be careful how STMs are presented as part of the larger missions movement. Statements such as "If you are serious about missions, then you need to take a short-term mission trip" are common. This is a vast overstatement, as many, many folks serve in missions long term without an STM experience. Furthermore, such messages can give a false impression about what it really takes to do serious missions or community development work.

Have a substantial presentation for prospective team members of at least several hours that clearly explains what the trip is and is not about. Give people time to think about what they heard in this first meeting and to "count the cost" before committing to the trip.

Require potential trip members to demonstrate a serious interest in missions by being active in their church and its local outreach efforts. Doing so could increase participation in your church's local ministry as well as decrease the number of people who go on expensive trips as their first testing ground for involvement in ministry. Moreover, the fact is that many of us are better equipped to minister closer to home, as there may be fewer cultural and contextual barriers, although these barriers can still be significant as we start to cross even local socioeconomic divides. In addition, engaging in local ministry that is development focused helps one experience the ups and downs of long-term change. Understanding this dynamic is very helpful for adding a dose of realism about what an "outsider" can and cannot accomplish in the short span of a week or two on an STM trip.

Training for Success

"Experiential learning" is a powerful tool. It is the core reason we must work hard to improve STMs so that this learning gets leveraged for further action. Research is showing that a central factor in increasing the potential for STMs to have positive, long-run impacts on the team members is for there to be a training process that includes pre-trip, on-the-field, and post-trip components.[11] While not a solution to all the problems associated with STMs, particularly for materially poor host communities, well-designed training programs are part of the success formula for the team members. You need to develop a sound training program. Underinvesting in training or having misfocused training messages are a significant contributor to harmful STMs.

Make pre-trip learning a requirement, not a suggestion. Simply wanting to go and coming up with the money is not sufficient to qualify somebody to join the team. If people do not want to spend the time to learn before they go on the trip, are they really going to have a learner's mind-set during and after the trip?

Include in the training at least a summary of the basic concepts presented thus far in this book. Emphasize in particular that we are all poor, just in different ways. This content should be offered in addition to the typical training that is offered on team-building, spiritual preparation, and country-specific information, including some basic language skills.

Schedule training time on the field for two items. First, ask team members to reflect and discuss the ways they might be seeing ideas from their pre-trip training coming alive. Second, provide deeper learning tasks concerning the topics introduced in the pre-trip training.

The post-trip learning is absolutely crucial. Have a well-planned, mandated, learning journey *for at least one year following the trip.* Such follow-up uses a discipleship approach to help translate the costly mountaintop experience into an actual, life-changing event. Combined with a well-designed and executed trip, intentional and required ongoing learning will improve the impacts of STMs for those who go.

Funding the Trip

Who pays, and what they pay for, matters.

Require every member of an STM to pay for a portion of the expenses from his or her own pocket. Why? Remember, this is a learning experience, not a trip to save the world. Learners are more likely to value their training if they are paying for a portion of it. Participating for a few hours in a fund-raiser is probably not a large enough sacrifice for people to have a sufficient stake in their educational experience.

Consider donating as much money to organizations that are pursuing sound community development in the host community as you do for your team's expenses. This could include paying the salaries for indigenous missionaries or community development workers, but it is typically best not to support an indigenous pastor of a church, as this can undermine the congregation's responsibility to pay the pastor's salary. It is usually best not to channel such a large amount of money to small churches or to individuals, but to organizations that have demonstrated track records of long-run, developmental ministry with strong financial and managerial accountability systems.

STMS CAN BLESS

We have tried to help you think about some of the issues surrounding STM trips in order for you to see that they are not a "neutral" endeavor. Good can come out of them, but they can also do harm. If your church or ministry seriously considers the pros and cons of STMs, commits to deeply asking what role they should or should not play in your overall missions strategy, and implements many of the suggestions of this chapter, then you will go a long way toward maximizing the potential benefits and minimizing the possible harm of STMs.

The next two chapters will describe some other possible ways for your church to minister to materially poor people both at home and abroad, focusing on various "economic development" strategies, interventions that seek to increase people's incomes and wealth.

REFLECTION QUESTIONS AND EXERCISES

Please write responses to the following:

1. Reflect on your answers to the questions in the "Initial Thoughts" at the start of this chapter. Have your views changed at all? If so, how? Be specific.

2. Think about the STM trips that your church is planning for the future. List three or four specific things you can do to improve these trips. How will you accomplish these changes in your church?

3. Can you think of any alternative things you could do with your missions or ministry budgets that might have greater impact than STMs? What are some specific actions you will take to investigate those alternatives?

INITIAL THOUGHTS

Consider the following questions:

1. What factors—historic or contemporary—caused your church to be located where it is?

2. What factors caused you to live in your neighborhood?

3. Do you know of any poor people who live near your church or near the neighborhood in which you live?

CHAPTER 8

YES, IN YOUR
BACKYARD

Johnny Price is a forty-four-year-old, unemployed African American. Johnny's father died when Johnny was only six years old, leaving Johnny's mother to support ten children on her meager wages as a house servant. Divorced, Johnny struggles to raise his two kids alone, receiving an unemployment check of only $1,168 per month. With a monthly mortgage of $700, Johnny cannot make ends meet. And Johnny is not unique; the poverty rate in his community is 14.4 percent.

Poverty in North American inner-city ghettos is devastating, but that's not where Johnny lives. If you live in the suburbs, then Johnny might live in your town. Indeed, today's suburban population is full of people like Johnny, including Jodi, who earns $6.25 per hour and depends on a food pantry for her survival; Rosa, who lives in an unheated garage and says that half of the people in her church are in a similar situation; and Juanita, a recent immigrant, who works seventy hours per week as a domestic servant at wages that amount to $4.03 per hour.[1]

For the first time in US history, more poor people live in suburbs than in cities.[2] Both traditional inner-city residents and new immigrants are moving to the suburbs in large numbers, due to the greater availability of cheaper housing and low-skill jobs than exist in urban centers. Hence, many suburban churches now find themselves on the front lines of America's war on poverty without even realizing it. Bob Lupton, who has more than thirty years of experience working in inner-city Atlanta as the Director of Family Consultation Service Urban Ministries, describes this new reality as follows:

> In the past, suburban church folk—those with a social conscience—have commuted into the city to serve the poor. They have partnered with our urban ministry to build houses, tutor kids, [and] donate used clothes. They journeyed into the city because that's where the poor were concentrated. All that is now changing. There are still plenty of needy neighborhoods in the city, to be sure. But poverty is gradually, relentlessly suburbanizing. . . . The old commuter model of ministry, though still necessary, is in decline. New methods of serving must be devised to accommodate these "different" newcomers who are appearing in once-secure bedroom communities, in the classrooms of once-homogenous schools.[3]

One of the tricky features of the new suburban poverty is that it is less visible than traditional, inner-city poverty. We are all familiar with the large-scale, urban housing projects that seem to announce their residents' poverty to the world. In contrast, the suburban poor tend to be less densely concentrated and are scattered about in older apartment complexes, pockets of mobile homes, subdivisions of circa-1950 brick units, and low-income housing built behind strip malls.[4] The suburban poor are easy to overlook.

Of course, eventually these poor suburbanites will become more apparent. As they do, will middle-to-upper-class, evangelical churches flee the suburbs, thereby repeating the mistakes of the twentieth century when these churches fled the poverty and racial mix of urban centers?[5] Will these churches' message to the poor again be, "Not in my backyard!" as they load the pews into moving vans and relocate even farther away from those for whom Jesus cares so deeply? Or will suburban, evangelical churches embrace the ministry opportunities that are landing on their doorsteps, as poor people from every tongue, tribe, and nation move in across the street? Will they say, as the early church did, "Yes, in my backyard!"

Of course, in addition to the new suburban poor, poverty continues to manifest itself in everything from inner-city ghettos to rural Appalachia. Hence, regardless of where your church is located or where you live, it is very likely that you do not have to travel very far to find materially poor people. What can North American Christians do to address this myriad of poverties? While each context is different, the following chapter describes several strategies of economic development that can work in a wide range of settings. But first we will consider the general economic environment contributing to poverty in North America. Throughout the discussion, it is important to keep the overall goal in mind:

> **MATERIAL POVERTY ALLEVIATION:**
> **Working to reconcile the four foundational relationships so that people can fulfill their callings of glorifying God by working and supporting themselves and their families with the fruit of that work.**

BROKEN SYSTEMS AND BROKEN INDIVIDUALS

Poor people are often at the mercy of systems created by the powerful. Hence, poverty-alleviation efforts need to address both broken systems and broken individuals, using highly relational approaches wherever possible. What does this look like in the North American landscape?

As discussed in chapter 3, centuries of broken systems—some intentionally oppressive and some not—have contributed to poverty in the African-American experience. And most readers are well aware that historic oppression has also been a major contributor to Native Americans' poverty. As a result of these histories, the playing field is not level at the start of the twenty-first century. Even if there were no present discrimination—and there is—many people enter this century with distinct disadvantages, some of which greatly hamper their ability to function in an increasingly integrated, global economy.

Globalization is exposing North American workers to increased competition from low-wage workers across the Majority World. Emerging economies are expanding their manufacturing sectors, thereby creating much-needed jobs for the poorest people on the planet. Corresponding to this, North American production is shifting away from basic manufacturing into services and knowledge-intensive sectors, increasing the demand for highly educated workers in North America. Unfortunately, the job opportunities and wages for blue-collar workers in such sectors are lower than they were in traditional manufacturing jobs. Hence, blue-collar workers in North America are getting squeezed, and this trend is very likely to continue and even accelerate in the coming decades. Moreover, the interconnectedness of the global economy is creating increased volatility.

Johnny Price, the man mentioned at the start of this chapter, is a prime example of these dynamics. Johnny worked for nineteen years for a textile manufacturer about thirty minutes outside of Greensboro, North Carolina. His wages of fifteen dollars per hour plus benefits were sufficient to enable him to get a mortgage and to raise his family in a middle-class neighborhood. But company-wide layoffs forced Johnny to return to school at the local community college, where he hopes to develop sufficient skills to avoid working as a low-paid clerk in a nearby department store.[6] Unemployment and low-wage, service-sector employment taking the place of higher-wage jobs is a major contributor to poverty in North America today.

Of course, the employment problems of poor people are not solely due to national and international economic systems. Many poor people have behavioral problems that make them less than ideal workers. Moreover, historically some of these behaviors were exacerbated by a welfare system that penalized work by removing benefits as people's earnings increased. Welfare reform legislation of 1996 greatly increased work incentives by lowering continuous welfare assistance to two years and lifetime welfare assistance to five years. In addition, receiving welfare benefits was made contingent upon working, looking for work, or getting additional education or job training. As a result of these reforms, being able to work is once again crucial for economic survival, making it imperative that workers overcome any behavioral traits that undermine their employability.

SKILLS THAT WORKERS NEED

Economic globalization highlights the need for a strong educational system that produces workers not just with vocational training but also with sufficient general skills and the basic capacity to learn so that they can adapt to a rapidly changing, global economy. The job that a person has today could easily vanish tomorrow, so people need to be able to adjust, get retrained, and learn new skills.

Unfortunately, there is arguably no greater perpetuation of historical injustice in the United States than funding for the public educational system. Because public schools are largely dependent upon state and local tax revenues to meet their budgets, schools in poorer states and localities necessarily have fewer resources per pupil. Moreover, the formulas used to dispense national, state, and local funds have been shown to allocate significantly fewer resources to poor school districts, exacerbating the economic disparities that already exist.[7] The end result is wide variations in expenditures per student, with some school districts spending 300 percent more per pupil than others.[8] Inadequate funding of schools in poor communities is one contributor to unprepared graduates, who then go on to earn low wages and to pay little in school taxes. And then the vicious cycle repeats itself.

Of course, a lack of money is not the sole problem in failing schools. Sinful hearts, distorted worldviews, and bad values, many of which may be transmitted via "cultures of poverty" such as ghetto nihilism, significantly contribute to poor student performance. But let us not forget that local, national, and even international forces, including hundreds of years of racial discrimination, contributed to the formation of these ghettos in the first place. Even if there were not any current racial discrimination—and there is—the plague of historic discrimination is perpetuated via the American educational system.

THE IMPORTANCE OF WEALTH ACCUMULATION

Economic globalization also highlights the need for wealth, not just income, in the fight against poverty. Income is the *flow* of revenue that a household receives from its wages, interest, and dividends. Wealth is the *stock* of assets that a family has from its savings or inheritance, including such things as bank accounts, stocks and bonds, and equity in houses.

Accumulating wealth plays three distinct roles in poverty alleviation. First, wealth provides the buffer that people like Johnny Price need in order to survive when they have been laid off from a job. In most recessions, poor people are the first to get laid off but have the fewest resources to survive. In an increasingly volatile economic climate, wealth is needed to ride out the storm. Second, wealth generates additional income: stocks and bonds pay dividends, houses appreciate in value, and cars enable people to get to work to earn wages. Third, the process of saving and managing wealth develops positive attitudes and self-discipline, requiring people to replace a "live-for-today," survival mentality with a "live-for-the-future," investment mentality.[9]

Unfortunately, while public policy has historically encouraged wealth accumulation for middle-to-upper-class people, it has often discouraged wealth accumulation for the poor. Middle-to-upper-class people are encouraged to accumulate wealth through such things as tax-deferred (and often employer matched) retirement savings (IRAs, 401[k]s, 403[b]s) and mortgage-interest tax deductions. At the same time, poor people have been forced to deplete their assets before qualifying for welfare assistance and have been penalized with the loss of benefits if they somehow manage to save and invest too much! The end result is that many poor families are highly vulnerable to economic shocks and unable to even think about their financial futures.[10]

Of course there is no better example of an economic shock than the subprime mortgage crisis that rocked the world in late 2008, a crisis that illustrates another feature of the broken economic system: unscrupulous lenders, mortgage brokers, and appraisers taking advantage of financially ill-informed borrowers. Indeed, inadequate money management skills—budgeting, planning for the future, and understanding financial transactions—hamper many poor people from getting the most out of their incomes and building their wealth.

HOUSING AND HEALTH CARE

The subprime mortgage crisis also highlights another systemic reality facing people like Johnny Price: a shortage of affordable housing. While wages and employment opportunities for blue-collar workers are decreasing, long-run housing expenses have continued to rise. Even before the subprime mortgage crisis hit, 47 percent of low-income households in the United States were "severely burdened" by housing costs, meaning that they spent more than 50 percent of their incomes on housing, leaving them with, on average, only $257 per month to spend on food, $29 for clothing, and $9 for health care.[11]

And this leads us to the final major systemic problem facing the poor in North America: inadequate access to affordable health care. In 2007, 42 percent of working adults in the United States were either uninsured or underinsured, and 37 percent reported going without needed care because of rising costs.[12] Moreover, considerable socioeconomic disparities exist. Minorities and poor people experience significantly inferior health care compared to the rest of the population.[13]

In summary, poor people in North America could benefit from all of the following: (1) the ability to work at jobs with living wages, (2) the capacity to manage their money, (3) the opportunity to accumulate wealth, and (4) a greater supply of quality education, housing, and health care at affordable rates. Moreover, like all of us, poor people need highly relational ministries—delivered through the body of Jesus Christ—that help them to overcome the effects of the fall on their individual hearts, minds, and behaviors.

ADDRESSING THESE NEEDS

The following discussion focuses on ways to address the first three needs listed above—employment, financial management, and wealth accumulation—because they all fall squarely within this book's focus on helping poor people to work and to support themselves and their families with the fruit of that work; that is, they are all part of the "economic development" sector of poverty alleviation. Moreover, these interventions are typically easier for churches to pursue than increasing the supply of education, housing, and health care. Nonetheless, we recognize that increasing the supply of these services is profoundly important and that some churches and ministries have successfully pursued these strategies.

While each of the economic development interventions discussed in the rest of this chapter play unique roles, they are similar in that they all:

- Use development rather than relief, because the vast majority of poor people in North America are capable of participating in the improvement of their lives;
- Improve some aspect of the economic system or enable poor people to use the existing system more effectively;
- Use an asset-based approach that builds upon the skills, intelligence, labor, discipline, savings, creativity, and courage of poor people;
- Have the potential to be designed, implemented, and evaluated in a participatory manner;

- Provide an opportunity to use biblically based curricula, allowing for a clear presentation of the gospel and the addressing of worldview issues;
- Use church-based mentoring teams that can offer love, support, and encouragement, thereby providing a relational approach that seeks to restore people's dignity (relationship to self), community (relationship to others), stewardship (relationship to the rest of creation), and spiritual intimacy (relationship to God);
- Are implemented over fairly long periods of time, thereby creating space for "development," the process of ongoing change and reconciliation, for both the "helpers" and the "helped."

Jobs Preparedness Ministries

Clive grew up in a housing project in the Cleaborn and Foote neighborhood in inner-city Memphis, Tennessee, one of the poorest neighborhoods in the United States. Clive followed the stereotypical path of many ghetto residents, getting involved in gangs, drugs, violence, and prison. At one point Clive nearly died from a gunshot wound. Today, Clive is the "employee of the month" at the warehouse where he has worked for the past year. He is also a follower of Jesus Christ.[14]

Clive is just one of more than one hundred people to graduate in 2008 from the Jobs for Life (JFL) training program offered by Advance Memphis, a Christian ministry that has brought hope to the Cleaborn and Foote neighborhood for the past ten years. During the first ten months of 2008 alone, eighty-three of Advance's JFL graduates found jobs; and without any marketing, Advance is turning away poor people from its jobs preparedness classes because the demand is greater than the number of seats available. Poor people want jobs!

Advance Memphis is one of 130 affiliates of the nationwide Jobs for Life network, which mobilizes churches and Christian ministries to help poor people find and keep jobs. A JFL affiliate like Advance coordinates three ministry components:

1. Classroom training for poor people that emphasizes the development of "soft skills" from a biblical perspective. Soft skills are general, nontechnical abilities such as a solid work ethic, the ability to function in a team, and

strong communication skills. In contrast, "hard skills" include the technical knowledge needed for specific jobs; for example, an auto mechanic needs to know how an engine operates. JFL develops soft skills using a biblically based curriculum that addresses such issues as career planning, the inherent value of work, good attitudes, personal integrity, respect for authority, conflict resolution, responsibility, punctuality, appropriate dress, etc.

2. Mentors, called "champions," provide support and encouragement to JFL participants, helping them to overcome obstacles that hinder their ability to complete the class, to get a job, or to cope with life. While one-on-one mentoring is possible, mentoring teams from churches are likely to be able to sustain relationships over longer periods of time, as the mentoring process can be overwhelming.

3. Businesses covenant to provide interviews, job opportunities, and supportive work environments to JFL graduates. This represents a tremendous opportunity for Christian businesspeople to serve the kingdom by helping poor people to get a fresh start on fulfilling their God-given callings. Ideally, employers will be in contact with the mentors so that they can work together to nurture the JFL graduate through the ups and downs of the job.

JFL represents a powerful example of how a jobs preparedness ministry can address brokenness in both systems and individuals in order to foster reconciliation of the four key relationships, thereby enabling people to glorify God through work. By imparting soft skills, offering support structures, and providing networks for job opportunities, JFL makes the economic system accessible to poor people. Moreover, the biblically based training and highly relational approach address brokenness at the individual level. The result is that more than 80 percent of JFL participants nationwide maintain employment for at least one year after graduation, a remarkable success rate.[15]

The soft skills training in jobs preparedness ministries offers a crucial first step in getting poor people employed. A nationwide survey asked businesses to list the qualities they were seeking in welfare recipients who applied for entry-level positions. From a list of twelve positive qualities, employers were asked to choose the three that they considered to be the most important. Figure 8.1 summarizes the responses, the figures next to each quality specifying the percentage of employers who listed that quality as one of the three that they consider most important.[16] Note that having job-specific knowledge, the type of knowledge that would be acquired through "hard skills" training, was listed as the least important quality, while the qualities that can be obtained through "soft skills" training were listed as the most important.

Qualities Rated as Most Important in Job Candidates

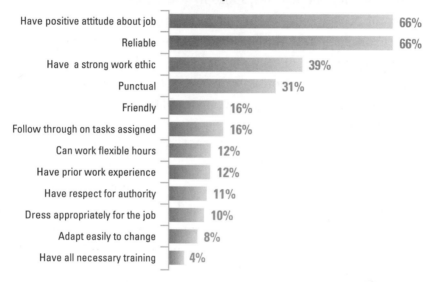

FIGURE 8.1

Marsha Regenstein, Jack A. Meyer, and Jennifer Dickemper Hicks, *Job Prospects for Welfare Recipients: Employers Speak Out* (Washington, D.C.: Urban Institute, 1998), New Federalism Issues and Options for States, Series A, No. A-25, August.

Entry-level positions do not pay well, so poor people often need additional hard-skills training to be able to increase their wages. Although churches typically do not have the capacity to provide such training, they can help people to identify their long-term vocational goals and assist them in furthering their education in community colleges and vocational schools. Of course, going back to school costs money, a problem that will be addressed further in the section on wealth accumulation.

Financial Education Ministries

Isaac, an African American in his late twenties, drives up to Title Brokers in a rusting minivan that needs a new muffler. In exchange for handing over his car title and a set of keys for the repo man, Isaac receives a check for $600. At the end of the month, he will owe $750, which amounts to an annual percentage rate (APR) of 300 percent. Should he fail to repay within ninety days, he will owe $1,172, reflecting an APR of 381 percent. "If I wasn't in such a desperate situation, I wouldn't come back. I'm embarrassed to be here because these guys rip people off. This is [money] I should be investing for my children."[17]

Isaac's story is becoming all too common. Poor neighborhoods are teeming with mortgage brokers, rent-to-own stores, payday and tax refund lenders, pawnshops, and car title loan dealers, all of which charge very high interest rates, often burying people in a cycle of debt. For example, a two-week loan of two to three hundred dollars from payday lenders charges interest averaging more than 400 percent APR, and the majority of payday borrowers have to roll over their loans multiple times, incurring additional fees in the process. The average payday borrower spends $800 to repay a $325 loan.[18]

Many poor people do not understand the terms of the loans from these sources, leaving them open to abuse from unscrupulous lenders, many of whom engage in outright fraud. Indeed, research has found that a lack of financial education significantly contributes to people's falling prey to such schemes.[19]

Of course, even without the recent explosion in the number of predatory lenders, many poor people—and many people in general—lack the knowledge and discipline to manage their money well. This creates a tremendous opportunity for churches and ministries to provide basic financial education using any number of biblically based curricula that are available. Topics typically covered include Christian stewardship, budgeting, goal setting, saving, debt reduction, record keeping, tithing, taxes, banking, managing credit, and more. A solid financial education curriculum should be part of the tool kit of every church deacon and counselor. Training can be done one-on-one or in group settings, and a team of mentors can provide accountability and relational ministry, walking with trainees across time to foster long-term development.

Choosing the best curriculum is not easy. It is crucial that your church or ministry understands its target population's educational level, training needs, cultural characteristics, learning styles, and worldview issues. If you are ministering to a range of populations, you may need to use multiple curricula.

Ideally, the biblical content of these curricula would be designed to address the particular spiritual and worldview struggles of the trainees in a culturally affirming way. Curricula full of pictures of middle-class Caucasians is not the best way to build up the dignity of poor African Americans, Hispanics, or Native Americans. Your church or ministry may want to spend some resources contextualizing existing curricula to best fit its target population.

Financial education ministries can help to mitigate the problem of low-wage employment by helping trainees to use the US government's Earned Income Tax Credit (EITC). Started in 1975, the EITC gives low-income workers a tax credit for every dollar of wages earned. Moreover, even if the worker does not owe any income taxes, he is still eligible for the EITC and can receive these funds as a refund check from the federal government. At present, a low-income worker with two or more children is eligible for a credit at a rate of 40 percent, meaning that a worker earning eight dollars per hour can get an additional $3.20 from the federal government. The rate of subsidy decreases as one's earnings rise, but the overall impact can still be quite dramatic. For example, a household head who works full-time at eight dollars per hour earns $16,000 per year, which is below the poverty line for a family of four. The EITC gives this family another $4,536, enabling them to live above the poverty line.[20]

The EITC changes the economic system so that a poor person can work and support himself and his family through that work. Enjoying strong bipartisan support, the EITC has been dramatically expanded and is now the largest federal program providing assistance to low-income working families. In 2003, the EITC lifted 4.4 million people's financial status above the poverty line, with more than half of these people being children. Without the EITC, it is estimated that the poverty rate for children would be 25 percent higher.[21]

Unfortunately, an estimated 15 to 25 percent of people who are eligible for the EITC fail to claim it.[22] Many people are simply unaware of the EITC or do not know how to access it. Churches can provide a tremendous service to poor people by helping them to file for the EITC as part of a financial education ministry.

Wealth Accumulation Ministries

Veralisa was struggling to get off welfare and to support herself and her two children by making jewelry. But her income for the year totaled less than six thousand dollars, and then she received the heartbreaking news that she had developed cancer, possibly as a result of the harsh chemicals she was using in her jewelry business. A government agency referred Veralisa to Covenant Community Capital, a faith-based organization in Houston, Texas, that helps low-income, working families to escape the cycle of poverty by building money management skills and by helping them to acquire assets that grow in value over time.

Veralisa enrolled in Covenant Community Capital's Individual Development Account (IDA) Program, which rewards the monthly savings of working-poor families by providing a two-to-one savings match. Veralisa earned her match by saving some of her hard-earned dollars and by attending personal finance education and home-buyer preparation classes that were a required part of the IDA program.

Veralisa graduated from the program fifteen months later, buying her first home for $52,000 with a down payment that came from her own savings plus matching funds from Covenant Community Capital and additional matching funds from several other organizations. With a renewed confidence, Veralisa went on to increase her income and enrolled at the University of Houston. Three years later, Veralisa's cancer is in remission, and she has paid off her mortgage.[23]

IDA programs seek to build the wealth of poor people by encouraging them to save money out of their earned income. People's savings are matched in ratios that typically range from one-to-one to three-to-one as long as the savings and matched funds are used to acquire an asset such as a house, business capital, education, a car, etc. The matching funds are released to the vendor of the asset—for instance a mortgage lender—to ensure that the funds are used for their intended purpose. Matching funds for IDA programs can come from churches, individual donors, foundations, financial institutions, and federal and state governments.

During the time that the participants are saving—a period that averages two to three years—they are typically provided with financial education that seeks to improve their capacity for budgeting and managing their resources. In addition, there is usually training related to the asset the participant wants to purchase, such as small-business management training or home ownership courses.

Clearly, IDAs can only work if the poor are able and willing to save. This issue has been examined extensively in a systematic study that followed 2,364 IDA participants in fourteen programs for four-and-a-half years. The study found that the average monthly net savings deposits per participant amounted to $19.07, and that participants made deposits in about six out of every twelve months. With their matching money, participants accumulated approximately seven hundred dollars per year. When poor people are given savings incentives that are similar to those of the non-poor, for example in defined contribution 401(k) plans, they can and do save in large enough amounts to acquire much-needed wealth.[24]

IDA programs can also be used to minister to youth, helping young people to develop savings patterns and to plan for their futures. Dynamic entrepreneurship and financial education curricula targeting youth can be used to augment the matched savings portion of the ministry.

IDAs are within the capacity of most churches because they can be operated on a very small scale of even one to five participants. Deacons or ministry leaders can administer the program, and matching funds can come from the individual congregation or from other churches in its denomination or networks.

IDA programs can be powerful wealth accumulation strategies for people of all ages, but they are much more than this. Because participants are in the program for several years, mentoring teams and program staff have ample opportunity to walk with them in restorative relationships, helping both the poor people and the mentors to have a renewed sense of dignity and hope, to develop new patterns of behavior, and most important to experience the healing of Jesus Christ.

REFLECTION QUESTIONS AND EXERCISES

Please write responses to the following:

1. Reflect again on the questions in the "Initial Thoughts" at the start of this chapter. Is your church's location a symptom of the "white flight" of the twentieth century in which middle-to-upper-class families and churches fled the inner cities to the suburbs? If so, how should you and your church respond to this situation in terms of a biblical understanding of justice for the poor?

2. Find out where the nearest poor people live to your church. Good people to ask include local government social service providers, nonprofit ministries, and real estate agents. You can even find data for your church's census tract from online data. A tutorial for accessing this data is available at the following URL maintained by FASTEN: http://www.fastennetwork.org/Display .asp?Page=Census.

3. Once you have located poor individuals or communities, start to think about ways to begin developing relationships with them using the concepts and approaches described in chapters 5 and 6.

4. Ask any Christian businesspeople you know if they would be willing to provide an employment opportunity to a poor person. Find out what steps you could take as a church to make this idea more palatable to these businesspeople.

5. Could your church provide temporary employment to poor people by opportunities to do yardwork, cleaning, repairs, etc.?

6. Visit a poor neighborhood and list the number of mortgage brokers, rent-to-own stores, payday and tax refund lenders, pawnshops, and car title loan dealers. Ask some of them to explain to you their loan terms.

7. Consider getting additional training on jobs preparedness, financial education, and wealth accumulation ministries. Explore the training resources and opportunities that are available from the Chalmers Center for Economic Development (www.chalmers.org).

INITIAL THOUGHTS

Ask a church, missionary, or small ministry that is working
in the Majority World the following questions:

1. Have you ever lent money to a poor person in the Majority World?

2. Did you have any trouble getting the loan repaid?

3. What are the successes and failures you experienced in this process?

AND TO THE ENDS
OF THE **EARTH**

In 1976, a virtually unknown economics professor was visiting a village in rural Bangladesh during a devastating famine. There he encountered Sufiya, a very poor woman who was struggling to support her family by weaving bamboo stools. Sufiya was trapped. She needed to borrow twenty-two cents per day to buy materials, but banks would not lend to her because she did not have acceptable collateral and her desired loan size was too small. As a result, Sufiya was forced to borrow from loan sharks, whose exorbitant rates of interest left her with only two cents of profit at the end of a twelve-hour workday. Sufiya's neighbors expressed similar frustration, facing interest rates ranging from 10 percent per week (520 percent per year) to 10 percent per day (3,650 percent) per year. The professor reached into his pocket and lent Sufiya and forty-one of her neighbors a *total* of twenty-seven dollars. To the amazement of observers, the loans were fully repaid on time.[1] Contrary to the received wisdom, it was possible to lend money to very poor people and get it paid back!

Thirty-five years later, that economics professor, Dr. Muhammad Yunus, is a Nobel laureate, and the Grameen Bank, which he established to provide credit to the poorest people of Bangladesh, has 7.58 million poor borrowers and has lent $7.4 billion since its inception in 1976. More than 98 percent of Grameen's loans have been repaid, meaning that Grameen's money can be lent and re-lent to poor people over and over again![2] Moreover, Dr. Yunus's work has spawned the global microfinance (MF) movement, which aims to reach 175 million of the world's poorest families with loans and other financial services (e.g., savings and insurance) by the end of 2015.[3] Indeed, MF, which is sometimes also referred to as "microenterprise development," has become one of the premier strategies for bringing economic empowerment to poor people in the Majority World.

HARDER THAN IT LOOKS

Grace Fellowship Church is located in the suburbs of a North American city. For decades Grace has been working with a network of churches in western Uganda, trying to help this network to minister to the spiritual and physical needs of their congregations and communities. Over the years, Grace has spent a lot of money helping them to construct church buildings, to run orphanages, and to pay the pastors' salaries.

As a businessman, John had been growing frustrated about Grace's approach in Uganda. Although John believed that the Bible called Grace to share its wealth with its sister churches in Uganda, it was all starting to feel like a black hole. After decades of help, the reality is that the churches in Uganda were not even remotely close to being financially self-sufficient. The congregations were still poor; the communities were still poor; and the pastors and staff needed ongoing donations from Grace. It seemed like it would never end.

After reading about the Grameen Bank, John got very excited. Perhaps Grace could help the network of Ugandan churches to emulate the Grameen Bank by making small loans to poor people both inside and outside their congregations. In addition to being great ministry, this could help everyone's incomes to go up and increase the amount put into the offering plate. Eventually, there would be enough money to fund the pastors' and staff members' salaries and to pay for the churches' ministries. Best of all, because the money could be lent and re-lent over and over again, the program could last perpetually. John felt like he had found the solution to the black hole.

John discussed his strategy with the other missions committee members, and they soon shared his excitement. A few months later, John took a two-week trip to Uganda to help the churches there to put together a business plan for a MF program. John left them with a check for twenty thousand dollars to start making loans. Six months later, all of the money had been lent out. Twelve months later, almost none of the money had been paid back, and the churches in Uganda were now asking Grace for more money to replenish their MF program. The black hole was bigger than ever before.

Although there may be some exceptions in particular contexts, Grace Fellowship's experience is very common. Many churches, missionaries, and ministries from North America have been trying to use MF as part of their global outreach. Unfortunately, they usually find that emulating the Grameen Bank is far more difficult than they imagined. Loans are often not repaid, putting a drain on ministry budgets and causing some programs to collapse entirely. Everybody gets hurt in the process: the North American churches, ministries, and missionaries; the partner churches and ministries in the Majority World; and—most important—the poor themselves.

This chapter examines the economic environment facing the poor in the Majority World and suggests three highly strategic ways for churches, missionaries, and ministries to use economic development to impact the lives of the materially poor in the Majority World: (1) Use appropriate forms of MF; (2) Support training in small-business management, household financial stewardship, and related topics; and (3) Pursue "business as missions." Throughout the discussion, it is important to keep the overall goal in mind:

> **MATERIAL POVERTY ALLEVIATION:**
> **Working to reconcile the four foundational relationships so**
> **that people can fulfill their callings of glorifying God**
> **by working and supporting themselves and their families**
> **with the fruit of that work.**

BROKEN SYSTEMS AND BROKEN INDIVIDUALS

Broken economic systems contribute to material poverty, and nowhere is this more true than in the Majority World, where unemployment is rampant and an estimated 2.6 billion people live on less than two dollars per day.[4] The vast majority of this poverty is chronic, requiring long-run development, not relief (see chapter 4).

Most economists believe that the key to economic growth for countries in the Majority World is for these countries to establish large-scale manufacturing firms. As this happens, there will be more jobs available for poor people, and material poverty will eventually dissipate. The problem is that the creation of manufacturing firms in the Majority World is not happening rapidly enough to absorb the burgeoning populations. As a result, many poor people depend upon self-employment on small farms or in microenterprises, simple businesses employing fewer than ten people.

Many researchers and practitioners believe that the primary constraint facing poor farmers and microentrepreneurs is a lack of access to capital to purchase equipment and other inputs. Traditional banks are not available in many regions, and those banks that do exist typically find it unprofitable to provide loans or savings accounts to very poor people. As a result, the poorest people on the planet do not have access to the typical savings and loan services that the rest of us take for granted, services that they need in order to acquire the capital for their farms and microenterprises.

In the absence of such banking services, poor people like Sufiya are often forced to borrow money from loan sharks at extremely high interest rates. Alternatively, they can try to accumulate capital by saving their money under their mattress, but such money can be easily stolen. Moreover, secrets are hard to keep in slums, and "long-lost cousin Jake" seems to show up needing financial assistance every time any capital is accumulated. Desiring to get their savings out of the house, poor people will sometimes give their money to a "savings shark," who will keep their savings in a "safe place" until they need it. The savings shark does not provide this service for free, charging as much as 80 percent interest for simply holding people's money.[5] Imagine saving ten dollars over the course of the year and then having only two dollars left after paying the bank for holding your deposit!

Why would poor people be willing to pay so much? Borrowing or saving are necessary to accumulate the capital that the poor need to operate their farms or microenterprises, which are often their only source of income. And without capital, they cannot purchase the medicine to save their baby from dying, pay for a wedding or a funeral, invest in their children's education, or patch the leaky roof over their heads. Accessing capital—through either borrowing or saving—is a matter of life and death.

In summary, the systems are broken for poor people in the Majority World, often preventing them from being able to support themselves and their families by working. But it is important to remember that it is not just the systems that are broken. Like all of us, poor individuals often suffer from their own rebellious hearts, faulty worldviews, and immoral behaviors. A failure to address these by focusing only on the fallen systems surrounding poor people will fail to bring about the reconciliation of relationships that is at the heart of poverty alleviation. The gospel and its implications for humans' relationships to God, self, others, and the rest of creation must be clearly presented and modeled in all poverty-alleviation strategies. In particular, many ministries in the Majority World need to confront the lies of animism, a belief system that often entraps poor people in a self-defeating fatalism, as we saw in chapter 3.[6]

THE MICROFINANCE REVOLUTION

Muhammed Yunus's Grameen Bank demonstrated that it was possible to fix at least part of the broken economic system. By placing poor people in borrowing groups of their own choosing and then requiring the group members to guarantee one another's loans, Grameen showed that it was possible to obtain high rates of loan repayment from poor people. Moreover, Grameen showed that if enough money was lent to poor people, there would be enough interest revenue coming back to Grameen to enable Grameen to pay the cost of its operations. In short, Grameen created a viable "bank" for lending money to poor people.

Like John at Grace Fellowship Church, the response of the donor community to Yunus's invention has been understandably euphoric. Rather than give money away for, say, an orphanage, which requires ongoing subsidies, donors saw the opportunity to give money that would be recycled perpetually as MF programs lent and re-lent their loan funds. As a result, microfinance institutions (MFIs) like the Grameen Bank have sprung up all over the Majority World. MFIs lend money from donors and investors to poor people, collect the money back, and then lend it out again. In the process, many poor people have been able to access capital at lower interest rates than they could have from loan sharks.

What makes MFIs like the Grameen Bank work? There are many technical issues, but a key feature of their success is that the MFI, like any bank, must convince borrowers that it will exist over the long haul. If borrowers do not believe the MFI will be there tomorrow, they will not worry about repaying their loans today, as the MFI will not be around to penalize them for not repaying. And if borrowers do not repay their loans, the MFI will go broke.

The Pros and Cons of MFIs

Well-functioning MFIs provide a remarkable service and should be seen as a tremendous asset in poor communities. They are very good at quickly injecting capital into microenterprises, and some MFIs are creatively adding new financial services such as health or life insurance. However, MFIs have some shortcomings that must be noted:[7]

- *Difficulties in providing savings services.* Research has found that many poor people would rather save than borrow. This is particularly true for the "extreme or destitute poor," whose income is well below the poverty line (see figure 9.1 below).[8] Such people are particularly vulnerable, making savings very attractive to them, since saving is less risky than borrowing.[9] Unfortunately, MFIs have historically focused on lending money and have not provided options for poor people to save. While this is changing in some places, many MFIs are still prohibited by government regulations from holding people's savings.[10]

- *Failure to reach the extreme or destitute poor.* It is difficult to find MFIs that can provide loans of less than forty dollars, and many cannot even provide loans that small. Unfortunately, the extreme or destitute poor typically cannot handle loans this large, usually desiring loans in the five- to twelve-dollar range. Recall that Sufiya wanted a loan of only twenty-two cents per day! Loan sizes that are too large and the absence of savings services make MFIs incapable of ministering to the extreme or destitute poor. Hence MFIs are better able to help the "moderate poor" or "vulnerable non-poor," whose income levels are just below or just above the poverty line, respectively.

- *Failure to reach the rural poor.* It is much cheaper to lend money in areas with high population density because transportation costs per client are lower; hence, MFIs struggle to reach the poor living in rural areas, who account for nearly 75 percent of the total poor in the Majority World.[11]

- *Exclusive focus on businesses.* Poor people need capital for their microenterprises, household improvements, emergencies, and life-cycle events such as weddings and funerals. MFIs tend to focus narrowly on finance for microenterprises, overlooking the fact that the poor need capital for a wide range of reasons.

- *Lack of evangelism and discipleship activities.* The pressure to stay in business is pushing most MFIs to reduce costs by cutting out all services other than loans and other financial products. Unfortunately, this trend has sometimes caused the MFIs operated by Christian relief and development organizations to reduce their evangelism and discipleship activities. But loans alone cannot reconcile people to God, self, others, and the rest of creation. "Faith comes by hearing," not through borrowing money!

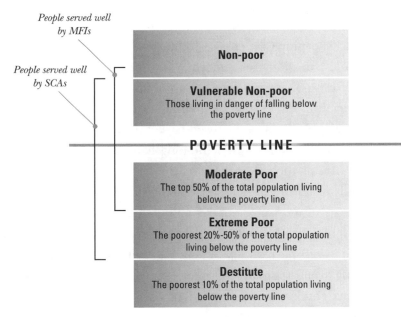

FIGURE 9.1

Adapted from Monique Cohen, *The Impact of Microfinance*, CGAP Donor Brief (Washington, D.C.: CGAP, July 2003), 1.

BEING "THE BODY" IN THE MAJORITY WORLD

How can missionaries and Majority World churches use economic development to minister in word and deed, bringing material poverty alleviation to their communities? Since missionaries and Majority World churches are on the front lines of poverty alleviation in these contexts, the appropriate role of North American churches is to support and strengthen the ministries of these missionaries and Majority World churches. The last section of this chapter suggests appropriate ways for North American churches to provide such support, focusing on strategies that are consistent with avoiding paternalism, building upon local assets, and using participatory approaches.

The MF Provider Model: Don't Try This at Home!

Many missionaries and churches (and small ministries) in the Majority World pursue the "Provider Model" in which they try to emulate the Grameen Bank by setting up a small MFI to provide loans to poor people. This is what the Ugandan churches mentioned earlier were trying to do with the money provided by Grace Fellowship Church.

Unfortunately, missionaries and churches are particularly ill-suited to provide loans for two reasons. First, they do not have the technical, managerial, and financial resources to get big enough to make their loan program financially sustainable. And as discussed earlier, when borrowers sense that the program is not sustainable over the long haul, they stop repaying their loans, thereby causing the program to go broke. To be viable, successful MFIs need thousands or tens of thousands of clients, a number that is simply beyond the capacity of most missionaries and churches. Second, missionaries and churches find it very difficult to balance their culture of grace with the discipline needed to enforce loan repayment. How many missionaries or pastors would be willing to enforce loan repayment—by confiscating collateral—from a widow with five children who failed to repay her loan? But if the missionary or pastor will not enforce loan repayment for this widow, other borrowers will believe that they do not have to repay their loans, and the program will fail. MF is a tough business.

Many missionaries and churches ignore this warning and believe that they can successfully pursue the Provider Model. But the landscape is covered with the carcasses of failed loan programs started by well-meaning missionaries and Majority World churches (and small ministries). The story of Grace Fellowship Church is extremely common. Do not try the Provider Model.

The MF Promotion Model: Microfinance without Donor Money!

Maria walked to the front of God's Compassion Church (GCC) in a Manila slum and testified to the congregation, "My child would have died had it not been for the help of the members of [this church's] Savings and Credit Association. I was able to get a loan for the medicine, and they also prayed for me, and visited my sick child." Camilla then stood up and explained how the SCA members had encouraged her to borrow some money so that she could start a small cookie-selling business. As a result of this business, she has been better able to meet the daily needs of her children.

The Savings and Credit Association (SCA) associated with God's Compassion Church dispensed a total of forty-one relatively low-interest loans, enjoying a 100 percent repayment rate. Moreover, the interest paid on the loans enabled the SCA members to earn dividends on their savings that averaged 50 percent in annual terms.

But the blessings were more than economic in nature. The SCA members prayed for each other and their families, and God steadily answered their prayers: husbands found jobs, children were healed, and broken relationships were mended. Neighbors of the SCA members commented about the love and concern that the members showed to one another, so the SCA members invited these neighbors to attend their weekly meetings and Bible study. These nonmembers were allowed to borrow money from the SCA at an interest rate much lower than that available from local loan sharks. And when the SCA started its second savings-and-loan cycle, these nonmembers were allowed to become members.[12]

God's Compassion Church's SCA represents a powerful word-and-deed ministry to the household of faith and beyond, called the "Promotion Model." Quite remarkably, this SCA, which reflects an alternative approach to MF, did not require a dime of donor money or management by outsiders. A SCA is a very simple credit union in which poor people save and lend their own money to one another. Each member contributes an agreed-upon savings amount to the group's fund at a weekly meeting. The SCA members decide how much of the group's fund to lend, to whom it will be lent, and the terms of the loans. At the end of a predetermined length of time, usually six to twelve months, each member's savings are returned along with dividends they have earned from the interest charged on loans. It is microfinance without outside managers or money!

The role of the indigenous church or missionary in this model is simply to promote the group by facilitating its formation. The church or missionary does not manage the group or handle the money. Rather, the church or missionary empowers the poor to do this for themselves, equipping them to create and manage a system for saving and borrowing the lump sums of money that they need. In addition, the group meetings provide an excellent context for evangelism and discipleship activities that may be offered by the missionary, the church, or by the group members themselves.

Promoting SCAs has proven to be a highly effective and strategic intervention for indigenous churches and missionaries in the Majority World for the following reasons:

- SCAs are simple to facilitate, can work on a small scale, and do not require the churches or missionaries to lend and collect money.
- In addition to providing loans, SCAs offer a way for poor people to save and even to earn interest on their savings.
- SCAs can work in both urban and rural areas.
- Loan sizes in the five- to twelve-dollar range are entirely feasible, as are loan sizes amounting to hundreds of dollars; hence, SCAs can minister to multiple levels of poverty, including the extreme poor.
- Lump sums from SCAs can be used for the full range of households' needs, not just financing business investments.
- Because SCAs were originally developed by poor people, promoting them builds upon local knowledge. This fact, combined with the use of local savings, makes the promotion of SCAs consistent with an asset-based approach.
- SCAs can be promoted using highly participatory methods, allowing group members to make their own policies rather than prescribing such policies for them in a blueprint fashion.[13]

- The fact that the SCAs can originate from the ministries of churches and missionaries makes it relatively easy to maintain evangelism and discipleship activities, thereby addressing brokenness at the individual level.

There are numerous examples of individual churches and ministries promoting SCAs as part of an effective word-and-deed ministry on a small scale, but large-scale programs are also possible. For example, the Anglican Church of Rwanda is currently trying to include eighty thousand people in church-centered SCAs as part of its nationwide, holistic outreach.

What are the downsides of promoting SCAs? Two problems stand out. First, poor people sometimes struggle to manage their groups well, to keep accurate records, and to enforce discipline. Many MFIs perform better in all of these functions. Second, SCAs do not mobilize large amounts of loan capital as quickly as MFIs do. Group members can grow impatient with the process of saving money for loan capital, particularly if their businesses can handle larger loan sizes. Nevertheless, the Promotion Model is a viable alternative for addressing brokenness at both the systemic and individual levels for all ranges of poverty in the Majority World.

The MF Partnership Model: Linking Arms in the Fight against Poverty

When both MFIs and churches/missionaries have a holistic vision, they can join hands in ministry, with each party providing a component of what is needed to address the effects of sin at both the individual and systemic levels.

During the savage civil war in Liberia, a Christian MFI sought to minister to those suffering from the carnage. The MFI provided loan services and then actively partnered with local churches, soliciting their help in ministering to the spiritual needs of borrowers. The MFI loan group meetings were intentionally held in or near local churches in order to make it easier for the churches to be able to minister to these groups. Pastors and church staff played significant roles in leading Bible studies at group meetings, visiting and counseling individual group members, and reminding borrowers of their need to repay their loans as a matter of integrity. The pastors expressed a great deal of "ownership" of these groups, seeing them as an integral part of their churches' ministries.

The comprehensive impacts of this partnership were quite amazing. The civil war victims were able to generate enough income from their businesses to avoid starvation. As one borrower explained, "Before [the MF program], I prayed to God to take my life because I didn't want to suffer anymore. My children were malnourished and complained of headaches. When they were hungry, they frowned and couldn't smile. [Now] we always have something to eat."[14] There was also evidence of improvements in borrowers' educational investments, health care, sense of dignity and responsibility, intertribal relationships, and spiritual maturity.

The pastors expressed joy over the way that this partnership has strengthened their churches. The MFI borrowers who were church members used their increased skills, confidence, spiritual maturity, and incomes to advance the full range of their churches' ministries. As one pastor stated, "Every week during our church's testimony time, I hear praises and expressions of gratitude to God for [this MF ministry]."[15]

The Partnership Model can be a powerful method for bringing reconciliation to both financial systems and individuals, as long as the target population is not the extreme or destitute poor, who are unable to handle MFI loans. The MFI provides the financial services such as lending money and monitoring repayment. The churches and missionaries can offer a range of complementary services that the MFI typically cannot provide, such as evangelism and discipleship; individual counseling; emergency assistance; and training in small-business principles, household financial management, and related subjects from a biblical worldview perspective.

Unfortunately, while the Partnership Model can be a powerful strategy for ministering in word and deed, it is not commonly observed in practice. Many churches and missionaries lack a holistic vision, believing that they are to care only for people's spiritual needs. In addition, some churches and missionaries dislike the banking culture of MFIs, seeing loans, interest, repayment discipline, and business as somehow dirty, unspiritual, and unmerciful. Theological groundwork concerning the comprehensive nature of Christ's kingdom can address these matters. Similarly, MFIs often lack a holistic vision, believing that poverty alleviation can be achieved just by making capital available. Moreover, MFIs are understandably leery of churches, whose cultures of charity and grace have often resulted in horrible loan repayment rates on the part of church members. Nevertheless, these obstacles can be overcome, making the Partnership Model a viable strategy for addressing brokenness at the systemic and individual levels in many contexts.

The Complementary Training Model: Man Does Not Live on Capital Alone

The MF movement is based on the premise that a lack of access to capital is the primary constraint facing poor entrepreneurs. Hence, relatively little effort has been made to offer small-business training to poor entrepreneurs. However, some are now questioning the standard MF approach, arguing that poverty is multifaceted and cannot be overcome through capital alone. Indeed, a growing body of evidence suggests that complementing savings and loan services with appropriate training topics and methodologies can improve the businesses and lives of poor people.[16]

The Chalmers Center for Economic Development, the organization at which the authors work, has integrated biblical worldview messages into technical curricula originally developed by a highly respected, nonsectarian development organization. In addition to training poor people in basic principles of small-business management, household financial literacy, and health-care topics (malaria, HIV/AIDS, diarrhea), the worldview messages apply a biblical understanding of the four key relationships to the lies of animism by emphasizing the themes of dignity, stewardship, and discipline.

While these curricula are suitable for many Christian ministry contexts, they are specifically designed to be used in SCA group meetings, thereby augmenting the holistic nature of the Promotion Model. Furthermore, churches and missionaries pursuing the Partnership Model could provide this complementary training to MFI client groups, resulting in a more holistic approach to poverty alleviation than the MFIs can offer on their own.

Business as Mission

A related intervention that has gained renewed popularity in the past decade is called business as mission (BAM). BAM finds its roots in the ministries of Paul, Aquila, and Priscilla, who used tent making as a means of supporting their missionary work. Today, BAM takes on many forms, but its defining feature is that the missionary owns and operates a legitimate, for-profit business that he or she uses as a vehicle for ministry.[17] In contrast, the other interventions described in this chapter, the Provider, Promotion, Partnership, and Complementary Training Models, all focus on helping poor people to own and operate their own microenterprises.

BAM offers an opportunity for businesspeople to participate in the missions movement by using their entrepreneurial ability, managerial talent, and financial resources for cross-cultural ministry. BAM enterprises are typically small-to-medium-scale businesses, employing anywhere from a dozen to a thousand workers.

While BAM can be used for a variety of reasons, such as gaining access to a closed country, providing the income needed for a ministry, or offering a natural context for developing relationships, a number of missionaries are using BAM as a means of poverty alleviation. Given that one of the primary problems in the Majority World is a lack of employment opportunities, it makes sense to start and operate businesses that can directly provide jobs for poor people. And by intentionally developing relationships with employees, suppliers, and customers, opportunities for evangelism and discipleship abound.

While BAM is as old as the New Testament, there has been very little systematic research concerning its effectiveness as a poverty-alleviation strategy for the twenty-first century; hence, it is difficult to compare its pros and cons to MF. However, a few observations are possible:

- BAM is likely to impact fewer poor people *directly* per ministry dollar than the Promotion, Partnership, or Complementary Training models. Explaining all the reasons for this assertion is beyond the scope of this book. However, note that BAM enterprises are more sophisticated than microenterprises, requiring greater technical expertise and larger amounts of capital per employee than in microenterprises. This is not to say that the "kingdom bang for the buck" is necessarily less in BAM. Jesus only had twelve disciples, and they changed the world! But one does have to ask whether BAM has advantages that justify its added expense per poor person directly impacted.

- Compared to microenterprises, BAM enterprises bring greater enhancement to workers' productivity through improved technology and larger amounts of capital. Hence, while fewer people are directly impacted in BAM, those who are impacted are likely to experience a far greater increase in their incomes than in MF.

- BAM is not for everyone. Many churches and missionaries are not gifted at running businesses. Moreover, even a person who is gifted at operating a business in North America will not necessarily be successful at doing so in a Majority World country. The culture and business climate in some contexts may make North American business skills not completely transferable. The Promotion, Partnership, and Complementary Training Models are all much simpler to pursue than BAM, thereby reducing the risk of harm.

- Churches and missionaries pursuing BAM need to be careful to avoid dependency-creating subsidies. For example, when missionaries operating businesses in the Majority World transport and market handcrafts to churches in North America, they create a dangerous situation. When the missionary retires, it might be impossible for the business to pay for the management, transportation, and marketing services that the missionary was providing. As a result, the business may fail, and poor employees may be left with nothing. BAM enterprises must be real businesses, covering *all* of their costs, both explicit and implicit.

THE ROLE OF THE NORTH AMERICAN CHURCH

Both the biblical mandate (1 Cor. 12:12–31) and asset-based community development require that the North American church encourage—not squash—the parts of the body that are already at work among poor people in the Majority World. In particular, note that missionaries and Majority World churches are fully capable of implementing the Promotion, Partnership, and Complementary Training Models.

What then is the appropriate role of North American churches? Here are some suggestions:

- Financially subsidize the training of missionaries and Majority World churches so that they can implement the Promotion, Partnership, and Complementary Training Models. Do not pay all the costs of this training, however, as people usually place greater value on things that they have paid something to receive.[18]

- Become a trainer of trainers. Although missionaries and indigenous churches are better positioned for frontline ministry to the poor than Christians living in North America, some North Americans have sufficient training gifts to help expose those on the front lines to new models, tools, and curricula. We have found that training teams comprising both North American and Majority World trainers can be a powerful means for supporting and encouraging those on the front lines.[19]

- Provide funds for MFIs to add evangelism and discipleship components to their programs. If a MFI is already financially sustainable, do not donate money for loan capital, since a financially sustainable MFI can raise such funds on international capital markets.

- Consider investing financial and human resources in support of a BAM enterprise.

- Become an advocate for MF and BAM by finding organizations that share your vision and supporting those organizations through prayers, networking, and financial assistance.

REFLECTION QUESTIONS AND EXERCISES

Please write responses to the following:

1. If your church has a relationship with missionaries or indigenous churches that are ministering to poor people in the Majority World, ask them if the Promotion, Partnership, or Complementary Training Models would be of interest to them. If so, encourage them and appropriate members of your church to get additional training in these models. Training resources and opportunities are available from the Chalmers Center for Economic Development (www.chalmers.org).

2. Do you have any gifts as a trainer? If so, prayerfully consider what role you might play as a trainer of trainers.

3. Ask businesspeople in your church if God might be calling them to consider pursuing or supporting BAM.

PART

4

GETTING STARTED
on HELPING
WITHOUT HURTING

INITIAL THOUGHTS

Please take a few minutes to write down your answers
to the following questions:

1. *Think of a time in which you took actions to effect positive change
   in your life. What caused you to take those actions?*

2. *Think of an individual(s) who has had a significant, positive
   impact on your life. How did they do this? What did you appreciate
   about their approach?*

CHAPTER

10

EXCUSE ME, CAN YOU
SPARE SOME **CHANGE?**

"**T**hanks so much, Jerry! I don't know what I would have done without
you. I am sure this will be the last time." As Tony left his office, Jerry
thought, *No, it won't be the last time. You will be here* again *next month, and* again *the
month after that . . . It will never end.*

Jerry put his head in his hands and thought about quitting his job . . . *again.*
For the past eight years Jerry had been serving as the Mercy Coordinator for
Parkview Fellowship, a thriving congregation located on one of the main thor-
oughfares of a mid-size, American city. Parkview is largely a commuter church,
visibly situated in an economically vibrant part of the city. For years, Parkview's
senior pastor had been trying to move the congregation away from an unhealthy inward focus, urging the congregation to show the love of Christ in
"Jerusalem, Judea, Samaria, and to the ends of the earth." Although it had
taken a while for the congregation to buy into the vision, once they did, there
was a renewed sense of energy and excitement. In particular, the young professionals in the congregation were enthusiastic about making a difference in
their city and beyond. They were determined to be part of creating a different
kind of church than the congregations in which they had been raised.

Jerry was on the front lines in Parkview's "Jerusalem," serving as the primary
liaison to the many needy people who wandered into their church building

seeking help. Jerry really bought into the pastor's vision for outreach, but he was growing increasingly disillusioned. His life seemed to be an endless cycle of people like Tony, people who for a variety of reasons, *consistently* struggled to pay their electric bills, *consistently* needed help buying their groceries, and *never* seemed to change. Jerry felt like a human ATM machine, dispensing an endless stream of money to the same group of repeat "customers." Jerry had begun to wonder if he was just enabling people like Tony, actually hurting them in the very process of trying to help them. *We've got to change what we are doing,* thought Jerry. *But how? Where do we begin?*

Just down the hall from Jerry, a related drama was unfolding. A group of people from the congregation was sitting in the church's conference room with Dan, Parkview's foreign missions pastor.

One of them spoke up. "Dan, we love you, but something has to change. We have been writing checks to pay for short-term teams for years, but the people in those African villages are just as poor as they were before we started going over there. We have dug wells, built latrines, handed out used clothing, and donated to their new church building, but they just keep asking us to send more teams and more money for more projects. If anything, they seem more dependent on us than ever before. This is bad stewardship of the money we are donating to this church. Something has to change! We've had enough."

Dan had been dreading this conversation for some time. His marching orders from the pastor were to get the church members engaged in missions, and the pastor had been elated with the number of people going on short-term trips. But Dan knew that before long the congregation would question the level of impact of these trips and of the projects the church was funding. Businesspeople in the congregation were particularly frustrated, questioning the "returns on the investment" from their donations. *We've got to change what we are doing,* thought Dan. *But how? Where do we begin?*

Parkview is not alone. Many North American churches and ministries are reconsidering the approaches they have been taking toward the materially poor. Many are realizing that they have been applying "relief" inappropriately and want to shift toward "development" in their work at home and abroad. But how do they get started? What should they actually do when the alarm clock goes off? What are the very first steps to getting going?

Unfortunately, because each situation is different, there is no "one-size-fits-all" formula for jump-starting successful "development" work; however, this chapter presents some core principles that can help churches or ministries to get started using an asset-based, participatory development process that was introduced earlier in the book. The next chapter then outlines some concrete steps to follow to get your church or ministry moving in the right direction.

Principle #1: Foster Triggers for Human Change

Recall that "development" is a process of *ongoing change* in which people move closer to being in right relationship with God, self, others, and the rest of creation. This begs the question: How do people actually change? Ultimately, lasting, positive change is impossible without the power of the Holy Spirit, so praying for change is *the* central tool in the development process. In addition, scholars and practitioners have observed some fairly regular patterns in the way that human beings experience change, patterns that can be used to encourage the kind of changes that are at the core of the development process.

Change Cycle for Individuals and Communities

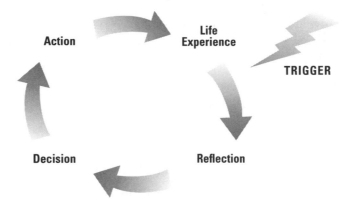

FIGURE 10.1

Adapted from David A. Kolb, *Experiential Learning: Experience as the Source of Learning and Development* (New Jersey: Prentice Hall, 1983).

As pictured in figure 10.1, the context for change is the current life experience of the individual or group. Change begins when something triggers the individual or group to reflect upon their current situation and to think about a possible future situation that they would prefer. This reflection can then lead to a decision to take some action that they hope will move them closer to the more desirable future situation. If they take action, it will lead them to some new life experience. The cycle needs to repeat itself over and over if humans are to continue to make positive changes in their lives. Hence, a central feature of development is looking for opportunities to foster the triggers for positive change.

Three common triggers for change for individuals or groups are: 1) a recent crisis; 2) the burden of the status quo becoming so overwhelming that they want to pursue change; or 3) the introduction of a new way of doing or seeing things that could improve their lives. The role of the helper with respect to each of these triggers is different.

For example, a person who is arrested for a crime is facing a crisis that may make them open to reconsidering their current lifestyle. The role of the helper in this situation may simply be to ask questions to get the person to examine themselves and to provide encouragement when they start to consider making positive changes. Never waste a crisis!

Fostering the second trigger might involve stopping the provision of "handouts" to people who are not destitute so that they can feel the burden of their current situation more acutely and be triggered to take actions that will improve their lives. For example, Jerry may need to stop paying Tony's electric bills and offer to work with Tony to find more lasting solutions.

Yesterday, just as Steve and I finished discussing the previous paragraph, I heard a knock on my kitchen door. A shabbily dressed man said, "Hello, my name is William. I was wondering if I could rake the leaves on your lawn in order to earn some gas money. I really need the cash, and your lawn really needs raking." We negotiated a fair price, and he completed half the work before the sun went down. I paid him for the portion he had completed, and he promised to come back and finish the job today. But then late last night, William knocked on my door, asking for a handout. (I was tempted to hand him a draft copy of this chapter!) I refused, but I also assured him that if he came back and finished the job, I would pay him the remaining money.

This morning I learned that William has been going door-to-door in my neighborhood for weeks, asking for handouts. My neighbors have been turning him down, so now he is apparently willing to work to earn some money. By refusing to give handouts to William, our neighborhood has been successfully fostering the second trigger for change: allowing the burden of William's current situation to induce him to work. William's behavior last night showed that he is clearly still interested in handouts, so we will need to be consistent in insisting that he work for money if we want the trigger to continue to operate.

Today, William returned and finished the raking job. I asked him if he wanted full-time work and he said, "Yes, I have experience as a crane operator, forklift driver, and airplane fueler, but I cannot find work right now." I told William he could come back and ask me for jobs to do in the future, but he was not welcome to knock on my door at 10 p.m. asking for handouts. He apologized for his late-night visit and gave me his phone number, asking me to call him when I needed more work done. My prayer is that our neighborhood will continue to allow the second trigger to operate.

There are many ways to foster the third trigger. Any of the economic development interventions discussed in chapters 8 and 9 could be used to introduce new possibilities for individuals and communities. And the basic approach of ABCD discussed in chapter 5 provides simple but powerful tools that can be used to encourage people to consider new possibilities. For example, when people feel a profound sense of inferiority, there can be a huge impact from asking the simple question, "What gifts and abilities do you have?" And when people live in cultures that have been devoid of hope for centuries, a powerful trigger for change can be found in asking, "What are your dreams?"

Note that once a trigger causes some reflection, it is *not* at all automatic that the rest of the cycle will result in major actions or significant changes or even that the cycle will proceed at all. Indeed, there are a host of obstacles that can get in the way of significant change, and a major part of the development process is coming alongside of materially poor individuals or groups to help them remove obstacles to change that they are incapable of removing on their own.

One of the most significant obstacles to change is a lack of supportive people. We all do better when we have people cheering us on, supporting us through prayer, offering a listening ear, and lending a helping hand when we need it. Unfortunately, many times when people start to pursue positive change, the people around them feel threatened or jealous, and they actually start to fight against the person's efforts to change. This leads to the next principle that is essential in pursuing asset-based, participatory development.

Principle #2: Mobilize Supportive People

Diane got laid off from her union job and ended up waiting tables. "I just felt a lot of shame. I think anybody in poverty does feel it, because I worked really hard, am really smart, and am a good person, but I just can't make it." Seeking help, Diane joined a "circle of support," a team of "allies" who came alongside of Diane, providing her with encouragement, community, and networks. A few months later, she got a job, but that did not end her commitment to her circle of support. "I would drive an hour to work, work for eight hours, drive an hour home to get my kids, and we would drive about another forty-five minutes to get to Circles." The circle provided Diane with a context to make friends and to develop leadership skills. Diane explains, "Circles gives you the opportunity to give back to the project and to other people, where other social service programs don't offer that." In her circle, Diane learned budgeting and money management skills. "It was a no-blame, no-shame environment. You say, 'This is where I am...' I made decisions that were not all smart ones, but I knew I had to take responsibility for [my situation] if I wanted to make things better."[1]

Diane's story illustrates the power of supportive people for individuals and families that are seeking to go through the change that is inherent to the development process. As a group of people who are being transformed by the gospel and who are called to be ministers of reconciliation (2 Cor. 5:18–20), the local church *should* be the ideal community for highly relational nurturing of hurting individuals and families.[2]

But reality often falls far short of the ideal. *Typically, the biggest challenge that ministries face is an insufficient number of people who are willing to invest the time and energy that it takes to walk through time with a needy individual or family.* Finding armies of people to volunteer one Saturday per year to paint dilapidated houses is easy. Finding people to love the people, day in and day out, who live in those houses is extremely difficult.

In addition, such relationships are not automatically healthy and can do considerable harm when they perpetuate the god-complex-low-self-esteem dynamic that is so often in play when materially non-poor and materially poor people interact. Indeed, even the oft-used language of "mentor" and "mentee" can start the relationship off on the wrong foot. Hence, Jobs for Life (www.jobs forlife.org) uses the term "champions" for these supportive people, and the National Circles Campaign (www.movethemountain.org) calls them "allies." Remember, the goal is that everyone grows and overcomes elements of their own brokenness. This calls for humility and reciprocity for all involved in these relationships.

How can churches and ministries mobilize supportive people and foster mentoring relationships that are consistent with the principles and goals of participatory, asset-based development?

There are a number of approaches and helpful resources on mentoring,[3] but Diane's story illustrates the power of the circles of support model that is gaining momentum across North America.[4] A circle consists of two to five volunteers—called "circle allies"—who come alongside one materially poor family or individual—called the "circle participant" or the "circle leader." The "allies" are people who are willing to use their time, talents, social and professional networks, and possibly financial resources to help the family or individual to escape material poverty. The "participant" (sometimes called the "leader") commits to use the circle to move forward toward a more positive future, including overcoming the shame and social isolation that is at the root of much of material poverty.

Although there are different ways of forming and maintaining circles, the approach of Beyond Welfare, a nonsectarian organization in Ames, Iowa, has several appealing features.[5]

• *Large Group Gathering:* Every week, allies, participants and their children, and any interested people meet to eat supper together. After dinner, the kids play while the adults meet. The content of the meeting consists of reaffirming their core principles, sharing about positive developments in their lives, and learning about a relevant topic. The latter could include training on jobs preparedness, financial education, or individual development accounts (see chapter 8).

• *Forming Circles of Support:* If and when a participant wants to form a circle of support, they ask the allies of their choice if they would be willing to join their circle. Allies are free to accept or decline. This approach has several appealing features to it. First, it overcomes the awkwardness of many approaches to mentoring in which mentors and mentees, who have never even met before, are simply preassigned to one another and told to make it work. What if they don't like each other? Second, this approach also has the advantage of using a team of people rather than just one ally per participant. A team-based approach has significant advantages including helping prevent volunteer burnout since the "load" is shared; mobilizing a broader diversity of gifts and capacities; and increasing the number of volunteers' social networks that a participant can access.[6]

• *Circle of Support Meetings:* Each circle meets monthly. The participant has been taught to lead the circle by presenting their "dream path," often in the form of a visual, about their future goals. The participant and allies then brainstorm together to help the participant create the steps they would like to take to reach their goals. The participant then decides on a concrete step to take and may describe whatever assistance they would like from the allies. The allies are free to decide if and how they would like to respond. The participant, with the help and support of their allies, then acts on their decision. Their life will then become different, and hopefully improved. This process is an application of the Change Cycle in figure 10.1.

Note that these dream paths could be tied to the topics of the large group gathering. For example, if the large group is going through a financial education class, the person's dream might focus on getting out of debt. The allies can then assist the participant with budgeting, opening a savings account, etc.

From a Christian perspective, the participant's "dream" is something that should be open to discussion. On the one hand, it is crucial that the chosen dream is something that the participant really "owns." It is their life! Allies must avoid paternalistic tendencies to impose their dreams and goals on the participant. On the other hand, all of us are prone to sinful goals and desires that need correction. If the participant states a dream that is ungodly or that is simply unrealistic, true love requires the allies to speak into the person's life, helping them to set more godly or realistic goals.

One of the appealing features of the circle meetings is that they have some structure to them. Research by Amy Sherman, one of the leading experts on holistic ministry in North America, has found that mentoring meetings that have a directed focus are less awkward and nebulous for everyone involved than those that are completely free of any structure or stated purpose.[7] Clearly, when used by churches or ministries, the circle of support provides an excellent opportunity for evangelism and discipleship.

Helpful resources on forming circles of support include *One Candle Power: Seven Principles that Enhance Lives of People with Disabilities and Their Communities*[8] and *All My Life's a Circle, Using the Tools: Circles, MAPS & PATHS.*[9]

It is important to highlight that circles of support and other forms of mentoring should not be seen solely as helping materially poor people to overcome their personal brokenness. Recall from chapter 2 that it is not just individuals that are broken: economic, social, political, and religious systems are broken as well. This systemic brokenness can manifest itself in outright oppression—e.g., the Jim Crow era in the United States—or in more subtle forms of exclusion from the networks that are essential for getting out of poverty. For example, most people get jobs through their social networks. They learn of job openings and get referrals from friends who are already employed in the company or organization. Those of us who have access to such social networks are typically unaware of how important those networks really are to our success.

As highlighted in figure 10.2, one of the key roles of allies is to use their networks of relationships to help make connections for participants to the larger systems of society and to address the injustices that often exist in those systems. Sometimes just a phone call to the "right person" can result in a job interview, a mortgage application being considered, or an unjust decision being reviewed. Middle- and upper-class North American Christians need to be aware that their networks constitute an enormous resource that they can bring to bear on the lives of materially poor people, not just as an act of "mercy," but also as an act of "justice" in addressing the broken systems that oppress and marginalize many materially poor people.

If poverty is rooted in broken relationships that result from both individual and systemic brokenness, then highly relational approaches are needed to alleviate poverty. Mobilizing teams of supportive people and their social networks are an essential component of any ministry seeking to overcome a Poverty of Being, a Poverty of Community, a Poverty of Stewardship, and a Poverty of Spiritual Intimacy.

Allies Connect Participants to Networks and Systems

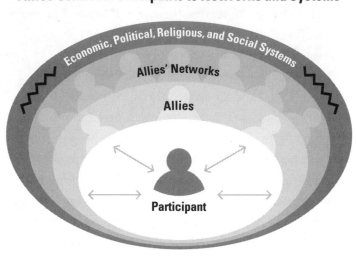

FIGURE 10.2

Principle #3: Look for an Early, Recognizable Success

Change is difficult. In order for people to be willing to go through the pain of change, they must have adequate enthusiasm and drive to motivate them to make initial changes and to sustain them throughout the process. As discussed in chapter 6, people's enthusiasm and drive are directly related to the degree that they are participating in the selection, design, implementation, and evaluation of the planned intervention. But participation alone will not give people the enthusiasm and drive to persevere for very long. Indeed, we have all participated in things that seemed to be going nowhere, causing us to give up.

To motivate people, participation typically must be accompanied by something else: *early and recognizable success toward the goals that the participants deem to be important.*[10] Think about what happens when you start an exercise program in order to lose some weight. It is a whole lot easier to get back on the treadmill when you lose a few pounds after the first week than when you don't!

Note that achieving an early and recognizable success is not just important to generate enthusiasm and drive for the materially poor but also for those who are helping them, including staff, volunteers, donors, and those watching the process to see if they would like to join in. To build adequate momentum, it is important to get the ball rolling in the right direction as soon as possible.

A good rule of thumb for achieving an early, recognizable success is to "start small, start soon, and succeed." *Start small,* because it is difficult to generate an early success in big, complex projects that take a long time to implement. Moreover, it is hard to be truly participatory in big or complex projects because participants often lack the skills necessary to manage them, thereby requiring the "professionals" or "experts" to make all the decisions. *Start soon,* because if too much time is spent gathering information, analyzing the situation, and talking about what might be done, people will lose interest and will begin to doubt that real change will ever happen.

One way to start small and start soon is to look at what you are already doing to determine if there are some ways to make it more developmental. You may not need to scrap everything and start all over.

For example, I (Steve) talked with a man who had been using donated material and labor, often provided by short-term teams, to do small-scale rehabilitation work on the homes of poor people in his community. After reading the first edition of this book, he was concerned that he was engaging in harmful paternalism and was questioning his entire approach. We met and talked through the situation. I simply asked if there might be ways that poor households could be required to significantly contribute, whether in money, materials, or labor, to the rehabbing of their own homes. He adjusted his ministry to move out of an inappropriate relief program to a more asset-based, developmental approach in which the poor households added some of their own resources to those from the outsiders to improve their own homes.

Similarly, Creekside Community Church, described in chapter 2, eventually adjusted their approach to Christmas by allowing materially poor parents to buy donated toys at low cost. The parents then gave the toys to their children, thereby building their dignity in the eyes of their kids.

And Jerry might find some tasks that need to be completed on the church's property or for the elderly or shut-ins, thereby offering Tony the opportunity to work for pay rather than giving him a handout.

Alternatively, if you feel led to start a new intervention, do so with just a few participants at first. For example, chapter 8 discussed the possibility of using jobs preparedness training, financial education, or individual development accounts to minister holistically. Rather than starting a huge program or founding a new nonprofit organization, a church or ministry could start using

one of these interventions with just a few people. By starting small and starting soon, early recognizable success is more likely to happen. This in turn will
then generate the enthusiasm and drive to grow the program over time.

Principle #4: Learn the Context as You Go

Some readers may be confused by the apparent contradiction between the advice to "start soon" and the advice of earlier chapters not to rush in too quickly
with outside ideas, skills, and resources. There is a delicate balance here.

On the one hand, the speed of the intervention must not be so fast that we
do not take the time to listen well, that we fail to identify the gifts and resources
of materially poor individuals or communities, or that we take charge of all
aspects of the intervention. The speed must be slow enough to allow for the
identification and mobilization of the ideas, skills, resources, and dreams of
the materially poor individuals or groups. Remember, most North Americans
have a bias to rush in and fix problems too fast, thereby crushing local ownership and initiative.

On the other hand, we must not overcorrect for this tendency by thinking
that we need to know everything about everybody in a community before we
can get going. If we spend too much time gathering and analyzing data, the
people involved—the materially poor, collaborating organizations, staff, volunteers, donors—will lose enthusiasm and drive.

The theory of change is helpful here. The cycle pictured in figure 10.1 is
assumed to be a spiraling cycle of action and reflection, a "learning as you go"
process: walk with people, trying something *together*; reflect on the experience,
together; decide to try something additional, *together*; reflect again; try again;
etc. You do not need to know everything to start the process. Having the attitude of a humble learner throughout the process is far more important than
having comprehensive knowledge at the start of it.

Principle #5: Start with the People Most Receptive to Change

Development can only occur with people who are willing to change. If people
do not believe that they are responsible to take actions to effect positive changes in their lives, it is very difficult to make progress with them.

Note, the previous paragraph should not be interpreted to mean that materially poor people are always to blame for the situations in which they find themselves. American slaves did not choose to be in chains. The people in Indonesia did not ask for a tsunami to hit them. Remember, due to the fall of humanity into sin, *both* systems and individuals are broken. However, regardless of how individuals or communities ended up in a bad situation, faithful stewardship on their part requires them to take whatever actions they can to use their gifts and resources to effect change. And faithfulness on our part requires us to do what we can to help them remove the obstacles that they cannot move completely by themselves.

As table 10.1 illustrates, individuals and communities have varying degrees of receptivity to change. Of course, we are called to love people in all degrees of receptivity, but the way that we love them is necessarily different, because they are different.

At the lowest end of the continuum are people who simply have no desire to change. *Some*, but not all, members of America's homeless population fit into this category. If, as we get involved with people, it becomes clear that they are simply unwilling to even consider any changes, then it is *not* loving to enable them to persist in sin by providing them with handouts of food, clothing, or shelter. Rather, the loving thing to do is to allow them to feel the burden of their choice in hopes that this will trigger positive change. One caveat to this would be if the person is so mentally ill that they do not have the capacity to make responsible choices.

Some readers might object to the idea of withholding material assistance, arguing that the Bible forbids us to say no when people ask us for help. Space does not allow for a full treatment of all that the Bible says on this difficult issue, and readers are encouraged to consult other sources that have dealt with these matters extensively.[11] However, there are two points that can be made here.

First, individual Bible verses must be interpreted and understood within the entire story line of the Bible, i.e. the creation-fall-redemption (now and not yet) motif. As explained in chapters 2 and 3, when applied to the plight of the poor, this overarching narrative means helping to restore materially poor people to what God created them to be: *people who can fulfill their callings of glorifying God by working and supporting themselves and their families with the fruit of that work.* Because God is consistent, each individual command in the Bible about the poor must be supportive of that overarching goal.[12] And any action that undermines this grand work of God in the lives of the poor is contrary to God's purposes.

Continuum of Receptivity to Change

Attitude of the Materially Poor Person	Approach to Moving Forward *with* Them
7. "I'm willing to demonstrate the solution to others and to advocate for change."	These responses are from people who are increasingly open and confident and who are eager for learning, information, and improved skills. It is relatively easy to move forward with them in pursuing positive change, i.e. "development." It will be relatively easy to "start soon" with them.
6. "I'm ready to try some action."	
5. "I see the problem, and I'm interested in learning more about what I could do."	
4. "I see there is a problem, but I'm afraid of changing for fear of loss."	This person has fears, often well founded, about the potential social or economic losses if they try to change. Their lives are often highly vulnerable, and they may understand the risks of potential solutions better than you do. Working with them will require listening well to their fears and concerns, modifying solutions to reduce risks, and creating a highly supportive environment.
3. "I see there is a problem, but I have my doubts that change is possible."	This person is skeptical that positive change is even possible. Their doubts may include legitimate concerns about the effectiveness of a proposed solution in their context or even the capacity of the helper. Or perhaps they have tried to change in the past and found it too difficult. Working with them requires listening well to their fears, working to build trust, and demonstrating to them that change is possible by giving examples of positive changes by others in a similar context or situation.
2. "There may be a problem, but it's not my responsibility to do anything about it."	This person believes the cause of the problem and its solution lie in the lap of the gods, or with the government, or with some outside agent. Although outside forces may be partly or even wholly responsible for their current situation, it will be extremely difficult for this person to take positive actions until they embrace their own responsibility to act in order to improve their situation.
1. "There is no problem."	This person is satisfied with things as they are, seeing no problem and no reason to change. It is impossible to make somebody change, but enabling them to persist in this condition through handouts is harmful. You need to allow them to experience the painful consequences of their decisions in hopes of triggering a desire for positive change. It may take much time and energy to help people change these attitudes, and there is no guarantee that change will occur.

The left vertical axis reads from bottom to top: DECREASING RECEPTIVITY TO POSITIVE CHANGE ↓ ↑ INCREASING RECEPTIVITY TO POSITIVE CHANGE

TABLE 10.1

Adapted from Lyra Srinivasan, *Tools for Community Participation, A Manual for Training Trainers in Participatory Techniques* (Washington, DC: PROWWESS/UNDP, 1990), 161.

This perspective can help us to sort through texts that might—at first glance—appear to be contradictory. For example, on the one hand, there are many passages in which God instructs His people to care for the materially poor in general and for widows in particular (e.g. Lev. 19:9–10; Deut. 14:28–29; Matt. 25:31–46; James 1:27; 1 John 3:17–18). Yet, that same God also instructed the New Testament church *not* to provide material assistance to widows who had children or grandchildren or to any widows who were not over sixty years of age, whether they had descendants or not (1 Tim. 5:3–16). Commentators believe that sixty was likely the maximum age at which individuals in those days could reasonably be expected to work and to support themselves.[13] Note that even material assistance for the older widows without descendants was not automatic, as they had to be known for their good deeds before they could receive material assistance.

Was God unloving toward widows? How can we reconcile these passages? If we interpret them in the context of the overall narrative, the mystery goes away. God wants us to be generous to the materially poor with both our time and our money. We are to "spend [ourselves] in behalf of the hungry and satisfy the needs of the oppressed" (Isa. 58:10a). But as we do so, we must proceed in a way that does not undermine the ultimate goal of restoring them to what they were created to be.

In fact, 1 Timothy 5:13 indicates that it was this ultimate goal that led God to command the New Testament church to withhold material support from all widows who were not over sixty, lest such support would cause them to become "idlers, but also gossips and busybodies" rather than productive kingdom servants. The Bible does *not* command mindless "generosity," but rather the use of wisdom and prudence that keeps the end goal in mind: restoration of people to what they were created to be.

Second, refusing to provide nondestitute people with "handouts" of material resources is *not* turning away from them. On the contrary, our message to them should be this: "We love you enough to give you far more than you are asking from us right now. We want to be part of your life and to walk with you as we get to the root cause of your present situation, *together*. This is going to cost us far more than the little bit of money you are asking us to give you right now. We are willing to take this much more costly path with you because you are worth it in God's eyes." This is not turning away from them! If they refuse such help, *they are turning away from us*! And if they do so, the proper response on our part should be to pray for them, to remain open to their return, and to make the offer to *truly* help them again in the future. But to give them material assistance when they do not need it is not the loving thing to do, and we are called to—truly—love our neighbors.

Returning to table 10.1, the people in categories 3 and 4 are open to change but have concerns that may be well-founded. As discussed in the section on "knowledge paternalism" in chapter 4, sometimes interventions that seem good to us as outsiders could be very harmful or risky. It is important to listen carefully to materially poor people who express these concerns. They are not always right, but neither are we. The intervention or approach might need to be modified in light of the information they are sharing with us.

Categories 5–7 represent those with whom it is easiest to embark on the development process, as they are the most open to pursing the proposed changes. As we try to get an early and recognizable success in order to generate enthusiasm and drive, it is often advisable to start working with people in these categories. And as they experience success, it can help the people in categories 3–4 to overcome any unwarranted fears and concerns. And it might even open up the people in categories 1–2 to new possibilities they had not considered before.

It is very useful to have tools that measure and reveal people's receptivity to change. These tools need to uncover at least two things. First, does the individual or group understand their part—whether large or small—in causing themselves to be in this situation? As discussed in chapter 2, poverty can be the result of structural injustice, natural disasters, personal sin, or some combination thereof. It is crucial that people identify any portion of the problem that is of their own making so that they can begin to address these issues. Second, does the individual or group understand that they have the responsibility to take some actions to improve their situation, even if not all aspects of the situation are within their power to change? The tools and methods described in the next chapter can help readers to discern these two dimensions of receptivity to change.

Remember, it is not only the materially poor who need to change. We all need to change, because we are all poor in different ways. Indeed, like many other North American churches and ministries, Parkview Fellowship is experiencing its own triggers of change, triggers that can propel it into a far more transformative and empowering approach to ministry. The next chapter outlines the steps Parkview can take to apply the principles described in this chapter to move ahead with asset-based, participatory development in the various contexts in which it is ministering.

REFLECTION QUESTIONS AND EXERCISES

Please write responses to the following:

1. Think about the ways that your church or ministry has been working with materially poor people. How have you been fostering triggers for positive change or undermining them?

2. What has been your church's or ministry's history of using a team of supportive people to help individuals and families to change? What are some things you have learned? If you are not using teams of supportive people, what could you do to change this?

3. Think of how you or those around you obtained their jobs. What role did their social networks play in their getting this job? What are some other ways that your social networks have helped you to make positive changes in your life? How could you use your networks to help materially poor people?

4. Think back to some initiative that your church or ministry tried to begin that never got off the ground. Did you fail to "start small" or to "start soon"?

5. Are there people in your life whom you have been trying to help who are simply not open to change? Stop and pray that the Holy Spirit would touch their hearts so that they would become more open to positive change.

6. Are you receptive to the positive changes that God wants to make in your life? Stop and pray that God would make you more open to the changes that He wants to make in you.

ON YOUR **MARK,**
GET SET, **GO!**

As Jerry, Dan, and the rest of Parkview's leadership team explored the best way to move forward, they realized that Parkview was actually ministering in three distinct settings (see figure 11.1). First, although Parkview was not situated in a materially poor community, its visible location on the main thoroughfare made it a natural stopping point for people from all over the city or for those who were just passing through. These people could be solitary individuals, but more likely they were parts of nuclear or extended households. Second, for

Contexts of Parkview Fellowship Church's Ministry

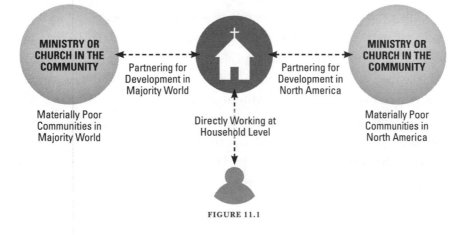

FIGURE 11.1

many years Parkview had been providing financial support and volunteers to a ministry that was located in a materially poor neighborhood about two miles away from Parkview in the same city. Finally, for many years Parkview had been sending teams to work with churches, organizations, and missionaries in materially poor communities in the Majority World.

With the framework of this book and the principles from the previous chapter in view, this chapter outlines paths that Parkview Fellowship and its partners can follow to pursue a more asset-based, participatory approach in all three settings.

DIRECTLY WORKING AT THE HOUSEHOLD LEVEL IN NORTH AMERICA

Directly Working at
Household Level

FIGURE 11.1A

Like many churches in North America, Parkview Fellowship is located in an area that is not materially poor overall; nevertheless, Parkview does have materially poor people—both members and nonmembers—asking for financial assistance. These poor people may live close to Parkview Fellowship's building, but they may also come from all over the city or even just be stopping in off the highway. Given the diversity of locations in which these materially needy people live and the fact that the area in which Parkview is located is not generally poor, Parkview may very well decide to focus on developing these individuals and their households rather than on pursuing broad-based development of the community in which Parkview is located. Parkview can use the following steps to move ahead with asset-based, participatory development for these individuals and their households:

Step One: Assess and Mobilize the Gifts of the Church or Organization

It is important to know the gifts, abilities, and resources that are present *and* available in Parkview's congregation, as well as any weaknesses that may hinder those assets from being mobilized effectively. Although financial resources may be helpful, the biggest challenge will be identifying and mobilizing supportive and humble people who are willing, ready, and able to engage in lasting and empowering relationships with materially poor people. As described in chapter 10, there are a variety of approaches to mentoring, but it is usually good to use some form of a mentoring team, such as a circle of support. It is crucial that mentors have been identified and are willing and ready to engage in long-term relationships before Parkview can play a significant role in the development process with materially poor people.

One approach to identifying and mobilizing Parkview's resources is to simply ask congregants to complete a short questionnaire in which they list their gifts *and* availability to help. A more comprehensive approach would be to assess the church's experiences, vision, attitudes, overall capacities, and weaknesses for engaging in holistic ministry. In either case, Heidi Unruh, one of the leading experts on holistic, church-based ministry in North America, has developed a very helpful resource entitled *Ministry Inventory Guide: Assess Your Church's Ministry Capacity and Identity*.[1] Remember, although a comprehensive assessment can be useful, it is important to "start small and start soon" so that enthusiasm and drive are not lost.

Step Two: Learn About the Existing Organizations and Services in the Area

It is likely that there are many organizations that are already providing services in Parkview's area. By finding out what is already available, Parkview can avoid "reinventing the wheel" and can help materially poor people to access those services. Note, Parkview should not simply refer materially poor people to these other services, thereby ushering them out the door. Remember, the goal is to develop long-term relationships that can bring about lasting change. Jerry should be saying, "Hey Tony, as we went over your budget *together*, I noticed that you were paying a lot for your electric bill each month. Let's jump in my car and go down to the electric company to see if they have any suggestions for things we could do to cut down on your costs." And then Jerry should walk with Tony through the process of figuring out how to implement some or all of the electric company's suggestions.

An excellent source of information about existing services is the *United Way 2-1-1 Resource Guide* that is available in many areas. If that publication is unavailable for Parkview's city, Parkview can examine the yellow pages, search the Internet, talk to well-known social service agencies (e.g. Department of Social Services, Salvation Army), speak with other churches and ministries, and just talk to people, including the materially poor people that Parkview knows. Helpful resources that include forms and tips to help with this process are available from the Asset-Based Community Development Institute at Northwestern University.[2]

Step Three: Adopt Asset-Based, Participatory, "First Encounter" Policies

Every church or ministry needs to have policies and procedures in place that guide them during their first encounter with materially poor people who ask for assistance. These policies and procedures, which are sometimes called "benevolence polices," need to outline the conditions and parameters under which material assistance will be given and the procedures that will be followed to move toward deeper engagement. The implementation of these policies requires a diagnostic tool that assesses the following for each individual or household: 1) Do they need relief, rehabilitation, or development? 2) Are they receptive to change? and 3) Are they open to an ongoing, supportive relationship with the church or ministry?

An outstanding set of resources can be obtained from Diaconal Ministries Canada. See in particular their *Guidelines for Benevolence*, which uses an "action plan" as the diagnostic and basic planning tool to use with those seeking material assistance. The structure of this tool is consistent with an asset-based, participatory approach, as evidenced by the following sample of questions:[3]

- What are your goals and dreams for your life?
- What strengths, abilities, and resources can you use to achieve those goals?
- What is the first action you will take to use your gifts to achieve your goals? By what date will you take this action?
- How could we support you in achieving your goals?
- Would you be willing to have a support person encourage you in meeting your goals?
- When can we meet with you again to check on how things are going?

The point of benevolence policies is to engage the person in a guided conversation that helps both them and you to better understand their life situation, to consider what could be done to improve that situation, to gauge their readiness to move forward, and to explore the role of your church or ministry in that process. If a *life-changing* crisis is not at play and the person is unwilling to engage in constructing an action plan, then *they, not you*, are refusing help.

As summarized in table 11.1, this action plan provides an opportunity to apply the five principles described in chapter 10.

Action Plan and the Principles of Asset-Based, Participatory Development

Principle	Application in Action Plan
1. Foster Triggers for Human Change	The action plan can serve as a trigger by asking people to consider—possibly for the first time—their future goals and the gifts and resources they can use to achieve those goals.
2. Mobilize Supportive People	The action plan asks materially poor people if they are open to the church or ministry bringing supportive people alongside them. If the person agrees, "allies" can be assigned or a more organic process can be used as in Beyond Welfare's use of large-group gatherings to form circles of support (see chapter 10). It is crucial that allies have been mobilized in advance so that they are ready to engage as soon as a materially poor person expresses an openness to deeper engagement.
3. Look for an Early, Recognizable Success	The action plan should start with some short- and medium-term goals that are likely to succeed: "Let's start by having you sign up your kids for flu shots"; "I'll pay you to rake the leaves and that will give you some immediate cash."
4. Learn the Context as You Go	The information that the person provides in their action plan enables you to learn a lot about them very quickly. You will learn more as you engage in an ongoing relationship with them.
5. Start with the People Most Receptive to Change	People who are unwilling to create an action plan are not receptive to change. Pray for them, but remember that you are not rejecting them; they are rejecting your help.

TABLE 11.1

Step Four: Explore the Possibility of Starting a New Ministry

As it goes through the previous steps, Parkview may see the opportunity to introduce a new ministry to help bring lasting change to the materially poor individuals and households it is encountering. For example, as the members of Parkview walk with people through the action plans they have developed, seeking to access existing services in the city, it is likely they will soon begin to see gaps between the services that are available and the assistance that materially poor people need to move forward. These gaps provide an opportunity for Parkview to find a niche for a new ministry.

Note that these gaps may be due either to a service simply not existing or to the service being inadequate for accomplishing the objectives of gospel-focused, asset-based, participatory development. For example, there are likely to be financial education programs in the community already, but the existing programs may not teach financial stewardship principles from a biblical perspective, thereby failing to address the underlying worldview issues that are often at the root of people's broken relationships with God, self, others, and the rest of creation.

Churches and ministries should "outsource" to existing service providers those features of the process in which they do not bring any distinct value added; however, they make a huge mistake when they "subcontract out" to secular service providers those features of the development process in which they have a unique opportunity to develop intentional relationships, to share the gospel, or to disciple people in a biblical worldview. For example, one feature of helping people with their finances is to encourage them to open up savings accounts. It would be silly for Parkview to start a bank if there are existing banks in the area that can provide savings accounts to materially poor people. As a church, Parkview is not particularly gifted at owning and operating banks. However, Parkview is clearly more capable of teaching biblical principles of financial stewardship and of discipling materially poor people than a secular service provider. It would be a mistake for Parkview to miss the opportunity for deep impact in this portion of the development process.

Of course, Parkview may also discover churches or Christian organizations in its community that are already ministering in very gospel-focused ways. If so, it should do its utmost to connect to and support those ministries rather than starting something redundant. For example, there may be an organization that is already offering biblically-based, financial education training that Parkview could support with mentors, trainers, etc. Collaborating with other believers is good stewardship of kingdom resources, is part of our testimony to the world, and pleases our heavenly Father.

As discussed in chapter 8, there are three economic development interventions that are likely to be good options for Parkview to consider: jobs preparedness training, financial education, and individual development accounts. The Chalmers Center's (www.chalmers.org) and Jobs for Life (www.jobsforlife.org) have training and curricula on these interventions that Parkview might want to consider. As mentioned in chapter 10, the large-group gathering in the circles of support model provides an excellent forum in which to use these three interventions.

As part of the exploration process, Parkview should pursue a very targeted asset mapping related to the intervention it is considering implementing. For example, if Parkview is considering starting a jobs preparedness ministry, it needs to discover the existing services in the community related to jobs training in order to create its unique niche and to leverage the services that are already present. Note that this targeted asset mapping is much more focused than some comprehensive asset mapping exercises which try to identify, mobilize, and connect the full range of existing organizations, associations, institutions, and resources in a community. Table 11.2 illustrates this point from a targeted asset mapping that was conducted to discover the existing jobs training and placement services in a particular community. Resources at the Asset-Based Community Development Institute at Northwestern University can help with designing and implementing a targeted asset map.[4]

PARTNERING FOR DEVELOPMENT IN MATERIALLY POOR COMMUNITIES IN NORTH AMERICA

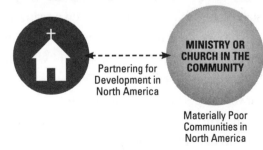

FIGURE 11.1B

As Parkview's leadership team considered ways to be more developmental in all of its ministries, it began to reflect on its historic partnership with the

Jubilee Center, a Christian ministry located in Westside, one of the poorest neighborhoods of the city. Westside has all of the common features of a North American ghetto: unemployment, crime, single-parent households, failing schools, deteriorating houses, gangs, and—worst of all—an absence of hope. For years Parkview had been supporting the Jubilee Center by sending volunteers to do things *for* Westside under the auspices of the Jubilee Center. Once every quarter, Parkview's volunteers spent a Saturday repairing and painting houses, picking up trash, and delivering baskets of food door-to-door. Given that Parkview consisted of Caucasian, middle- and upper-class professionals and that Westside consisted of low-income, African Americans, there was usually considerable awkwardness between the volunteers and the residents. However, the staff of the Jubilee Center, who had all grown up in Westside, had always welcomed the volunteers, so the volunteers had continued to go, figuring that the awkwardness was a small price to pay for serving the Jubilee Center and its community.

But now the leadership of Parkview was having second thoughts. They realized that there were similarities between paying the electric bill every month *for* Tony and the material assistance their volunteers were providing *to* the residents of Westside. They even began to wonder if their volunteers were actually undermining the work of the Jubilee Center, whose stated purpose was to foster "empowerment, dignity, and self-sufficiency."

Jerry called Michael, the executive director of the Jubilee Center, to share these concerns. After Jerry finished explaining, there was a long pause on the phone. Then, with his voice quivering, Michael responded, "Jerry, for the past several months the staff of the Jubilee Center has been praying about what to do. You see, for years we have been less than honest with you. We don't really want your volunteers doing all of this stuff for our community. In fact, we think the volunteers actually hinder our ministry. But Parkview is our largest donor, and we knew you wanted your volunteers to have something to do each quarter. We have been afraid to tell you the truth for fear that you would stop giving to us. And we really need your money to help cover our expenses. I am so sorry for being less than truthful with you, but I do believe your phone call is an answer to our prayers."

Jerry was sorry too. He remembered how the Jubilee Center had seemed a bit hesitant when he had first suggested sending in teams of volunteers

Example of a Targeted Asset Map
Percentage and Number of Local Associations Involved in Job Training and Placement

Community Benefit Activity	Have Done Work in This Area	Willing, but Haven't Done Work in This Area	Not Willing to Do Work in This Area	Willing to Collaborate with Other Groups
Start a job training program in the neighborhood	15% (13)	35% (30)	48% (41)	39% (33)
Participate in an existing job training program in the neighborhood	14% (12)	39% (33)	46% (39)	42% (36)
Participate in an inventory of the job skills and interests of local residents	8% (7)	44% (37)	45% (38)	42% (36)
Assist employers in job placement efforts	15% (13)	33% (28)	48% (41)	41% (35)
Recruit residents for local jobs	19% (16)	33% (28)	44% (37)	45% (38)
Inform members of neighborhood jobs through postings/announcements	29% (25)	29% (25)	39% (33)	48% (41)
Inform nonmembers of neighborhood jobs through postings/announcements	25% (21)	31% (26)	44% (37)	47% (40)
Help local teenagers find jobs	24% (20)	38% (32)	36% (31)	49% (42)
Connect unemployed residents to the available jobs of employed residents	29% (25)	29% (25)	38% (32)	45% (38)
Have members mentor unemployed and/or recently employed residents	19% (16)	34% (29)	44% (37)	41% (35)

Total Number of Respondents = 85

TABLE 11.2

Nicol Turner, John L. McKnight, and John P. Kretzmann, *A Guide to Mapping and Mobilizing the Associations in Local Neighborhoods* (Evanston, IL: The Asset-Based Community Development Institute at Northwestern University, 1999), 40.

many years ago. But he had insisted. He had been under orders to get more members "engaged" in ministry, and every volunteer represented "success" in meeting his goals. Jerry apologized to Michael, and the two agreed to meet soon to determine the best course of action.

After Jerry hung up the phone, he put his head in his hands, and then the tears began to flow. The Jubilee Center was just one of the many "partnerships" that Parkview had with ministries all over the city, ministries that had all "welcomed" Parkview's volunteers—at Jerry's insistence. *I just wanted to help these ghettos change,* thought Jerry. *But I've got to change before* they *can change.*

How can the Jubilee Center use a more asset-based, participatory approach in its community? How can Parkview Fellowship truly be of service to the Jubilee Center? What are the proper roles of each organization? In what follows, we will consider two good options that a church or ministry that is located in a low-income neighborhood—like the Jubilee Center—can pursue and the proper role of supporting churches from outside the community, churches like Parkview Fellowship.[5]

Partnering for Development at the Household Level in North America

The first option for the Jubilee Center is to minister at the household level in Westside. If Jubilee chooses this approach, it can get started in a more asset-based, participatory direction by simply following the same four steps that were outlined for Parkview in the earlier section entitled: "Directly Working at the Household Level in North America." This will likely result in the Jubilee Center running a ministry—e.g., jobs preparedness training—in which it seeks to use asset-based, participatory approaches with the individual households it is seeking to help.

Parkview's role in this should primarily be a supportive one, letting the Jubilee Center take the lead, because Jubilee's staff members are the ones who are working, and often living, in the community every day. Those staff members are usually in the best position to understand the community and to develop the long-term relationships that are essential to bringing the lasting change that is at the heart of the development process.

This does not mean that Parkview can never ask any questions of the Jubilee Center or make suggestions. But it does mean that Parkview needs to embrace the idea that the most visible and enduring presence in the community needs to be the Jubilee Center, not Parkview Fellowship. And it does mean that Parkview needs to be extremely sensitive to the power dynamics involved with being a Caucasian church that is the major donor to a ministry, whose staff and community are primarily African American.

Some potential roles for Parkview include: prayer; financial support; words of encouragement; helping to conduct asset mapping exercises; supplying mentoring teams for low-income households; providing jobs to residents of the community; linking community members to their networks; serving on the board of Jubilee; and providing counsel—when asked—to the executive director of Jubilee.

There is a very important point that needs to be emphasized here. Some readers have misunderstood the message of the first edition of this book to be: "Individuals and churches with financial resources should stop writing checks." That is *not* our message. We do believe that individuals, churches, and ministries should rarely be simply "writing checks" or handing out cash or material resources directly *to materially poor people*. However, we also believe that individuals and churches that have been blessed with financial resources like Parkview should dramatically increase their financial giving *to churches and ministries that pursue gospel-focused, asset-based, participatory development*. The churches and ministries that are engaged in development work have a very difficult time raising the funds needed to pay for this highly relational, time-intensive approach, an approach in which there are not always clear measures of success or of the "return on the investment." Development ministries desperately need financial supporters who understand what poverty alleviation is really about—reconciling the four, key relationships—and who are willing to fund the long and winding process that must be used to get there. In short, Parkview needs to give more—much more—money to alleviate poverty, but it must do so more wisely.

Although ministering at the household level is a legitimate strategy, the Jubilee Center needs to be cognizant of the impacts its ministry is having on the community as a whole. Bob Lupton, the founder of Family Consultation Service (FCS) Urban Ministries in Atlanta and one of the premier Christian community development experts in North America, discovered that some of the interventions FCS was using to help individual families were actually hurting FCS's community. For example, many of the people that FCS enabled to obtain jobs and to get out of public housing left the community for "greener pastures," thereby weakening the community as a whole. As a result, FCS changed its approach from working at the household level to working at the community level, which is the next option for the Jubilee Center to consider.[6]

Partnering for Development at the Community Level in North America

The second option that the Jubilee Center might choose to pursue is a more comprehensive approach to developing the Westside community. Unlike Parkview Fellowship, the Jubilee Center resides in a well-defined geographic area whose systems—families, schools, businesses, churches, associations, and institutions—are simply not functioning at the level needed for a stable and flourishing community. In addition, a significant percentage of the residents in Westside are suffering from a sense of hopelessness and despair, feeling that they are incapable of affecting much change in their lives (see the "poverty of being" in figure 2.2). In such a situation, the Jubilee Center may decide to promote the transformation of the community as a whole through a "community organizing" process that develops the local leadership, relationships, and momentum to bring wide-scale change to the systems affecting the Westside community.

What does the process for community organizing look like? There is no single recipe, and the process will take on unique features as it unfolds in any particular setting. Hence it is important to keep the overall goal in mind. In essence, community organizing tries to build a "community partnership" (sometimes called a "community organization"), a group of individuals, associations, and institutions in a community that take actions together to mobilize the community's assets in order to address the community's problems over time. If the Jubilee Center chooses to use this strategy, it may have the opportunity to proclaim and demonstrate the implications of Christ's kingdom to the entire community and to "seek the peace and prosperity of the city" (Jer. 29:4–7). Indeed, Christians must engage with the community as a whole—including everything from the police department to the recreation center to the grocery store—if we are to bear witness to Christ's reconciliation of *all things.*

On the other hand, this approach will result in a process that the Jubilee Center will not ultimately control and in which it may simply be one of many voices "at the table" as the community partnership grows. This limited, albeit crucial, role for the Jubilee Center is reflective of the fact that God has created a diversity of legitimate institutions in society—families, businesses, governments, schools, etc.—each of which has its proper role to play. No single institution should seek to take on the responsibilities that God has given to other institutions. Families are not businesses, and churches are not governments. Each institution needs to fulfill the role that God has given to it, nothing more and nothing less.[7]

Indeed, as the community partnership unfolds, it will eventually pursue activities—e.g. building a playground, lobbying the city government, etc.—that may be good and legitimate but that do not fall into the category of what most churches would consider to be "ministry." At this point, any churches involved in the community partnership may simply choose not to participate directly in those activities, even while recognizing that such activities are legitimate for other institutions in the partnership to pursue. Space does not permit a full discussion of the issues involved in finding the proper limits of the institutional church's involvement with the larger community, and we recognize that sincere Christians disagree on this difficult issue. Here we simply note that while Christian individuals and groups can and should be involved in the full range of a community's life, one of the many things the institutional church must consider before corporately engaging in any activity is the extent to which such engagement allows the church to clearly articulate the gospel message.[8] Hence, Parkview Church will need to prayerfully consider the best ways for it to support and encourage the Jubilee Center's community organizing activities.

The appendix describes steps in the community organizing process that the Jubilee Center can use to catalyze the overall development of its community. In addition, the Jubilee Center may want to use the resources of the Communities First Association (http://communitiesfirstassociation.org), a Christian organization that promotes community organizing in North America, and those available from the Chalmers Center (www.chalmers.org).

As an outsider to the community, Parkview's role in the community organizing process is one of being supportive of the Jubilee Center and of the community partnership including such things as prayer; financial support; words of encouragement; helping to conduct asset mapping exercises; supplying mentoring teams for low-income households; providing jobs to residents of the community; linking community members to their networks; serving on the board of Jubilee; and providing counsel—when asked—to the Jubilee Center and the community partnership.

PARTNERING FOR DEVELOPMENT IN MATERIALLY POOR COMMUNITIES IN THE MAJORITY WORLD

FIGURE 11.1C

Looking for some answers in its international ministries, Dan, the foreign missions pastor at Parkview, decided to spend some time on the ground overseas, looking for an alternative to Parkview's missions program. He knew the people at Parkview were right. Parkview needed to find something that brought sustainable progress on the ground, something that reduced the dependency on Parkview, something that was truly empowering . . . something that was very different from handing out shoes, conducting vacation Bible schools, building things, and then coming home.

While in Kenya looking for models, somebody suggested that Dan visit a small church of the Masai Tribe that was doing some interesting things. As Dan traveled over the dusty and bumpy roads to this church, he spent some time reading about the Masai. Although there was much to admire about their long and distinguished history, Dan was disturbed by the way that Masai women are often treated in this culture. Viewed as the property of their husbands, Masai women are subjected to backbreaking work, female genital mutilation, polygamy, and low levels of education.

Thus, as Dan arrived at the church, he was pleasantly surprised to see a group of Masai women who were singing and dancing together. The woman leading the group explained to Dan that this was the weekly meeting of their savings and credit association (SCA), a meeting in which these women came together to save and lend their own money to one another, to encourage and support each other, and to pray and study the Bible together (see chapter 9 for a further description of SCAs).

The Masai women in this church held their heads high as they discussed how a community development worker from their denomination had equipped them to form this SCA, which they owned and operated themselves. The SCA was enabling them to save and lend their own money and was providing them with the dignity they needed to start and expand their own small businesses. One woman testified, "I bought a cow with my loan of 20,000 Kenya shillings (approximately $300) and then sold it. I got good profit! When I finished this loan, I took another loan of 20,000 shillings. I am so happy. This has really uplifted me. I have now started another business of selling practice tests to students to help them prepare for the national exams. With the profits, I am able to pay the school fees for my children."

Dan asked the women how their husbands viewed this group. One lady, who has become a cattle trader as a result of the SCA, beamed as she explained, "Because we are born-again Christians, the Lord has helped this group of ladies. My husband is very proud of me. The Masai men don't think we women can do anything. But because I have been working so hard, my husband sees that I am a very important person."

And Masai women outside the church are taking note. Seeing the hard work and rising incomes of these ladies, unbelieving Masai women are asking if they can join this SCA as well.

Dan took furious notes throughout the meeting. As he got up to leave, one of the Masai women said, "But you haven't heard our vision for the future yet. Please sit down." Dan obediently took his seat again as the woman continued, "I am a pure Masai. Some Masai women look at all my business activities and wonder if I am a pure Masai. They do not believe that a Masai woman can do all these things. But I am a pure Masai. My prayer is that in the future I will be able to help the Masai girls far away from this road in the interior regions. The Masai fathers do not want to invest in their daughters' education because their daughters will be lost to other families when they get married. I want to teach the girls living in the interior regions, so that I can empower them to be just like us."

During the long drive back to Nairobi, Dan reflected on these remarkable women. They had progressed from being their husbands' property to a new status in which they were respected by their husbands and praised by their children. They were productive in the marketplace and even wanted to become missionaries, helping Masai girls to understand that they too had dignity and capacity. *These are Proverbs 31 women*, thought Dan.[9]

This appeared to be just the sort of model that Dan was seeking: local empowerment, no dependency, lasting change. When Dan got back to Nairobi, he spent some time speaking with the leaders of the denomination of which the Masai congregation was a member. He learned that this was not an isolated story, but rather part of a large-scale initiative that the denomination was using to equip hundreds of poor churches throughout Kenya to use their own resources—human, financial, spiritual, and social—to bring lasting change to their members and their communities.[10] Dan was struck by how invisible foreigners were in all of this. Everywhere he looked he saw Kenyan people doing all of the work in this ministry. Even the loan capital in the SCAs came from the Masai women themselves, women who were on the lowest rungs of society. As Dan explored further, he found that the Western church had played a pivotal role in all of this, just a different one than Parkview was accustomed to playing.

Dan returned to the United States and was determined to apply what he had learned to a new relationship that Parkview was forming with Shekinah Church, a congregation of roughly eighty people located in a small town in West Africa. Both the congregation and the town were very poor, with more than half of them living on less than two dollars per day. As Dan began to share his ideas with Jerry, they realized that there were enormous similarities between the approaches that Parkview needed to take with the Jubilee Center and with Shekinah Church. And although the ghetto in Westside was very different from the town in West Africa, the general processes and principles that the Jubilee Center and Shekinah Church needed to use were actually very similar.

Before explaining those similarities, it is important to highlight three issues that Parkview will need to pay more attention to in its Majority World partnerships than in its partnerships in North America.

What Time Is It?

As discussed in chapter 7, there are considerable differences in notions of time between Parkview Fellowship and its partners in the Majority World. Although such differences may also exist between Parkview and the Jubilee Center staff and the Westside community, they pale in comparison to the gap between Parkview and its Majority World partners. The implication of this is that Parkview needs to really slow down its expectations of how fast things will move on the ground in the Majority World. If it does not, Parkview will tend to get frustrated and will be tempted to take charge in areas where it should not, erroneously assuming that a lack of movement means a lack of ability on the part of their brothers and sisters in the Majority World.

From I to We

As chapter 7 mentioned, coming from an individualist culture, Parkview will need to be aware of both the challenges and possibilities of the more collectivist cultures in Majority World contexts. One implication of this is that Parkview needs to be particularly sensitive to the role of community leaders in collectivist cultures. A failure to recognize their authority can quickly cause any initiative to be rejected. Another implication is that people in collectivist societies are very accustomed to discussing things and doing things in groups, meaning that there is typically a more ready source of "supportive people" than in many settings in North America.

The Donald Trump Effect

Imagine that Donald Trump, one of the richest people in America, shows up at the annual congregational meeting of your church in North America. He sits in the back and listens as your church leadership presents its plans for your church for the next year. Just before the congregation is asked to vote about whether or not to adopt the plan, Mr. Trump raises his hand and says, "I'd like to make a small suggestion. I know of some churches that have built gymnasiums as a means of community outreach. It seems to me like that strategy might work for your church as well."

If your church is like most churches, a gymnasium would suddenly become part of your annual plan even if it had not even been on the radar screen a few minutes before! Why? Because everybody assumes that Mr. Trump might be willing to pay for this gymnasium. And who knows, as he engages more with your congregation, he might be willing to pay for even more things, including the things that you really wanted in the first place.

So you add a gymnasium to your annual plan, and sure enough, Mr. Trump pays for it. But then he moves on, and now your church is saddled with a gymnasium it didn't really want and that it does not have sufficient financial or human resources to maintain. As a result, the ministries that your church really wanted to pursue suffer, and the gymnasium deteriorates over time. All of this because Donald Trump simply made a suggestion!

Here is the punch line: Even the *average* North American who walks into most materially poor churches or communities in the Majority World is Donald Trump in that context. That's right, *you* are Donald Trump! "Suggestions" become "new directions" very quickly, and the results can be as harmful over time as the gymnasium was. Note that although this dynamic was present in Parkview's relationship to the Jubilee Center, it is far, far more pronounced in Parkview's relationship with its partners in the Majority World.

What is the solution to this? There are no easy answers, but here are a few suggestions:[11]

- Work hard to develop truthful and transparent relationships with your partners over time. Sticking with them, even when they fail, builds trust.
- Be less visible. Support indigenous trainers of indigenous churches so that "Donald Trump" is not seen or heard.
- Be extremely hesitant to make "suggestions." Listen more and talk less.
- Make sure that the local people—both your ministry partners and the people they are serving—are contributing their own time, money, or other resources to the project. This helps to measure their receptivity to change and their degree of enthusiasm and drive. When it costs people to participate in something, they have "skin in the game" and are less hesitant to say yes to something that they do not really want. Even the poorest people should be asked to contribute something of value to

them if they are to receive some sort of benefit from the project. The gymnasium might not have been pursued if every member of the congregation had been required to contribute $500 toward its construction.

The Beauty of Partnership Study Guide and videos are excellent resources to prepare North Americans for the joys and challenges of cross-cultural partnerships.[12] In addition, *The Lausanne Standards: Affirmations & Agreements for Giving & Receiving Money in Mission* provide very helpful guidelines to foster healthy transfers of material resources cross-culturally within the body of Christ (www.lausannestandards.org).

Partnering for Development at the Household Level in the Majority World

Similar to the Jubilee Center, one option for Shekinah Church is to minister at the level of households inside and outside its congregation rather than trying to affect its community as a whole. The general process for Shekinah is similar as well:

1. Assess and mobilize Shekinah's own gifts and resources.
2. Assess the existing assets in Shekinah's community.
3. Design a project or ministry.
4. Implement the project or ministry.
5. Evaluate and celebrate.

Shekinah Church can use the tools of participatory learning and action (PLA) to guide this process. PLA, which was formerly called participatory rural appraisal (PRA), is both a methodology and a mind-set, using techniques that seek a reversal of power from those who have it to those who do not, thereby allowing the voices of the voiceless to be heard. For example, PLA uses visual techniques (e.g., pictures drawn on the ground) rather than techniques requiring verbal skills or literacy (e.g., written charts on walls) in the planning process, thereby enabling even shy or the illiterate people to participate.[13] Given the power dynamics that exist between Parkview and Shekinah and the ones that may exist within Shekinah or its community, PLA can be a useful approach to encourage asset-based, participatory development.

The Umoja ("togetherness" in Swahili) Initiative of Tearfund, a Christian relief and development organization in the United Kingdom, has produced downloadable resources that use PLA tools to help churches and ministries in the Majority World through the five-step process described above.[14] Focus on "Stage 1: Envisioning and Equipping the Church" to help Shekinah minister at the household level. Additional downloadable PLA tools can be found in *Empowering Communities Participatory Techniques For Community-Based Programme Development.*[15] Training in PLA and related techniques is available through online courses from Village Earth (villageearth.org). In addition, when Shekinah gets to "Step 3: Design a Project or Ministry" above, it may need additional technical assistance. For example, if Shekinah decides that its project will be to use savings and credit associations like the one used by the Masai Church, it may need additional training and curricula to start these associations.

What is the role of Parkview Fellowship in this process? Again, Parkview should be in a supportive rather than a lead role, encouraging Shekinah to use its own gifts and resources to minister. Appropriate roles for Parkview include:

- Subsidizing the training of Shekinah in the PLA process. Shekinah should pay something for the training it is receiving. Options for training include relief and development organizations working in the area, training organizations in the region that specialize in PLA, local government agencies, or North American missionaries or community development workers who have been trained in the theory and practices of PLA.
- Prayer support and encouragement.
- Helping to find additional technical assistance if needed in the design of the project or ministry (step 3).
- Providing limited financial assistance for projects only when local resources are insufficient. Some local contribution should be mandatory.

This is largely the role that a Norwegian missions organization took to its relationship with the Kenyan denomination to which the Masai Church belonged. In response to a request from the Kenyan denomination for technical assistance, the Norwegians paid for a consultant who equipped a member of the Kenyan denomination, a community development facilitator, with the knowledge and skills she needed to help poor congregations across the denomination to use their own gifts and resources. The Norwegians provided some financial assistance to help pay this Kenyan facilitator's salary and expenses, enabling her to come alongside of the Kenyan churches as they developed their own ministries with no outside financial support.[16, 17]

Partnering for Development at the Community Level in the Majority World

An alternative strategy for Shekinah Church is to try to catalyze a process that may bring change to the entire town in which it is located, not just to the individual households to which Shekinah is ministering. This approach is similar to the second option described above for the Jubilee Center, i.e., the strategy of fostering a "community partnership" that seeks to mobilize the individuals, associations, and institutions of the community as a whole. Although this process will generally be slower and messier than if Shekinah simply works on its own, it can result in wider changes for the town, allowing Shekinah to represent Christ's love and reconciliation on a larger scale.

The process that Shekinah should use to catalyze such change is similar to that described for Jubilee Center in the appendix, the primary difference being that PLA is the primary tool rather than learning conversations and asset mapping.

The resources described earlier for Shekinah to use at the household level can also be used to work at the community level.[18] And Parkview's role is the same, taking a supportive rather than a lead role. In particular, Parkview may want to *help* pay for the salary and expenses of an indigenous community worker to facilitate the PLA process for Shekinah and its community, but only if there are also at least some contributions from Shekinah and any larger organizations or denominations which are involved in this process.

THE MOST IMPORTANT STEP

There is no magic formula that Parkview and its partners can use to ensure lasting change in any of the contexts in which they are working. Development is fundamentally a messy process that ultimately depends on the reconciling work of Jesus Christ (Col. 1:19–20) and the power of the Holy Spirit. Development is not something that can be "put into a bottle" and "poured out" whenever and wherever we want it to happen. However, the processes and resources described in this chapter can guide readers along the long and winding road of the development journey. But, as the "Final Word" at the end of this book reminds us, there is one more step—the most important step—that must be taken before that journey can begin.

REFLECTION QUESTIONS AND EXERCISES

Please write responses to the following:

1. Does your church or ministry have benevolence policies in place already? Are they consistent with an asset-based, participatory development approach? If not, what are the steps you could take to move in that direction?

2. Does your church or ministry partner with other churches and ministries in your area or in other parts of the world? If not, why not? What are the implications of John 17:20–23 and Philippians 2:1–11 on the importance of linking arms with other Christians and on the attitude that we should bring to such partnerships? What are some specific actions your church or ministry could take to be a better partner?

3. Have your church, your ministry, or you as an individual ever, perhaps unknowingly, brought the "Donald Trump Effect" into play in your partnerships? If so, what can you do to reverse this problem?

4. Does your church or ministry need to repent of any ways it has acted toward its partners? Consider ways you could ask your partners whether your church, your ministry, or you as an individual have put unwelcome pressures on them. How could you make it "safe" for them to tell you the truth?

5. Are there any ways that your church, your ministry, or your partners are helping individual households at the expense of the community as a whole? What could you or your partners do to work more effectively with the communities in which you are ministering?

6. Think about the three contexts pictured in figure 11.1. In which of those contexts is your church or ministry working or partnering? For each context, what are the specific steps you will take to follow the pathways described in this chapter to move in a more asset-based, participatory direction?

A **FINAL** WORD: THE MOST IMPORTANT **STEP**

This book has attempted to introduce readers to the principles and practices of poverty alleviation at the household and community levels. Along the way, the book has described a number of tools, techniques, interventions, and processes that churches and ministries can use to work with materially poor people more effectively. We believe that all of these methods are extremely useful, and we urge readers to diligently use them both at home and abroad.

But there is one step that is more important than using learning conversations, asset mapping, PLA, or any of the other techniques or tools that we have discussed. In fact, it is the most important step, the step that must be employed from the very start and repeated throughout the entire process of poverty alleviation. It is the step of repentance . . . *our repentance.*

In chapter 2 we described the equation that so often defines the relationship of the materially poor and materially non-poor, locking both parties into attitudes and behaviors that are typically destructive to both of them:

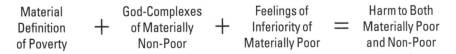

| Material Definition of Poverty | + | God-Complexes of Materially Non-Poor | + | Feelings of Inferiority of Materially Poor | = | Harm to Both Materially Poor and Non-Poor |

Recall that the first two terms in this equation require repentance on the part of the materially non-poor. Indeed, as described earlier, without such repentance, our efforts to help the materially poor are likely to do harm both to them and to us. Without such repentance, our efforts to help the poor will continue to be characterized by providing material resources *to* the poor, rather than walking *with* them in humble and relational ways as we call on King Jesus to fix the root causes of both of our poverties.

Note that such repentance is not solely a technique that we must use to help the materially poor; rather, such repentance is necessary for us to overcome our own poverty. Indeed, just as material poverty is a manifestation of deeper brokenness, we saw in chapter 3 that the "material understanding of poverty" and the "god-complexes" that so often characterize materially non-poor North Americans are symptoms of something deeper, something that strikes at the very core of our being: the modern worldview that has so profoundly damaged Western civilization without our even realizing it.

As described in chapter 3, too often the church in North America has syncretized biblical theism and the modern worldview, resulting in "evangelical gnosticism," a worldview that confines God to a spiritual realm that is disconnected from the rest of creation. At its core, evangelical gnosticism fails to understand who Jesus Christ really is, replacing the biblical Jesus with "Star Trek Jesus," who beams our souls up out of this world, a world in which He is fundamentally disinterested, a world from which He is fundamentally disconnected. "Star Trek Jesus" has nothing to do with our daily *human* existence, promising one day to transport only our souls out of here into some disembodied, new, nonhuman existence called heaven; an existence that, quite frankly, doesn't sound very appealing to most of us, because we are humans and can only imagine what its like to be, well, human!

In contrast, "Colossians 1 Jesus," is the Creator, Sustainer, and Reconciler of all things, the King whose kingdom is wiping out all of our diseases and all of our poverty. "Colossians 1 Jesus" doesn't ask us to stop being humans in this world or the next. Rather, "Colossians 1 Jesus" cares about our bodies, cares about our souls, and cares about the entire world that those bodies and souls are experiencing. As Tim Keller states:

Jesus, unlike the founder of any other major faith, holds out hope for ordinary human life. Our future is not an ethereal, impersonal form of consciousness. We will not float through the air, but rather will eat, embrace, sing, laugh, and dance in the kingdom of God, in degrees of power, glory, and joy that we can't at present imagine.[1]

If you are a North American Christian whom God has blessed with material resources, there is good news for you. For as you take the first steps in helping the materially poor—namely, repenting of the modern worldview—you may discover a solution for *your* own deepest hunger: "Colossians 1 Jesus," the King who is connected to your world, the King who heals all your diseases, the King who reconciles you to God, self, others, and the rest of creation: the King who can make both you and the materially poor truly human again.

You see, in a fallen world, we are all homeless beggars. As Keller explains, each one of us—whether we are materially rich or poor—is longing, like the Prodigal Son, to come home to a feast, a banquet in which all our physical needs are fully satisfied and all our relationships are completely restored, a banquet in which we experience all that it means to be human for the first time. We beggars can all come home to that wonderful feast, not through material resources or superior technology—the gods of modernism—but by embracing "Colossians 1 Jesus," the Master of the only banquet that can truly satisfy.[2]

> On this mountain the Lord Almighty will prepare
> > a feast of rich food for all peoples,
> > a banquet of aged wine—
> > the best of meats and the finest of wines.
> On this mountain he will destroy
> > the shroud that enfolds all peoples,
> > the sheet that covers all nations;
> > he will swallow up death forever.
> The Sovereign Lord will wipe away the tears
> > from all faces;
> > he will remove the disgrace of his people
> > from all the earth.
> The Lord has spoken. (Isa. 25:6–8)

THE COMMUNITY ORGANIZING
PROCESS IN NORTH
AMERICA

As pictured in figure A.1, the central dynamic of the community organizing process involves moving repeatedly through three interacting activities.[1] The goal of the process is to create a "community partnership," a group of individuals, associations (including churches), and institutions that cooperate to use the assets of the community to solve problems and to bring positive change to the community, i.e., to pursue "development." The size of the community partnership can start small and then grow over time, depending on the vision of its members. This appendix discusses the key steps involved in each part of this repeating process.

Discovering Care

"Discovering Care" refers to uncovering the issue(s) that people in the community are *motivated to act* to address. These issues are reflective of the concerns, dreams, and gifts of the community members themselves, not the outsiders trying to help them. Often, those seeking to help a community get frustrated when community members are not interested in acting upon their suggestions. In such situations, the helpers often conclude that the community member are simply unmotivated and are not interested in improving their own lives. That could be the case, but another possibility is that the community members simply care about—i.e., are willing to take actions to address—different issues than those suggested by the helpers.

The Community Organizing Process

FIGURE A.1

Adapted from Mike Green with Henry Moore and John O'Brien, *When People Care Enough to Act: ABCD in Action* (Toronto, Ontario: Inclusion Press, 2006), 93.

The steps to "Discovering Care" are as follows:

Discovering Care—Step One: Jubilee Center Conducts Learning Conversations

A staff member(s) of the Jubilee Center—sometimes called the "community organizer"—should begin to conduct learning conversations, which are the primary tool of community organizing.[2] A learning conversation is a highly relational, face-to-face, 45–60 minute interview of the individuals, associations, and institutions in the community that focuses on discovering what people care enough about to act on. In addition, these initial learning conversations enable the staff of the Jubilee Center to develop stronger relationships with the community, to explore mutual interests, to find more people to interview, and to identify "connector-leaders," who are discussed further below.[3] It is probably unwise for volunteers from Parkview Fellowship to help conduct these initial learning conversations, since it is important for the Jubilee Center's "face" to be clearly front and center in the early stages of relationship building.

Discovering Care—Step Two: Jubilee Center Forms a "Connector-Leaders" Group

By reflecting on the learning conversations, the Jubilee Center should be able to identify the community's "connector-leaders," individuals who are the key to mobilizing the community's assets in order to bring about wider change. Good connector-leaders have the following qualities:

- They have the ability to influence the community's individuals, associations, or institutions.
- They care enough to act about one or more of the top issues that are important to the community as whole.
- They are open to sharing their knowledge, connections, or power for the larger good rather than seeking to limit access in order to preserve their own status.

The Jubilee Center's community organizer should ask the connector-leaders if they are willing to work together to form a "community partnership" that will take on some issue to address in their community. The community organizer should share the results from the initial learning conversations concerning the top issues that the community (individuals, associations, and institutions) seemed to be most interested in solving. Typical examples might include such issues as violent crime, unemployment, low rates of home ownership, high school dropouts, predatory lenders, etc.

Discovering Care—Step Three: The "Connector-Leaders" Group Considers Conducting More Learning Conversations

It is imperative that the connector-leaders are very much in touch with the individuals, associations, and institutions that are willing to act and the issues they are willing to address. It may be that the original learning conversations and the knowledge of these connector-leaders is sufficient for them to mobilize the critical mass of people needed to get moving on addressing an issue. If not, then the connector-leaders, with assistance from the community organizer, should conduct more learning conversations in order to: 1) further identify individuals, associations, and institutions from the connector-leaders' networks and from the community in general to join the community partnership; and 2) gather further information to help identify the first issue—the priority issue—that the community partnership will seek to address.

Taking Meaningful Action

Again, it is important not to spend years collecting and analyzing data. Enthusiasm and drive are built when actions are taken that produce visible changes. It is important to take meaningful actions as soon as possible.

Taking Meaningful Action—Step One: Connector-Leader Group Chooses a Priority Issue

Based on the community's priorities as expressed in the learning conversations and on their own knowledge and willingness to act, the connector-leaders choose a priority issue for the community partnership to address. The facilitator from the Jubilee Center should encourage the group to choose a strategy that has the following characteristics:

- Has a high chance of an early and recognizable success. Remember, start small, start soon, and succeed. "Ending world hunger" is not a good priority issue. "Ending predatory lending in our community" is.
- Can mobilize and connect the individuals, associations, and institutions within the community more deeply than they were before.
- Can forge new connections with assets external to the community.

Taking Meaningful Action—Step Two: Connector-Leader Group Forms Community Partnership to Address the Priority Issue

Once the priority issue has been chosen, the connector-leaders group can use the information from the learning conversations and its own knowledge to invite people to join the community partnership to act on the priority issue. The community partnership will often have a name, e.g., "The Partnership for Hope," but it need not become a formal, nonprofit organization (501c3) at this point. The invitees represent individuals, associations, and institutions that have expressed a willingness to act on the priority issue. Again, it is not necessary to gather the entire community but rather a critical mass of people to get moving. In particular, it is important that materially poor individuals who are likely to have a stake in the priority issue are included in the partnership, as their voice needs to be heard.

Taking Meaningful Action—Step Three: Community Partnership Researches a Potential Strategy to Address the Priority Issue

With assistance from the community organizer, the community partnership needs to find out what others have done to successfully address the priority issue. For example, if the community partnership is addressing the issue of predatory lending, it can talk to banks and credit unions, consult with financial counselors, search the Internet for solutions, attend relevant conferences, etc. In the process, the partnership may discover particular strategies and interventions that might work well in their community. For example, in the case of predatory lenders, they may discover that other communities have successfully used financial education training to help low-income people to avoid these lenders. They may also identify some existing curricula and training programs that they might want to consider introducing to their community.

Taking Meaningful Action—Step Four: Community Partnership Conducts a Targeted Asset Mapping of the Community

Although the members of the community partnership will already be aware of some of the assets from the community as a result of the learning conversations and their own knowledge, the community partnership should conduct a targeted asset map of the community related to the strategy that they are considering. For a description of targeted asset maps, see "*Step Four: Explore the Possibility of Starting a New Ministry*" in the section in chapter 11 entitled, "Directly Working at the Household Level in North America." For example, in the context of addressing the issue of predatory lenders, a targeted asset map should look for the presence of more legitimate financial institutions in the community and the services they offer, existing financial education services, etc.

Note, the purpose of this targeted asset map is not to gather comprehensive information about all the resources that already exist in the community (Recall principle 4 from chapter 10: "Learn the Context as You Go"). Indeed, many asset mapping initiatives make the mistake of taking months or years to collect and process volumes of data that never get used. Rather, the purposes of this process are two-fold: 1) to make sure that the proposed intervention is not redundant with what already exists; 2) to enable the community partnership to develop relationships with relevant individuals, associations, and institutions, mobilizing them to address the priority issue. This is a good place for volunteers from Parkview Fellowship to assist with collecting and summarizing data.

Taking Meaningful Action—Step Five: Community Partnership Launches a Project

Taking into account all that it has learned from its research and from the targeted asset mapping, the community partnership designs and launches a project to pursue. This might involve starting a new organization, or preferably, having one or more existing associations (including churches) and institutions implement the project. It is imperative that the chosen project and its design be consistent with the principles of asset-based, participatory development. In particular, it would be terribly unfortunate if the community partnership chose a project that amounted to providing "relief" to people who needed "development," e.g., providing free food to able-bodied people on a regular basis.

The project might provide an opportunity for the Jubilee Center to engage more deeply in ministry. For example, if the chosen project is for the associations in the community to use financial education in order to increase people's ability to avoid predatory lenders, the Jubilee Center could offer to be one of the sites that offer these classes. And when it does so, the Jubilee Center should employ all of the principles of gospel-focused, asset-based, participatory development, including using a biblically-based curriculum that points to Jesus Christ as the reconciler of all things and church-based mentoring teams. In other words, when the project is implemented at the site of the Jubilee Center, it will look the same as it would have if the Jubilee Center had simply pursued the strategy of working at the household level rather than at the community level to begin with! The difference is that by developing the community partnership, the Jubilee Center may have catalyzed a process that can begin to address a host of issues to bring wide-scale change to the community over time.

Taking Meaningful Action—Step Six: Community Partnership Evaluates and Celebrates

At the end of the first cycle of the project, the community partnership should gather to evaluate how successful the project has been and to celebrate any successes. It is crucial that the voices of all members of the partnership have been heard, especially any materially poor people who have been participating in the project.

Making Connections

In the process of "Discovering Care" and of "Taking Meaningful Actions," the members of the community partnership will grow deeper in its relationships with one another and develop new relationships with others. These deeper and newer connections provide the opportunity to build upon what has happened in order to discover new "care," i.e., additional motivations to act that can lead to another round of the cycle.

WHAT'S NEXT?

At this point in the cycle, the community partnership must answer two questions.

First, should they address the initial priority issue at a deeper level, or should they take on an entirely new issue? Going deeper could simply mean impacting more people with the original intervention, or it could mean expanding the initial intervention. For example, if the initial project was to provide financial education training, going deeper could mean providing more financial education training per year, or it could mean adding individual development accounts to the financial education program. Either action would further reduce the leverage of the predatory lenders. Alternatively, the community partnership could decide to take on a whole new issue together.

Second, should they use the connections they have made to expand the size of the community partnership or should they keep the community partnership at the same size? Many theorists and practitioners argue that the goal is to continue to grow the size of the community partnership so that it will have the clout to effect large-scale changes in the institutions and social structures affecting the members of the community.

CONCLUDING **REMARKS**

We have covered a lot of ground, but this book is very introductory. Every topic that we have introduced needs to be unpacked and explored further. We strongly encourage you to pursue even deeper learning through the organizations and resources we have mentioned in the text and notes. In particular, the Chalmers Center for Economic Development at Covenant College provides additional resources and training on the topics introduced in this book (www.chalmers.org).

It is our prayer that God will use this book in some small way to equip His church to preach the good news of the kingdom of God—in both word and deed—to the poor, a group that includes, in some sense, each one of us.

The Authors

NOTES

CHAPTER 1
Why Did Jesus Come to Earth?

1. Portions of this chapter have been adapted with permission from a previous publication: Brian Fikkert, "Educating for Shalom: Missional School Communities," chapter 18 in *Schools as Communities: Educational Leadership, Relationships, and the Eternal Value of Christian Schooling* (Colorado Springs: Purposeful Design Publications, 2007), 357–76.

2. Timothy J. Keller, *Ministries of Mercy: The Call of the Jericho Road*, 2nd ed. (Phillipsburg, N.J.: Presbyterian and Reformed, 1997), 52–53.

3. Charles Marsh, *The Last Days: A Son's Story of Sin and Segregation at the Dawn of the New South* (New York: Basic Books, 2001), 44.

4. Robert Marsh, "The Sorrow of Selma," as quoted in *The Last Days: A Son's Story of Sin and Segregation at the Dawn of the New South* by Charles Marsh (New York: Basic Books, 2001), 51.

5. Dennis E. Johnson, *The Message of Acts in the History of Redemption* (Phillipsburg, N.J.: Presbyterian and Reformed, 1997), 87–89.

6. Jeffrey D. Sachs, *The End of Poverty: Economic Possibilities for Our Time* (New York: Penguin Press, 2005), 28.

7. Figures are in constant, 1993 purchasing power parity dollars. Figures are estimates using data from the World Bank, *World Development Indicators 2008* (Washington, D.C.: World Bank, 2008).

8. United Nations Development Programme, *Human Development Report 2007/2008* (New York: Palgrave Macmillan, 2007), 25.

9. Mark R. Gornik, *To Live in Peace: Biblical Faith and the Changing Inner City* (Grand Rapids, Mich.: Eerdmans, 2002), 73.

10. Rodney Stark, *The Rise of Christianity: A Sociologist Reconsiders History* (Princeton, N.J.: Princeton Univ. Press, 1996), 155.

11. Ibid., 166.

12. Ibid., 84.

13. Philip Jenkins, *The Next Christendom: The Coming of Global Christianity* (Oxford: Oxford Univ. Press, 2002), 92.

14. Marvin N. Olasky, *The Tragedy of American Compassion* (Wheaton, Ill.: Crossway, 1992).

15. George Marsden, *Fundamentalism and American Culture* (Oxford: Oxford Univ. Press, 1980).

16. James F. Engel and William A. Dyrness, *Changing the Mind of Missions: Where Have We Gone Wrong?* (Downers Grove, Ill.: InterVarsity, 2000), 23.

CHAPTER 2
What's the Problem?

1. World Bank, *Hear Our Voices: The Poor on Poverty,* DVD (New York: Global Vision, 2000).

2. As quoted in Deepa Narayan with Raj Patel, Kai Schafft, Anne Rademacher, Sarah Kock-Schulte, *Voices of the Poor: Can Anyone Hear Us?* (New York: Oxford Univ. Press for the World Bank, 2000), 65.

3. Ibid., 37.

4. Ibid., 70.

5. Ibid., 38.

6. Ibid., 39.

7. Ibid., 35.

8. Ibid., 43.

9. Ibid.

10. Ibid., 50.

11. There are many different locations and types of poverty in North America, including inner-city ghettos, rural communities, immigrants, and the new suburban poverty.

12. Cornel West, *Race Matters* (New York: Vintage Books, 1993), 19–20.

13. Defining what is a "sufficient" level of material things is a nontrivial exercise that goes beyond the scope of the present discussion.

14. There is solid scriptural support for the foundational nature of these four relationships. Matthew 22:37–40 teaches us to love God and then others as much as we love ourselves, saying that all the law and the prophets hang on these commands. And the first command

to humans in Genesis 1:28 is to steward the rest of creation.

15. Bryant L. Myers, *Walking with the Poor: Principles and Practices of Transformational Development* (Maryknoll, N.Y.: Orbis Books, 1999), 86.

16. Jayakumar Christian, *Powerlessness of the Poor: Toward an Alternative Kingdom of God Based Paradigm of Response* (Pasadena, Calif.: Fuller Theological Seminary Ph.D. thesis, 1994).

17. Robert Chambers, *Rural Development: Putting the Last First* (London: Longman Group, 1983).

18. Amartya Sen, *Development as Freedom* (New York: Anchor Books, 1999).

CHAPTER 3
Are We There Yet?

1. Alisa Collins's story can be viewed in Tod Lending, *Legacy*, DVD (Chicago: Nomadic Pictures, 1999).

2. Mark R. Gornik, *To Live in Peace: Biblical Faith and the Changing Inner City* (Grand Rapids, Mich.: Eerdmans, 2002), 170–73.

3. Ibid., 175.

4. Ibid., 177.

5. Scott D. Allen and Darrow L. Miller, *The Forest in the Seed: A Biblical Perspective on Resources and Development* (Phoenix: Disciple Nations Alliance, 2006), 15.

6. As quoted in Lending, *Legacy*.

7. David Hilfiker, *Urban Injustice: How Ghettos Happen* (New York: Seven Stories Press, 2002), 50.

8. LeAlan Jones and Lloyd Newman with David Isay, *Our America: Life and Death on the South Side of Chicago* (New York: Washington Square Press, 1997), 97.

9. Carl Ellis, "The Rise of Ghetto Nihilism," presentation given at the Second Annual Christian Economic Development Institute of the Chalmers Center for Economic Development, Covenant College, Lookout Mountain, GA, May 2004.

10. See Ruby K. Payne and Bill Ehlig, *What Every Church Member Should Know About Poverty* (Baytown, Tex.: RFT Publishing, 1999).

11. This story is taken from Disciple Nations Alliance, *Aturo Cuba's Ministry among the Pokomchi in Guatemala* (Phoenix: Disciple Nations Alliance, 2004), 2.

12. Jones and Newman, *Our America*, 141.

13. This section draws on the following: Hilfiker, *Urban Injustice;* William Julius Wilson, *The Truly Disadvantaged: The Inner City, the Underclass, and Public Policy* (Chicago: Univ. of Chicago Press, 1987); and William Julius Wilson, *When Work Disappears: The World of the New Urban Poor* (New York: Knopf, 1996).

14. Gornik, *To Live in Peace*, 45–46.

15. Michael O. Emerson and Christian Smith, *Divided by Faith: Evangelical Religion and the Problem of Race in America* (New York: Oxford Univ. Press, 2000).

16. Darrow L. Miller with Stan Guthrie, *Discipling the Nations: The Power of Truth to Transform Cultures* (Seattle, WA: YWAM, 2001), 31–46

17. See Myers, *Walking with the Poor,* chapter 8 for a helpful discussion of this point.

CHAPTER 4
Not All Poverty Is Created Equal

1. Jessica Murray and Richard Rosenberg, "Community-Managed Loan Funds: Which Ones Work?" Consultative Group to Assist the Poor, Focus Note No. 36, May 2006.

2. The Sphere Project, *Humanitarian Charter and Minimum Standards in Disaster Response,* 2004 revised edition, available from www.sphereproject.org.

3. Alvin Mbola, "Bad Relief Undermines Worship in Kibera," *Mandate,* Chalmers Center for Economic Development, 2007, no. 3, available at www.chalmers.org.

4. This is a modification of the definition of paternalism found in Roland Bunch, *Two Ears of Corn: A Guide to People-Centered Agricultural Improvement* (Oklahoma City: World Neighbors, 1982).

5. See Michael P. Todaro and Stephen C. Smith, *Economic Development,* 9th ed. (New York: Addison, Wesley, Longman, 2006).

6. Ruby K. Payne and Bill Ehlig, *What Every Church Member Should Know About Poverty* (Baytown, Tex.: RFT Publishing, 1999).

7. An excellent example of a church that has moved from relief to development in its ministry is described in Tara Bryant, "Broken but Beautiful," *Mandate,* Chalmers Center for Economic Development, 2007, no. 1, available at www.chalmers.org.

CHAPTER 5
Give Me Your Tired, Your Poor, and Their Assets

1. John P. Kretzmann and John L. McKnight, *Building Communities from the Inside Out: A Path Toward Finding and Mobilizing a Community's Assets* (Chicago: ACTA Publications, 1993).

2. Robert Chambers, *Whose Reality Counts? Putting the Last First* (London: Intermediate Technology Publications, 1997).

3. David L. Cooperrider and Suresh Srivastva, "Appreciative Inquiry in Organizational Life," *Research in Organizational Change and Development,* 1987, no. 1, 129–69.

4. Myers, *Walking with the Poor,* 179.

5. Bryant, "Broken but Beautiful."

CHAPTER 6
McDevelopment: Over 2.5 Billion People NOT Served

1. Roland Bunch, *Two Ears of Corn: A Guide to People-Centered Agricultural Improvement*, 18–19.

2. William Easterly, *The White Man's Burden: Why the West's Efforts to Aid the Rest Have Done So Much Ill and So Little Good* (New York: Penguin Press, 2006), 4.

3. Shaohua Chen and Martin Ravallion, "The Developing World Is Poorer Than We Thought, But No Less Successful in the Fight Against Poverty" (Washington, D.C.: World Bank Development Research Group, 2008), August, Policy Research Working Paper 4703, 20.

4. Anonymous, "Short-Term Missions Can Create a Long-Term Mess," *Mandate*, Chalmers Center for Economic Development, 2007, no. 3, available at www.chalmers.org.

5. Lissette M. Lopez and Carol Stack, "Social Capital and the Culture of Power: Lessons from the Field," chapter 2 in *Social Capital and Poor Communities*, ed. Susan Saegert, J. Phillip Thompson, and Mark R. Warren (New York: Russell Sage Foundation, 2001), 39.

6. Daniel Watson, "A Family's Journey Toward Restoration," *Mandate*, Chalmers Center for Economic Development, 2008, no. 2, available at www.chalmers.org.

7. See, for example, Laura Hunter, "A Participatory Party in Mozambique," *Mandate*, Chalmers Center for Economic Development, 2008, no. 2, available at www.chalmers.org.

CHAPTER 7
Doing Short-Term Missions Without Doing Long-Term Harm

1. Data in this paragraph are from Roger Peterson, plenary address at *Short-Term Missions Long-Term Impact?* a conference cosponsored by Interdenominational Foreign Missions Association and the Evangelical Missiological Society, 28 September 2007, Minneapolis.

2. Miriam Adeney, "When the Elephant Dances, the Mouse May Die," *Short-term Missions Today*, inaugural edition, 2000.

3. Peterson plenary address.

4. Myers, *Walking with the Poor*, 65–66.

5. Adeney.

6. Anonymous, "Short-Term Missions Can Create a Long-Term Mess," *Mandate*.

7. Peterson plenary address.

8. Rick Johnson, "Going South of the Border, A Case Study: Understanding the Pitfalls and Proposing Healthy Guidelines," *Mission Frontiers*, January 2000.

9. Kurt Alan Ver Beek, "Lessons from a Sapling: Review of Research on Short-term Missions, Study Abroad and Service-Learning," working paper at Calvin College, Grand Rapids, Michigan, 2006.

10. Ibid.

11. Randy Friesen, "The Long-Term Impact of Short-Term Missions," *Evangelical Missions Quarterly* 41 (4), 2005, 448–54.

CHAPTER 8
Yes, in Your Backyard

1. Eval Press, "The New Suburban Poverty," *The Nation*, 23 April 2007.

2. Alan Berube and Elizabeth Kneebone, *Two Steps Back: City and Suburban Poverty Trends 1999–2005* (Washington, D.C.: Brookings Institution, December 2006), Living Cities Census Series.

3. Bob Lupton, "Suburbanization of Poverty," *Urban Perspectives*, FCS Ministries, March 2008, available at www.fcsministries.org.

4. Ibid.

5. Harvie M. Conn, *The American City and the Evangelical Church, A Historical Overview* (Grand Rapids, Mich.: Baker, 1994).

6. Press, "The New Suburban Poverty."

7. Education Trust, *Funding Gaps 2006*, Washington, D.C., 2006.

8. U.S. Census Bureau, *Public Education Finances: 2006*, Washington, D.C., April 2008.

9. See Ruby K. Payne and Bill Ehlig, *What Every Church Member Should Know About Poverty* (Baytown, Tex.: RFT Publishing, 1999).

10. See Michael Wayne Sherraden, *Assets and the Poor: A New American Welfare Policy* (Armonk, N.Y.: M. E. Sharpe, 1991); and Thomas M. Shapiro and Edward N. Wolff, eds., *Assets for the Poor, the Benefits of Spreading Asset Ownership* (New York: Russell Sage Foundation, 2001).

11. Joint Center for Housing Studies of Harvard University, *The State of the Nation's Housing 2008* (Cambridge, Mass.: President and Fellows of Harvard College, 2008), 4.

12. Commonwealth Fund Commission on a High Performance Health System, *Why Not the Best? Results from the National Scorecard on U.S. Health System Performance, 2008* (New York: Commonwealth Fund, July 2008), 12.

13. Ibid., 36.

14. Michael Rhodes, "Jobs, Money, and Jesus: The Gospel in Inner-City Memphis" *Mandate*, Chalmers Center for Economic Development, 2008, no. 3, available at www.chalmers.org.

15. From Jobs for Life website: www.jobsforlife.com.

16. Marsha Regenstein, Jack A. Meyer, and Jennifer Dickemper Hicks, *Job Prospects for Welfare Recipients: Employers Speak Out* (Washington, D.C.: Urban Institute, 1998), New Federalism Issues and Options for States, Series A, No. A-25, August.

17. Dean Foust, "Predatory Lending: Easy Money," *BusinessWeek*, 24 April 2000.

18. *Predatory Payday Lending Traps Borrower* (Durham, N.C.: Center for Responsible Lending, 2005).

19. Danna Moore, *Survey of Financial Literacy in Washington State: Knowledge, Behavior, Attitudes, and Experience* (Pullman, Wash.: Social and Economic Sciences Research Center of Washington State University, 2003), Technical Report No. 03-39.

20. Bradley R. Schiller, *The Economics of Poverty and Discrimination*, 10th ed. (Upper Saddle River, N.J.: Pearson Education, 2008), 291.

21. Steve Holt, *The Earned Income Tax Credit at Age 30: What We Know* (Washington, D.C.: Brookings Institution, 2006), Metropolitan Policy Program, Research Brief, February.

22. Ibid., 11.

23. Stephan Fairfield, "A Penny Saved Is a Penny Matched," *Mandate*, Chalmers Center for Economic Development, 2008, no. 1, available at www.chalmers.org.

24. Margaret Clancy, Mark Schreiner, and Michael Sherraden, *Final Report: Saving Performance in the American Dream Demonstration* (St. Louis, Mo.: Center for Social Development, at the Washington University 2002).

CHAPTER 9
And to the Ends of the Earth

1. Muhammad Yunus, *Banker to the Poor: Micro-Lending and the Battle Against World Poverty* (New York: Public Affairs, 1999).

2. Grameen Bank, *Grameen Bank Monthly Update*, Statement No: 1, Issue No. 345, 11 October 2008.

3. See the Microcredit Summit Campaign website at www.microcreditsummit.org.

4. Shaohua Chen and Martin Ravallion, *The Developing World Is Poorer Than We Thought, But No Less Successful in the Fight Against Poverty* (Washington, D.C.: The World Bank, 2008), Policy Research Working Paper 4703, 20.

5. Stuart Rutherford. *The Poor and Their Money* (New Delhi: Oxford Univ. Press, 2000).

6. An excellent discussion can be found in Gailyn Van Rheenen, *Communicating Christ in Animistic Contexts* (Grand Rapids, Mich.: Baker, 1991).

7. For a helpful review of the issues facing Christian MFIs, see David Bussau and Russell Mask, *Christian Microenterprise Development: An Introduction* (Oxford, UK: Regnum, 2003).

8. The poverty line is the level of income that divides the "poor" from the "non-poor." The international poverty line that is commonly used is one U.S. dollar per day.

9. See Brian Fikkert, *Christian Microfinance: Which Way Now?* working paper #205, Chalmers Center for Economic Development at Covenant College, www.chalmers.org.

10. Sometimes MFIs claim to offer savings services when in reality the MFIs are requiring borrowers to place money on deposit with the MFI as collateral for loans. These "savings" are typically not accessible by the MFI clients until their loans are repaid, making this money useless in alleviating emergencies.

11. Martin Ravallion, Shaohua Chen, and Prem Sangraula, *New Evidence on the Urbanization of Global Poverty* (Washington, D.C.: World Bank, 2007), Policy Research Working Paper 4199.

12. Brian Fikkert, "Fostering Informal Savings and Credit Associations," *Attacking Poverty in the Developing World: Christian Practitioners and Academics in Collaboration,* ed. by Judith M. Dean, Julie Schaffner, and Stephen L. S. Smith (Monrovia, Calif.: World Vision and Authentic Media, 2005), chapter 6, 77–94.

13. See Laura Hunter, "A Participatory Party in Mozambique," *Mandate,* Chalmers Center for Economic Development, 2008, no. 2, available at www.chalmers.org.

14. As quoted in David Larson, *A Leap of Faith for Church-Centered Microfinance,* working paper #204, Chalmers Center for Economic Development at Covenant College, www.chalmers.org, 10.

15. Ibid., 13.

16. Dean Karlan and Martin Valdivia, *Teaching Entrepreneurship: Impact of Business Training on Microfinance Clients and Institutions,* working paper at the Department of Economics, Yale University, October 2008; Jennefer Sebatad and Monique Cohen, *Financial Education for the Poor,* Financial Literacy Project, working paper no. 1, Microfinance Opportunities, April 2003; Bobbi Gray, Benjamin Crookston, Natalie de la Cruz, and Natasha Ivans, *Microfinance Against Malaria: Impact of Freedom from Hunger's Malaria Education When Delivered by Rural Banks in Ghana,* research paper no. 8, Freedom from Hunger, January 2007.

17. See Tetsuanao Yamamori and Kenneth A. Eldred, eds., *On Kingdom Business: Transforming Missions through Entrepreneurial Strategies* (Wheaton, Crossway, 2003); Steve Rundle and Tom Steffen, *Great Commission Companies* (Downers Grove, Ill.: InterVarsity, 2003).

18. Training is available in multiple formats from the Chalmers Center for Economic Development (www.chalmers.org). Contact the Chalmers Center to find out ways of subsidizing training for missionaries and indigenous churches.

19. The Chalmers Center's Global Fellowship of Trainers program equips people to become trainers of trainers. Find more information at www.chalmers.org.

CHAPTER 10
Excuse Me, Can You Spare Some Change?

1. Scott C. Miller, *Until It's Gone: Ending Poverty In Our Nation, In Our Lifetime* (Highlands, TX: aha! Process, Inc. 2008), 19–20.

2. Unfortunately, many churches need to reconsider the extent to which their cultures—attitudes, styles of worship, dress, language, norms, and racial composition—make them highly inaccessible to materially poor people.

3. The Faith and Service Technical Assistance Network has many helpful resources. In particular, see the *Mentoring Programs Toolkit: Equipping Your Organization for Effective Outreach,* availableatwww.urbanministry.org/wiki/mentoring-programs-toolkit-equipping-your-organization-effective-outreach.

4. Miller, *Until It's Gone: Ending Poverty In Our Nation, In Our Lifetime.*

5. See Mike Green with Henry Moore and John O'Brien, *When People Care Enough to Act: ABCD in Action* (Toronto, Ontario: Inclusion Press, 2006), 44–53.

6. Amy L. Sherman, *Establishing a Church-based Welfare-to-Work Mentoring Ministry: A Practical "How-To" Manual* (Washington DC: Hudson Institute, 2000).

7. Amy L. Sherman, *The ABCs of Community Ministry: A Curriculum for Congregations* (Washington DC: Hudson Institute, 2001).

8. Cathy Ludlum, *One Candle Power: Seven Principles that Enhance Lives of People with Disabilities and Their Communities* (Toronto, Canada: Inclusion Press International, 2002).

9. Mary A. Falvey, Marsha Forest, Jack Pearpoint, and Richard L. Rosenberg, *All My Life's a Circle, Using the Tools: Circles, MAPS & PATHS* (Toronto Canada: Inclusion Press International, Second Edition, 2003).

10. This section draws heavily on Roland Bunch, *Two Ears of Corn: A Guide to People-Centered Agricultural Improvement* (Oklahoma City, OK: World Neighbors, 1982), 21–36.

11. See for example, Craig Blomberg, *Neither Poverty Nor Riches: A Biblical Theology of Material Possessions* (Grand Rapids, MI: Eerdmans, 1999).

12. For a discussion of the importance of interpreting individual texts within the context of the Bible's overall narrative, see Dan McCartney and Charles Clayton, *Let the Reader Understand: A Guide to Interpreting and Applying the Bible* (Phillipsburg, NJ: Presbyterian and Reformed Publishers, 2002).

13. Blomberg, *Neither Poverty Nor Riches*, 209.

CHAPTER 11
On Your Mark, Get Set, Go!

1. Heidi Unruh, *Ministry Inventory Guide: Assess Your Church's Ministry Capacity and Identity*, from the Congregations, Community Outreach, and Leadership Development Project, 2007, available at www.urbansermons.org/f/ministry-inventory-guide-assess-your-churchs-ministry-capacity-and-identity.

2. In particular, see Nicol Turner, John L. McKnight, and John P. Kretzmann, *A Guide to Mapping and Mobilizing the Associations in Local Neighborhoods* (Evanston, IL: The Asset-Based Community Development Institute at Northwestern University, 1999). See especially chapters 1–2.

3. Diaconal Ministries Canada, *Guidelines for Benevolence* (Burlington, Ontario: Diaconal Ministries Canada), available at www.diaconalministries.com/resources/pguidelines.html.

4. In particular, see Nicol Turner et al., *A Guide to Mapping and Mobilizing the Associations in Local Neighborhoods*. See especially chapters 3–4.

5. A more comprehensive discussion about effective partnerships in the North American context can be found in Ronald J. Sider, John M. Perkins, Wayne L. Gordon, and F. Albert Tizon, *Linking Arms, Linking Lives: How Urban-Suburban Partnerships Can Transform Communities* (Ada, MI: Baker Books, 2008).

6. Robert D. Lupton, *Compassion, Justice, and the Christian Life: Rethinking Ministry to the Poor* (Ventura, CA: Regal Books, 2007), 104–09.

7. Some readers may recognize this as the idea of "sphere sovereignty" developed by Abraham Kuyper.

8. For a helpful discussion of this point, see Tim Keller, "The Gospel and the Poor," *Themelios,* December 2008, 33 (2).

9. This story is adapted from Brian Fikkert, "Proverbs 31 Women in Tribal Dress," *Mandate,* Chalmers Center for Economic Development, 2007, no. 2.

10. Interested readers can learn more about this remarkable ministry in Roy Mersland, "Innovations in Savings and Credit Groups—Evidence from Kenya," *Small Enterprise Development,* "vol. 18, no. 1, March 2007, 50–56.

11. All of these principles are present in the Chalmers Center's ASSET (Advancing Stewardship, Social Enterprise, and Training) Program. For more information, go to www.chalmers.org.

12. Werner Mischke editor, *The Beauty of Partnership Study Guide, Standard Edition* (Scottsdale, AZ: Mission One, 2010), available at www.beautyofpartnership.org.

13. For more on this, see Robert Chambers, *Whose Reality Counts? Putting the Last First* (London, UK: Intermediate Technology Publications, 1997), 154–56.

14. Francis Njoroge, Tulo Raistrick, Bill Crooks, and Jackie Mouradian, *Umoja: Transforming Communities Facilitator's Guide and Co-ordinator's Guide* (Teddington, UK: Tearfund, 2011), available at http://tilz.tearfund.org/Churches/Umoja.

15. Bérengère de Negri, Elizabeth Thomas, Aloys Ilinigumugabo, Ityai Muvandi, and Gary Lewis, *Empowering Communities Participatory Techniques For Community-Based Programme Development, Volumes 1 and 2, Trainer's Handbook and Participant's Manual* (Nairobi, Kenya: The Centre for African Family Studies in collaboration with The Johns Hopkins University Center for Communication Programs and the Academy for Educational Development, 1998), available at http://pcs.aed.org/empowering.

16. See Mersland, "Innovations in Savings and Credit Groups—Evidence from Kenya."

17. The Chalmers Center is exploring a similar model in West Africa, albeit with some important modifications as well in its ASSET (Advancing Stewardship, Social Enterprise, and Training) Program. Go to www.chalmers.org.

18. See Francis Njoroge et al. *Umoja: Transforming Communities Facilitator's Guide and Co-ordinator's Guide.* Stages 2–5 in this guide are particularly relevant for guiding the community organizing process. Additional helpful PLA tools can be found in Jules N. Pretty, et al., *Participatory Learning and Action: A Trainer's Guide.*

A Final Word: The Most Important Step

1. Timothy Keller, *The Prodigal God: Recovering the Heart of the Christian Faith* (New York: Dutton, 2008), 104.

2. Ibid., 107, 132–33.

APPENDIX

The Community Organizing Process in North America

1. This section draws heavily on Mike Green with Henry Moore and John O'Brien, *When People Care Enough to Act: ABCD in Action* (Toronto, Ontario: Inclusion Press, 2006).

2. Ibid. 96–100 discusses the qualities of a good community organizer.

3. Ibid. 102–04 describes the key elements of a learning conversation and provides examples.

ACKNOWLEDGMENTS

The ideas in this book reflect a decade-long collaboration between the authors and the other staff members of the Chalmers Center for Economic Development, an interdisciplinary team that has been working together to help churches around the world to minister to the economic, spiritual, and social needs of the poor. We have greatly benefited from the "iron-sharpening-iron" process that naturally takes place when people with different strengths and weaknesses try to solve problems together, and we want to thank each member of the Chalmers Center staff, both past and present, for the host of ways that they have contributed to the ideas in this book.

Of course, numerous other voices have spoken into our lives for even longer periods of time, including researchers, scholars, practitioners, and poor people. We are extremely indebted to all of them for their continued patience in helping us to learn and to grow.

We wish to thank Covenant College, where both of us teach in the Department of Economics and Community Development. We are deeply grateful to the board, administration, faculty, staff, and students who combine to create a rich community that daily seeks to discover the implications of "Colossians 1 Jesus."

We are deeply thankful for the financial support that generous donors have given to the Chalmers Center over the years. Without such funds, many of the ideas in this book could not have percolated. In particular, this book was written with trust funds donated by Dick and Ruth Ellingsworth.

We would like to thank Uganda Christian University, which graciously hosted Brian Fikkert and his family for five months in 2006. Many of the stories and experiences described in this book emerged during Brian's research and travels on this sabbatical.

We wish to express our thanks to the entire team at Moody Publishers, especially Dave DeWit, Tracey Shannon, and our patient editor, Cheryl Dunlop.

Thanks to our wives and children for putting up with us both in ways that we recognize and in ways that we do not. There will be many jewels on our wives' crowns someday.

Finally, we are thankful to Jesus Christ, who is reconciling all things, even us.

Steve Corbett
Brian Fikkert
Lookout Mountain, Georgia
January 2012

CHECK OUT THE STUDY GUIDE
FOR WHEN HELPING HURTS!

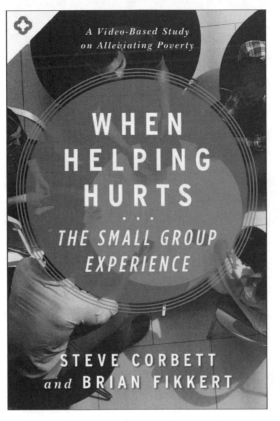

Also available as an ebook

From the Word to Life

Move your church forward in helping without hurting.

The Chalmers Center equips churches and ministries with gospel-driven tools designed to point the materially poor to Jesus and produce sustained transformation. Whether you are working with the poor in North America or the Majority World, the Chalmers Center has opportunities for you to be equipped for positive change.

The
Chalmers
Center

www.chalmers.org

Maria, a single mother, walks into your church's office asking for help paying her electric bill.

What do you do?

The Chalmers Center's *Faith & Finances* program

equips churches to empower people like Maria, fostering long-term transformation rather than merely providing temporary handouts. Through *Faith & Finances* classes, your church can train Maria in practical money management skills. In the process, both you and Maria can explore who God is, what gifts He has given you, and how your money is a part of His work in the world.

The Chalmers Center

Get your church trained, visit
www.chalmers.org/finances

CHECK OUT THESE OTHER
TITLES BY MOODY PUBLISHERS!

978-0-8024-1148-8

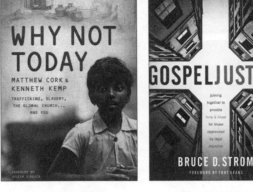

978-0-8024-1083-2

978-0-8024-0884-6

978-0-8024-0859-4

978-0-8024-0954-6

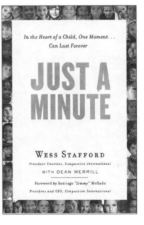

978-0-8024-0966-9

Also available as ebooks

MOODY
Publishers™

*From the Word **to** Life*

www.MoodyPublishers.com

MOODY
Radio™

*From the Word **to Life***

Moody Radio produces and delivers compelling programs filled with biblical insights and creative expressions of faith that help you take the next step in your relationship with Christ.

You can hear Moody Radio on 36 stations and more than 1,500 radio outlets across the U.S. and Canada. Or listen on your smartphone with the Moody Radio app!

www.moodyradio.org